SAMUEL BECKETT
Reading the Body in His Writings

SAMUEL BECKETT
Reading the Body in His Writings

nishi chawla

PRESTIGE

Published by
Prestige Books
3/28, East Patel Nagar
New Delhi 110 008

1999

ISBN: 81-7551-063-3

Photo Typesetting by
Pivot Computers
Delhi 110 006
Ph. 3981867

Printed at
Chaman Offset Printers
New Delhi 110 002

Contents

Acknowledgements

My deep gratitude to:

Professor James Maddox, Department of English, the George Washington University, Washington D.C., for making me rethink . . . and think again. . . .

And to Professor Gail Kern Paster, Jennifer Green-Lewis, Judith Plotz and Rajeshwari Sunderajan, all of G.W., for enabling an acuter discrimination of my ideas; and, finally, to all my students who will always remain the ultimate evaluation point of any worth this book holds.

For my husband
who taught me the quality of patience
and for my two sons
on whom i have to test it out

Introduction

There are more things in heaven and earth, Horatio,
Than are dreamt of in your philosophy
William Shakespeare, *Hamlet*

The primacy of the body in Samuel Beckett's writings is the foregrounding issue of this study. Loosely applied as a critical term, the "body" implies the physical and the social space it occupies as well as its discursive practices. The phenomenological dimensions of the body and the experiential issues it foregrounds are my subject. This study establishes that Beckett holds the natural processes of the body and mind as intrinsic to the tenement of the flesh since the mind and body function by the same principles of physiology. The living body is the fundamental phenomenological basis for apprehending self and society. The symbolic significance of the body has been defined in many ways in different fields of scholarship, but most of them relate to the notion of identity. The term "identity," deriving its roots from the Latin "idem," relates to a conception of "I" or "self," these words being used as synonyms in this study. I argue here that, for Beckett, the body is the prime agency for apprehending identity. Abandoning all dualistic ideas, Beckett believes that the body has a direct role in knowing and in perceiving reality. Also abandoning the essentialist perspective on human identity which locates the self as internal, as existing prior to social structures, Beckett opposes to the idea of the fixity of being or identity the body's becoming. In examining representations of the body in Beckett, I aim to show the role of the corporeal in Beckett's search for the sense of human existence and its multiple frames of reference in configuring identity. The primary aim of this project is to show how Beckett deploys the body as an instrument for annihilating the conceptual basis of identity.

In Beckett's writings, the investigation into the nature of the self blurs the distinctions between subject and object. While the self has traditionally been considered as subject, in Beckett, the self plays the dual role of subject and object. The self-conscious fictionalizing, the stories filling the fictional space of his narratives, engage with existential perplexities and questions of being and knowledge: who am I? why do I exist at all? how can I know myself? The philosophical search for answers to these queries is only an aspect of the existentially experienced scepticism concerning any essential or ultimate being. The I-centered notion of identity undermines the stability of character by reversal and self-contradiction. Names themselves subvert identity. The only relationship that offers any sense of legitimacy is the relationship between self and the corporeal frame, the fundamental sense of embodied existence in a physically experienced form. The body's presence is an integral element in the way one experiences living within it as well as the way it is deployed to destroy the idea of identity in a mental framework.

The body, considered both as tangible object and as signifier in a system of representations, social and political, has been devalued ever since Rene Descartes divided the universe ontologically, into two types of entities: the "res cogitans" which is mental, and the "res extensa" which is physical. Descartes's schizoid-like sense of alienation from anything outside the mind leads to a search for an epistemological assurance about the corporeal. In such a framework, the world can be realized and known only through mental representations, in which the body has no role to play. Hence, it has become a commonplace to claim the invention of the mind for the rationalist tradition set up by Descartes. What was new, however, in the Age of Reason was the location of the boundary between mind and body and the primacy of the mind in matters of knowledge. As Richard Rorty has pointed out:

> There were, to be sure, the notions of taking tacit thought, forming resolutions in foro interno, and the like. The novelty was the notion of a single inner space in which bodily sensations ("confused ideas of sense and imagination" in Descartes's phrase) and all the rest of what we now call "mental" were objects of quasi-observation. (*Philosophy and the Mirror of Nature*, 50)

What was novel about the Cartesian conception of the mind was that he divided states of consciousness from events in the external world—a distinction which resulted not only in the separation of the mind from the body, but also in a distinction between consciousness and what is not consciousness, between awareness and non-awareness. Consciousness then becomes a non-bodily substance. The notion of the mind as either a reflecting surface—a "glassy essence"—or an internal theatre is based on the perception of the mind operating on mechanistic modes of understanding and accounting for human knowledge. And it is well-known that the shadow cast longest of all philosophical systems on literary aesthetics is that of Cartesian idealism, designated as the subjective "cogito."

Beckett's writings evidence a consistent preoccupation with the cultural ramifications of Cartesian dualism as it has affected the conceptual formation and development of ideas about human physiology and the human body. A central concern in Beckett's work is his involvement with dualities. The paradigms of binary opposition—microcosm and macrocosm, intellect and emotion, mind and body—find a recurrent resonance in his works. However, it is my firm belief that, in spite of this deep engagement with Descartes, Beckett is not a Cartesian. Beckett perceives the world not as dualistic but as fragmented. His writings are so completely saturated with sentience, and yet engage so acutely with the parameters of the mind, that one gets the impression he is playing with the body-mind dualism. Through the constant evasions, the imminent revelation resting in the "I . . . my . . . mine . . . me" of his narrators, Beckett seems to struggle with the tension by which he finds himself caught in the epistemological trap laid by Descartes. However, Beckett believes only in the absence of any fixed hypostasis of self. He knows that the Cartesian problematic has misdirected and transformed the body into a standing "reserve" to be used by the mind for its own purposes. Hence, he rejects the cogito, the abstract reasoning of Cartesian Enlightenment.

Almost as if he were alienated by the Cartesian search for the systematic clarity which Beckett knew was totally foreign to his own temperament, Beckett "wisely" abandoned, as he phrased it in his 1934 poem, "Gnome," a career teaching the "loutishness of learning" (7). Again, signing his name for the "Poetry is vertical" manifesto framed by the editor of *Transition*, he consciously dissociated himself from "a world ruled by the hypnosis of positivism . . . the sterilization of the living imagination" (McMillan, 66). Repeatedly, Beckett parodies and mocks Descartes's well-known maxim: "Cogito ergo sum." His *Whoroscope* rewrites the Cartesian statement as "Fallor ergo sum"—I make mistakes, therefore I am:

> No I believe every word of it I assure you.
> Fallor, ergo sum! (lines 72-73)

In *Endgame* again, there is a subtle and indirect reference to the "ergo" of Cartesian thinking:

> CLOV: He's crying.
> [He closes the lid, straightens up.]
> HAMM: Then he's living,(62)

The shift from the Cartesian search of a stable mind in a world of dubious certainties to his own recognition of the lack of possibilities resting in the nature of the mind or the self is the fulcrum on which Beckett turns his own writings.

Beckett acquired his exhaustive knowledge of Cartesian philosophy in the course of writing his Master's dissertation on Descartes. But it is in his early poem *Whoroscope* that Beckett initiates his Cartesian literary program. It is extraordinarily appropriate that the poem, formally beginning Beckett's artistic preoccupation with Cartesianism, should be the first piece of writing Beckett published. It is also appropriate that I begin my study of Beckett by discussing the implications of his first published work to his concept of the body. Descartes's bifurcation of substance into mind and matter is the fundamental polarity that Beckett assails in his writings. By revealing Descartes as a wholly, fully bodily being in *Whoroscope*, Beckett, subtly and by clever inversion, explodes and cracks open the body-mind divide of Cartesian thought. The aesthetic of Beckett's poem demonstrates that the needs of the body are as valid as the needs of the mind. Based on the life of Rene Descartes, the Seigneur du Perron, *Whoroscope* borrows from Adrian Baillet's biography of Descartes, and focuses on a stream-of-consciousness presentation of the philosopher's physical eccentricities.

The title of Beckett's poem, *Whoroscope*, is a typical Joycean pun and has been derived from James Joyce's *Finnegans Wake*:

"How to pull a good Horuscoup even when Oldsire is Dead to the World" (105). Indeed, the whole of *Whoroscope* may be said to reflect the punning, allusive density of Joyce's final work. The term "horoscope" means hour-watcher. The empirical side of Descartes's personality distrusted the divination of the future by means of horoscopes. There is broad irony in the title as it relates to the last line of the poem. The antimetaphysical and antiabstractive side of Descartes, fearful of astrology and reposing faith in the present and the concrete, concealed his birthdate so that his horoscope could never be cast. Hence, his death was a "second/starless inscrutable hour." The Cartesian dualism is reinforced by the title of the poem although we soon find that the poem is based on Descartes's life and not his philosophy. The play on time is projected through the reductive narrative shifts from the fuller sense of the past to the more meagre sense of the reduced present.

Beckett's poem is also closely influenced by T.S. Eliot's *The Waste Land*. It shares the same dependence on a heavily allusive style replete with obscurities as well as the same use of a discontinuous form. In a typical Eliotian manner, Beckett attaches footnotes as an explanatory supplement to the deep obscurities found in his poem. The puns and parodic play, the wild blending of esoteric and colloquial elements in *Whoroscope*, the vigorous parade of knowledge in it, mimicking Eliot's *The Waste Land*— all these elements rollicking within the free associative structure of Beckett's poem focus on the rich and messy humanity of Descartes's pecadilloes.

Descartes speaks in the first person in *Whoroscope*. The poem is, in fact, entirely made up of references to events in his life. Conducted in the fashion of a monologue, the poem presents Descartes's stream-of-consciousness as he waits for his morning breakfast of omelettes. His predilection for "eggs hatched from eight to ten days" renders comic his very childish need, and in effect punctures the pompous gravity of his philosophical vision: "What's that?/An egg?/By the brothers Boot it stinks fresh./Give it to Gillot." The metaphorical locus of the poem rests in Descartes's fretful refusal to eat an egg that has not been hatched for more than eight days. He would rather have his valet, Gillot, have the egg which Descartes is wont to dump on him as easily as he dumps his easy analytical problems. Just as the Bloomian hunger dominates the imagery of "The Lestrygonians" episode in James Joyce's *Ulys-*

ses, Descartes's eggs, suggestive of dualism of course, hatch all through the poem which winds through the biographical details of his life. Beckett writes in his notes that "the shuttle of a ripening egg comb[ed] the warp of [Descartes's] days." The philosopher also has his anti-Aristotelian moments. This is immediately reinforced in the poem by the allusion to the two Dutch doctors, the Boot brothers, who had attacked Aristotle in a book they had published in Dublin in 1642. The close proximity in which Beckett wickedly places Descartes's physical penchants and his scholasticism ridicules the latter's pretenses toward mental cogitation. Eggs also point toward fecundity and the physical process of maturation as well as the inevitable deterioration of life. Most of the images and puns in the poem center on food, particularly eggs. "In the name of Bacon will you chicken me up that egg" (line 66), Descartes wails. There are other references to such vital sources of energy as "Porca Madonna," "a little green fry or a mushroomy one," the Joycean "prostisciutto," "hen-and-a-half ones," "burning liver," "fruit," "fish fork," and "a sack-of-potatoey charging Pretender." The elemental existence that Descartes has sacrificed at the altar of the "starless inscrutable hour," exists, in fact, not in the "cave-phantoms" (line 67) of the mind, but in the solid nourishment of eggs and bacon (line 66).

Thrown into the poem with its playful dialectical frame, one finds it hard to locate the speaker and the queries posed to him. The vivid effects of a man entirely controlled by his own subjective needs and hungers thwart the overpowering impact of the gigantic intellect that Descartes is known by. The ambivalent nature of Descartes's relationship with Galileo again brings him out as a man full of uncertainties. That Descartes found himself caught between the attachment to old certainties and his anti-Aristotelian moments; the "contempt" of the conservative Descartes for Galileo's "expedient sophistry concerning the movement of the earth"; the cursing of Galileo as a "vile old Copernican lead-swinging son of a sutler" (line 10) on the one hand, and his swearing "by the brothers Boot" who refuted Aristotle on the other; the Cartesian dualism in tension with Descartes's belief in transubstantiation and in Dante's "great high bright rose"—all of these details fix the philosophical inconsistencies of Descartes, caught in his historical moment. Although Beckett's Descartes swears "by the brothers Boot" who refuted Aristotle, he also curses Galileo for saying that the earth is in motion. The traditional anthropocentric understanding of the earth's motion was shattered by the heliocentric revolution in astronomy initiated by Galileo, the "charging Pretender." Later, in the eighth section of the poem, there is an allusion to Francis Bacon by whom Descartes swears just as he swears by the brothers Boot. As the author of the *Novum Organum*, Bacon, like Descartes, had dreamed of creating a new method in which Aristotelian logic would come under attack. At the same time, Bacon, like Descartes, expressed his reservations about the scholastic practice of subordinating scientific research to religious authority. The historical Descartes was divided between the medieval and the modern worlds. Beckett's Descartes, in *Whoroscope* and later, has his own philosophical inconsistencies.

Like the thoughts of Beckett's Malone, Descartes's thinking moves by associations—and associations prompted by the physical body, at that. Throughout the poem, the admirable Cartesian mind is thoroughly linked to the appetitive body. The admiration that his intellect elicits from famous mathematicians, such as the German Faulhaber, the rector Isaac Beeckman, and Peter the Red from Nuremberg, contrasts with the boyish triumph Descartes displays in "come now . . . and I'll pebble you all your hen-and-a-half-ones" (line 19). His interesting hypothesis about avalanches, and his honest assessment of the work of a fellow-colleague, Gassendi, about the "sun-red crystally cloud," emphasize his intellectual achievements. Playing against these mental gains are his triumphant aggressiveness in getting permission to stay in bed till late "or I'll pebble a lens under the quilt in the midst of day" (line 20), as well as the impulse to throw "Jesuits out of the skylight." All these are symptoms of a man divided between his mind and his body as he caresses the failures of life as well as its happinesses.

In the poem, Descartes's ties with other human beings leave their own impact upon his philosophical vision. In his childhood, Descartes had been fond of a girl who was slightly cross-eyed: "My squinty doaty!/I hid and you sook" (lines 29-30). This resulted in his life-long weakness for people who possessed this visual impairment. This relationship between sense impressions, emotions and intellect flouts the Cartesian injunction, inscribed in *Discourse on Method*, against those who "never lift their minds above tangible things, and consider things higher than corporeal objects" (57). Beckett emphasizes the life/philosophy disjunction further by connecting this recollection with another, that of the death of Descartes's illegitimate daughter, Francine, who was "scourged by a fever to stagnant murky blood." The deep lament for "my precious fruit," the pining for "a house-and-parlour foetus!" who suffered from such bodily pain—"What an exfoliation!/Her little grey flayed epidermis and scarlet tonsils" (lines 32-33)—is acute. Beckett exposes and implicitly critiques the Cartesian postulate that even though one may confuse the pure sensation of pain with an erroneous judgement about its physical causes a "res cogitans" can experience pain though he has no body whatsoever.

Descartes, conditioned by the mechanistic view of the universe, conceived of man's body as

> a machine, which, having been made by the hands of God, is incomparably better ordered . . . than any of those which can be invented by men. (*Discourse on Method*, 73)

Descartes was, of course, perfectly aware that this is not literally so, that the body is subject to pain and the machine is not. If the mind belongs to the realm of the spirit, and the body belongs to the material world, the spirit cannot be matter, nor can matter be spirit. If the distinction is so clear-cut, how could Descartes explain the mind's monitoring the activities of the body. The mind shares the material world with the body, just as much as the body's reporting of sensations to the mind makes it participate in the spirit. Hence, the body has to be something more than a perfectly assembled conglomeration of mechanical parts, an ideal arrangement of matter. What does the idea of subjectivity imply for the experience of pain and suffering? Beckett would have us reexamine the relation between the neurophysiological events occurring in the brain and the conscious experience of them, the correlation between the subjectively describable phenomena of consciousness and the physical phenomena occurring in the cerebral cortex. Is the relation a question of identity? Descartes's reduction of men to mere automata can be contradicted by pain-behaviour which is not just a complex of external stimuli and nerve agitation. Instead, one has only to imagine Descartes's own pain in order to refocus the identification between mental events and physical states as intersubjective transference. Seen in this perspective, the traumas and agonies of the body reduce consciousness to the limits of the physical. The "hot-cupboard" in which Descartes seeks intellectual solitude and stimulation leads to "a wind of evil" causing him pain on his right side, fatigue, and "the despair of ease" which made it difficult for him to walk. In this way Beckett reveals that one's being in pain can only be identical with the body's being in a certain state.

The image of "blood" has many resonances in the poem. Such was the stark impact of the image of blood upon Descartes that he refused the practice of blood-letting on his own dying body until the body had to relent. Within the framework of the poem, the "blood" image leads to Descartes's acknowledgment of William Harvey's blood circulation theory. The mention of Harvey's *De Motu Cordis* also leads to a recollection of the reception of Henry IV's royal heart at the Jesuit college of La Fleche, "the crypt of the arrow," during Descartes's student days there.

The recurrent blood motif in *Whoroscope*, of course, stresses the full presence of the body to Descartes. Descartes had his own transubstantiation theory about Christ's body and blood in the Mass: he believed that wine and wafer underwent a process of "natural transubstantiation" whereby the essence was transformed by miracle, though the surface remained the same. The preoccupation with transubstantiation can be called Descartes's attempt to transform the physical into the non-physical. Here he aligns himself with the Aristotle of primal matter and against those theologians who believe in "accidents reels." "The watery Beaune" is wine, and the wafer is "stale cubes of Hovis" (a whole-meal bread). However, as in Joyce's *Finnegans Wake*, there is a reversal, for "Beaune" can also refer to the body of Christ, and "Hovis," or "eau de vie" to His blood.

Descartes had hoped that his clever sophistry would enable his own explanation of transubstantiation to be accepted as the established one. The theologians had argued for "accidents reels" but Descartes had proposed the concept of surfaces under which the essence remains the same. Contact is made only with surfaces. Descartes emphasizes his conviction that all the senses are in reality forms of the sense of touch. The Aristotle of substantial forms comes alive in the real movement of the zigzag and the jig. The senses are made concrete as Beckett tropes on surface movements. The privileging of "touch" over other sense organs is such that "the nose is touched by the kiss of all foul and sweet air," the ears can hear "the drums, and the throne of the faecal inlet," the eyes move with the motion "of its zig-zags," and the taste buds relish as "we eat Him and drink Him" (lines 57-60). Reading through the eyes of Beckett, the Cartesian structure seems like hollow casuistry.

Beckett defeats Descartes at his own game. Reading Beckett's *Whoroscope* one wonders where does the "peeling of the onion" stop? Beckett would make his Descartes and his "cracked beater" stop at the body only. This is the message of the richly ironic verse of the young Beckett. The only truth resides in the real world of the senses. The sensual fabric of Descartes's embodied existence weaves through the blasphemous allusions to Madonna as "Porca Madonna," to Christ as both fish and hen: "Kip of Christ hatch it!" and the fusion of condiments and Catholicism in the reference to the Eucharist.

In the concluding sections of *Whoroscope*, Beckett parodies Descartes's philosophical axiom: "Cogito ergo sum" by fusing it with Augustine's less well-known "si fallor, sum." Descartes's defense of his axiom rests in his confession that he had said nothing that Augustine had not said before him. Beckett's version, "Fallor, ergo sum," is a neat way of bringing home the point to the "coy old frolier," Descartes, of the truth of "I am deceived." Thus *Whoroscope* disparages Augustinian conversion by replacing the Saint's affirmation of belief with an admission of self-deception. Typically, thinking becomes erring. The references to Augustine's conversion as "he buttoned on his redemptorist waistcoat," and the anglicized play on the phrase from the *Confessions*, "He toll'ed and legg'ed," undercut the process of conversion but not, in my opinion, what Augustine was converting from, namely, the pleasures of the table and the immoderate desires of the flesh. Beckett's *Whoroscope* affirms the submersion in things physical, the chaos of elemental human existence where Beckett's characters live, and which Augustine as well as Descartes deny and reject. The reference to Augustine's conversion is strategic because Beckett chooses to endorse the emotional affinities of Descartes and Augustine in regard to the "cogito." Both Descartes and Augustine prove the existence of God, in Beckett's ironic terms, "by exhaustion." On the subject of reconciling Descartes's dualism with the Church's dogma of transubstantiation in the Eucharist, the philosopher insists that he believes wholeheartedly in transubstantiation and in Dante's "great high bright rose," the mystical body of Christ as imaged in the last cantos of the *Paradiso*.

Beckett's poem follows Descartes to the court of Christina,

Queen of Sweden, where Descartes died from the effects of early rising and the inclement Swedish weather. "Christina the ripper," the "Rahab of the snows," "the murdering matinal pope-confessed amazon," who in the name of religious salvation killed men, invites the Catholic Descartes to her Protestant country and eventually proves instrumental in his death. The plea, "Spare the blood of a Frank," was made by the dying Descartes against the bloodletting to which his helpless body finally succumbed. It was also made by Descartes "who has climbed the bitter steps," an apparent reference to the image of the ladder or flight of steps Descartes had used to lead mankind to certain knowledge. In his *Rules for the Direction of the Mind*, Descartes explains that his method entails reducing involved and obsure propositions to simpler ones by the ascent on ladders. Beckett has used the ladder image again in *Murphy* and *Watt*. However, Beckett is obviously using it in ironic terms here in *Whoroscope* where he effectively exposes Descartes's absurd confidence in his ability to reason his way to "my second/starless inscrutable hour." Like the exile Dante describes in Paradiso, Descartes's loneliness reaches its climactic moment in his reference to himself as one "who has climbed the bitter steps."

Lawrence Harvey, who has written the only exhaustive treatment of Beckett's *Whoroscope*, asks the question: "Why Descartes? What did the great seventeenth-century philosopher mean to the avant-garde twentieth-century poet?" (33) Harvey's long and incisive analysis of Beckett's poem arrives at the point where I begin my study of Beckett. Like Harvey, I believe that in his poem, Beckett attacks the kind of abstract reasoning which made Descartes perceive a radical schism between thinking and being. Unlike Descartes, Beckett starts from the premise that there is nothing but the human body for one to be in, that the body's relationship to the mind begins from the fact that one is bound by the body one is claimed by. While Descartes posited the idea of a thinking mind, he blissfully neglected the fact that the mind is irrevocably tied to a physically decaying body with "grey flayed epidermis and scarlet tonsils," "stagnant murky blood," and the "sweet milled sweat of my burning liver" (line 12).

Descartes's own particular interest in studying the relationship between body and mind was to find out whether the body was an essential part of oneself. On one rare occasion, he admits that "Nature teaches me," as he declares in the *Sixth Meditation*,

> I am not only lodged in my body like a pilot in his ship, but, besides . . . I am joined to it very closely and indeed so compounded and intermingled with my body, that I form, as it were, a single whole with it. (159)

Descartes is really asking what properties are analytically contained in the concept of body in general. His underlying intent is otherwise, to discover what belongs to the concept of the mind. He merely uses the concrete examples as rhetorical means of showing that we will not "refuse to call something a body" if it lacks color or hardness or some such quality. For Descartes, however, one's sense of existence is not contingent on the body. Instead, one derives existence from the capacity for thought:

> from the mere fact that I know with certainty that I exist. . . . I rightly conclude that my essence consists in this alone, that I am a thinking thing, or a substance whose whole essence or nature consists in thinking. (156)

The essence of material things, Descartes holds, consists not in those qualitative features which are arrived at by sensory observation, but in their underlying structure. The sensory apprehension of material things is "obscure and confused," and Descartes suggests in the *Sixth Meditation* that "they are perhaps not exactly as we perceive them through the senses" (158).

Descartes's entire philosophical position is fraught with contradictions: he contradicts himself when he occasionally admits that the body can act on the mind, which is otherwise responsible for the cognitive faculties of pure intellect, senses, and imagination. How can sensations, which we are told require the activity of the body, arise in a mind whose essence consists in pure thought which exists independently of the body? For the union of the spirit and the body is made evident by sense.

Descartes's emphasis on the individual thinking man is the mainspring of his philosophy of epistemological individualism which attempts to answer the question of what man may know, rather than what men may know. Man's body and mind are, according to Cartesian philosophy, essentially distinct substances which separate at death. He takes his discussion of the wax to provide the basis for a more fundamental claim: namely, that nothing can be more evidently perceived than the mind. In the Cartesian form of dualism, the mental and the physical are logically distinct and neither can be reduced to the other. The subject-object relationship assumes the dimensions of the problem of consciousness and what is not consciousness. According to Cartesianism, consciousness is an ultimate given, and an unanalyzable form of awareness, and there is nothing one can prove or infer regarding its presuppositions. Descartes used "conscientia" in a radically new way: the Cartesian consciousness is bodiless and incorporeal. In his *Meditations*, Descartes distinguished not simply between mind and body, but also between consciousness and what is not consciousness. Alienated from anything bodily outside itself, consciousness becomes a non-bodily substance.

In furthering his thesis of the mind, Descartes argued that the conception of a disembodied mind is plausible. For Descartes, it is possible for one to imagine oneself to be a person with no body, to believe that one's idea of the body might be a case of false belief or of not exactly certifiable knowledge. The essential nature of the soul consists in its power of thinking—thought, being immaterial, is unextended. The classic formulation of the disappearance of the body as a philosophical issue has been stated by Descartes in the first of his *Meditations*: "I will consider myself as having no hands, eyes, flesh, blood or senses, but as believing wrongly that I have all these things" (100).

In his writings, Beckett takes up the fiction of the disappearance of the body and its relationship to the "transparency" of the mind. Beckett makes us think about what constitutes identity in terms of the mind-body problem by dislodging and disembodying the mind in many of his writings. He thereby forces us to ask how we are related to our bodies. Is the specific body that the characters inhabit no longer the basic thing that existed independently? Must immateriality and disembodiment be connected to expanses of the mind and imagination? On the Cartesian dualistic view that the mind and its contents are non-spatial rests the conviction that what is essential about people, is broadly speaking, mental. Descartes's argument based on the piece of wax, all of whose qualities change except its transempirical identity, is revealed by Beckett to be contingent. Beckett would argue that mental entities are also in space and that the mental is, therefore, a realm of the physical. Beckett would regard all categories of truth as identical, and reduce all a priori and a posteriori, all contingent and necessary truths.

Unlike Descartes, Beckett's interest in the body stems from the physical condition in which one is positioned and from which one knows the world. The coordinate body along with its sensory apparatus is an inescapable element in the working of the cognitive faculties of pure intellect, sense and imagination of the human mind. While Descartes holds that the body is not essential for constituting the identity of man, Beckett knows that this conception raises insuperable difficulties. He obviously does not take the knowledge of the existence of a thinking being to be a sufficient basis for a theory of the self. He rejects Descartes's "rationalist" epistemology because he rejects his method and logic of "certainties." In his own open-ended manner, Beckett questions Cartesian thinking without, however, pronouncing it philosophically incorrect. Beckett's own aporetic style refuses such a dogmatic formulation. Instead, he seems to perceive Descartes as having introduced a problematic which has forever fissured human perception of reality. Beckett knows that the Cartesian principles were mere hypotheses masquerading as statements of real essence. He also perceives the Cartesian method of deducing from true and immutable essences, distinctly perceived in intellectual God-guaranteed intuitions, a bogus means of discovery.

Of course, the existence of thinking is a given fact; consciousness would not be possible without it, to state it tautologically. In this respect, my understanding of the mind is closely connected to my conception of the brain as that part of the nervous system of the body which is responsible for the interpretation of sensory impulses, the coordination of bodily activities, and the exercise of emotion and thought. Just as the unity of a mind is not broken by the fact that a human brain has two hemispheres, so too the unity of a human body inherently contradicts any mind-body dualism. However, what I want to emphasize in my study is that, for Beckett, the body is the natural vehicle for envisioning the mind. For Beckett, a human being is, above all, a bodily being—one who can be identified only by virtue of his corporeality. It is the body's presence which forms a fundamental element in the way one experiences living within it. Beckett's real concern is with the fundamental ontology of human existence. Ontology is the theory of being, and Beckett's writings insistently make us think about our ontological commitments, about the nature of existence—how is essence to be distinguished from existence, and if there are any distinctions at all. If in the seventeenth century, Descartes encapsulated this thought in a single phrase, "I think, therefore I exist," Beckett makes us reexamine the ontological basis of such axiomatic conceptualization about identity. The ontology of human existence should include the lived experience of physical reality.

In foregrounding the contingencies of human biological constitution, Beckett focuses on rescuing materialism from the fallacy of dualism. The origin of everything is matter: matter as classically conceived is not the ultimate physical reality; but that would not prove that ultimate reality is immaterial or mental. In reconfiguring the relationship of the bodily with the mental, Beckett would have us believe that though the truth-conditions concerning identity may vary, the legitimacy of identity in pure bodily terms is a necessary a priori truth. Bodiliness is defined as well as experienced from within, but perceived from without as the spatial extension of bodily form. The issue of human identity, in other words, has to be associated with the boundaries of the body, on what is integral to the body and what is exterior to it. Deeply embedded as bodily identity is in Beckett, his texts invoke a sense of felt embodiment that is more fundamental than self-consciousness or cognition. The Cartesian split between the mind and the body as an object of sense perception, and between the mind as subject and as object of its own self-observation, is parodied and ridiculed in Beckett's refusal to ground identity solely in the mind's consciousness of its own processes.

The critical implications of the observation that Beckett's thinking is binary, and therefore Cartesian, have too often been challenged and even rechallenged to make my work absolutely ground-breaking viewed in terms solely of Beckett's exploration of the Cartesian dilemma. Although Beckett's writings are riddled with Cartesian splits and divisions—mind is divided from body, action from desire, self from the world, particularly nature—Beckett and Descartes meet in Beckett's writings only to part. It is true that Beckett evinces a life-time's obsession with the mind-body dualism, often, one almost begins to suspect, subscribing to the fatal power of the argument. However, opposed to Descartes's establishment of a thinking subject as invulnerable to scepticism, Beckett embraced scepticism, and proceeded always from that scepticism. Descartes's belief in the certitude of knowledge was, of course, motivated by the attempt to affirm the sovereign power of the mind.

Beckett's intrinsic disagreement is with Descartes's interpretation which somehow fails to capture the sense in which the certainty of the "cogito" is directly extruded from all doubt. In arriving at the existential truth of the cogito, the Cartesian construct entails a whole apparatus of fundamental concepts which can be manipulated and whose necessity is never questioned. If Descartes could create a new philosophy of the mind by making epistemology the center of his philosophical inquiry, Beckett examines the foundations of such an epistemology. The Cartesian formulation is known less for any explicit expounding of rationality than for the perspective in which it views the relationship between the mental and the physical. Beckett besets us with doubts about the epistemological status of the Cartesian argument whose contradictions and ambiguities are too well-acknowledged, though few have yet abandoned the Cartesian vision of the privileging of, and the possibilities of the mind against the body. For Beckett, the mind's a priori assumption of itself is as much an unverifiable hypothesis as Descartes posits it of the body.

The importance of Descartes's thought to Beckett was first documented in the Fall 1959 special issue of *Perspective* where Hugh Kenner and Samuel I. Mintz discussed Beckett's relationship to Descartes. Since then, there have been many specific studies of Beckett undertaken through the eyeglass of Cartesian philosophy, among which Hugh Kenner's analysis of Cartesian motifs and the Cartesianism so clearly demonstrable in *Murphy* in particular, is the most well-known.[1] Hugh Kenner's acclaimed Cartesian reading of Beckett's trilogy is, and remains, the watershed. Kenner's brilliant essay, "The Cartesian Centaur," depends on Cartesian principles to show how Beckett "carries the Cartesian process backwards, beginning with a bodily 'je suis' and ending with a bare 'cogito'" (128). The fundamental problem relates to the idea of a perfect machine and the facts of imperfection as they impinge on the human body. Beckett uses the simple mechanics of "man as machine" and "man using machine." The collapse of the distinction between the being of humankind and that of mechanical thinghood, res extensa, leads to the erosion of all sense of value and vitality with the organicity of the body embodied in the mechanical. Beckett's characters try to erase and obliterate their fundamental human identity by transmuting human beings into machines. The prosthetics of the body in Beckett leads to liminal beings when mechanical devices and body parts interact and merge into each other. But if man is a "machine made by the hands of God," and if the body is an extendable substance, how is it that it "defects"? Beckett's heroes suffer a gradual deterioration of the body. Certainly, the body is in itself the most uncertain kind of machine, and becomes more unstable as its members deteriorate. The Cartesian ideal of the perfect man-machine fails and is completely shattered, according to Beckett, who shows his Cartesian characters disintegrating in their bodies. Relentlessly engaged in his rational quest, Beckett's protagonist as "the Cartesian Centaur . . . riding a bicycle," is, as Kenner observes, "mens sana in corpore disposito" (134).

Kenner opines that, like Descartes, Beckett's characters are spectators in the "theatre of the world" (23). Beckett deliberately leads them into the "higher" regions only to bring them back to their senses after their apprehension of the causal interaction between mind and body. Most of his early protagonists particularly start from the Cartesian premise of absolute doubt, using the yardstick of reason to prove the truth of anything, and doubting the veracity and reality of that which cannot be established by sense perception. Beckett casts his characters as minimally epistemological agents with limits on their cognitive resources, and then proceeds to explore the cognitive system of beliefs and perceptions which govern our understanding of rationality. By putting them in unpredictable situations, he explores the validity of any neat divisions between mind and body. There being an element of uncertainty about even the most certain sense-based beliefs, Descartes-like they are convinced that one should concentrate on the mental sphere, and ignore the material world. The autonomy of the mental is thus repeatedly questioned by Beckett. Descartes's distinction between the domains of the physical, which is subject to deterministic laws, and the mental, which is free, is collapsed, thereby cracking and exploding the tacitly assumed conception of rationality.

Beckett's works compel us searchingly in the direction of the mind-body dichotomy as Beckett leads us to reexamine the possibilities of the mind, how far it is independent of the bodily. Beckett exposes the hollow interior of Descartes's mechanistic philosophy by presenting victims and casualties of Cartesianism who eventually return to their bodily selves after brief, though intense dalliances with the pure mental zones. Reason in the Cartesian landscape defined as the means to objectivity and certain knowledge, is challenged by a writer like Beckett, sensitive to designations of difference. Questioning the authority of reason and its certainties as it continues to dominate systems of interpretation and power, Beckett obliquely indicts Descartes and the Age of Reason for the cultivation of mythologies of power.

Beckett's interrogation of normative rationality puts limitations on the character as an epistemological agent, thereby condemning traditional Cartesian possibilities of the mind. The Cartesian dependence on mathematics is turned, in Beckett, into "a mania for symmetry." If Cartesian relationships are the basic necessities of the rational "Enlightenment," then the sciences are organically related to each other and can be explained by the supervisory science of mathematics. If matter extends, then how are human beings responsibly situated with respect to other objects. Such issues plague the Beckettian res cogitans. The process of reducing the number of sequences in which he may eat his biscuits to a "paltry six" is the puzzle with which Beckett's Cartesian Murphy occupies himself. Who is to be blamed when the body fails or when the mind fails to understand? These rational exercises reduce the Beckettian residual human as a specimen of the breakdown of the machinery, as mere empty verbal incantation. In Beckett's writings, then, is grounded the cognition that the mind can never singularly overcome the body nor can it resolve the schism between the inner self and outer reality. This is the key to Beckett's despair at the dilemma of Cartesian dualism and the epistemological postulates underlying Cartesian or rationalist assumptions. Beckett recognizes the fact that an exclusive devotion to the mental can create fissures in relating to the outside world. He questions and challenges Cartesian assumptions about a schizoid division into two selves, a conscious, mental self, and a bodily self of instincts and sensations. The biological nature of the body thus becomes a cognitive systematization. Beckett's anti-Cartesian fallibilism leads him to the belief that no beliefs are immune to challenge. He thus tests the concept of reason by presenting his schizoid characters with minimal rationalist conditions or no rationality restrictions in order to show that those who are beyond the bounds of reason also exist.

In exploring Beckett's critique of Descartes's fundamental postulates further, I hope to extend Kenner's reading, and break new ground in carrying out a sustained reading of the body in Beckett. I believe that by dismantling the concept of identity based on the mind, Beckett shores up the concept of man as a biological being. In the chapters that follow, I aim to demonstrate the groundedness of Beckett's characters in bodily processes, at the same time that I argue that Beckett's characters are shorn of any definitive sense of identity.

My theoretical polemic will trace the central "bodily" concerns that pervade Beckett's writings: the issue of the relationship between mind and body; the natural, instinctual elements of the body and the bodily processes as they decay and disintegrate; the disciplining and politicization of this body; the possibility of an ontology and an aesthetics based on negativity and absence; and the arbitrary role of sexual limits and the limits of language as systems of representation in the configuration of identity.

Stemming directly from these concerns is the problematic of identity. Besieged with questions of "who am I" and "what am I," Beckett's characters seem to return to their bodies in several ways in trying to resolve the uncertainty of their identity. Their body's creativity and productivity being repressed, his characters reveal the interface between the various selves of the body. The castrati, lobotomized vegetables, and alienated, often schizophrenic subhumans in Beckett exist within the interstices of identity as only schizophrenic doubles, multiples and fragments. A destabilized consistency of selfhood is, of course, an inescapable feature of Beckett's early works, more notably the prose trilogy. In his subsequent works, however, we are confronted, as Andrew Kennedy outlines, with "further and radical instances of dramatic lessness," with "the self moving towards existential and verbal extinction" (30). To expose the shaky and unstable premises of the identity of Beckett's characters is the thematic stake of this study.

The more I ponder my subject—what the body means—the more I am plagued by a discomfiture about arriving at any clear and singular definition of the body. That the ever-present material body grounds and delimits being and knowing is inescapable. That the body is the site for one's deepest desires and longings, including the desire for death and oblivion, becomes evident the more one reads Beckett keenly. Despite this understanding, I have kept my operative definition of body loosely general as the body means as well as implies so many different things at the same time. One major aspect of my argument is that our attitudinal relationship with our body is a reflection of our social beliefs and ideas. This is most evident in the way our sexuality, located within the body, is organized, controlled and expressed by the manner in which our social ideas impose and restrict our sexual bodies.

Finally, the overarching design of my study is governed by the query: does the body have any definitive relationship to selfhood? Often considered as something reflexive, private and possessive, the self has been taken by many thinkers to denote more an epistemological subject than an existential one. Beckett exposes the arbitrary nature of the symbolically constituted self, and inverts, or rather deconstructs, the humanist emphasis. In the course of this study, I will show how Beckett calls into question all a priori attachment to humanist entities like self and identity. The self is suspect, and one cannot transcend the phenomenal world in coming to terms with oneself. Beckett's perception of the contingent nature of the self includes the possibility of comprehending reality through the tangibly concrete.

Beckett's prime emphasis is on the physical. Although the body is the condition of existence for the category of mind, it has traditionally been constructed as the negative other of mind. Bodily activity can thus be dismissed as fundamentally alien to the mind, wherein lies the true essence of self. One consequence of the mind-body dualism is that the body is experienced as a "prison," a limitation and confinement. Many of Beckett's characters begin from this premise. They distance themselves so far from their bodies and live within the hollow interior of their minds that they are reduced to a nameless I. In Chapter One, I discuss at length this tendency, in Beckett's early novel *Murphy*, and to a lesser extent, in *Watt* and *Molloy*. My argument rests on the thesis that all the fictionalizing of Beckett's characters must return, eventually, to what is called in Beckett's "From an Abandoned Work," "the old half-knowledge of when and where, and of what" (49). The reassuring nature of a knowable world is an impossible construct without the recognition of the physical. Our thoughts and our knowledge can be derived only from the experience of our senses. I strongly believe that in a world where essentialist thinking is losing its sway, Beckett's work stands either as an ironic affirmation of bodily experientia, or else as a protest against those who have devalued the body completely.

The thematic reading of my argument, especially in Chapters Two, Three, and Four, draws closely on the writings of two body theorists, Mikhail Bakhtin and Michel Foucault. Bakhtin and Foucault ostensibly seem to theorize about divergent conditions of the body, but converge in their underlying intent of valorizing a free space for the body. The contrapuntal pull of Bakhtinian subversion and Foucauldian repression are two directions the discourse of the body takes. Bakhtin's concept of "carnival" operates as a centrifugal trope to oppose social impositions on the body. Deriving from the physical materiality of the human body, the "grotesque realism" of protuberances, excretions, and gargantuan appetites represents in gross and exaggerated form the fundamental ambivalence of all carnivalesque. The exaggerations and the grotesqueries of the bodily form persist in Beckett's writings as something like a late continuation of the late medieval period Bakhtin captures in *Rabelais and his World.* But Beckett's is a more modern grotesque form in which the bodies have dwindled and shrunk and reduced to an uncertain state of identity. The second chapter is an attempt to use Bakhtin to enlighten Beckett by showing Molloy as a very physical and an intensely Bakhtinian character. I return to Beckett's *Molloy* often in the course of this book as I consider the work paradigmatic and central to Beckett's philosophical valorization of the body.

Foucault's historicizing of power, knowledge and theatricality in his *Discipline and Punish* engages with a form of tyranny and bodily repression that can be closely applied to the play of power relations found in Beckett's writings. I have argued this in my third chapter where I have applied the Foucauldian paradigm to Beckett's *Molloy, Waiting for Godot*, and *Catastrophe.* Foucault is useful to my argument in another sense. His work on sexual ethics in *The History of Sexuality* offers insight, not only into the conceptualization of sexual desire, but also into the stringent policing of the sexual body. Foucault's notion of the subversive potential in discourses of sexuality is particularly relevant to developments in, and challenges to, sexual ideology. The layers of assumption under which sex, gender and heterosexual desire have been categorized and regimented have been tapped by Foucault as well as later feminist theorists like Judith Butler. I have used their arguments in my fourth chapter to trace the implications of the inscription of gender identity in Beckett's "Enough" and *Not I.* And, finally in the fifth chapter, I have analyzed the epiphenomenal implications of corporeal absence in *Not I, Footfalls*, and the later trilogy.

To chart the map of the critical scholarship relating to my subject, it must be stated at the outset that, while a great deal has been written on the body-mind dualism in Beckett, "the body in Beckett" has not been so exhaustively commented on. Despite the virtual explosion of body criticism, the body has only occasionally, and never intensively been studied and analyzed in Beckett's writings. From the seminal theoreticians—Michel Foucault, Alain Robbe-Grillet, Maurice Blanchot, Georges Bataille, Theodor Adorno—to the seminal critics, both early as well as recent, and whose number is great, the tendencies within the history of Beckett criticism have taken many directions and redirections. Nonetheless, there are two kinds of scholars who have discoursed on the subject of the body: those who would position Beckett as an "existential humanist"[2] and, increasingly of late, those who consider his work as Deconstructionist, an art of unmaking, a "literature of silence" (10) in Ihab Hassan's words. Deconstruction has also affected the shape of Beckett scholarship, and his writings have often been subjected to poststructuralist readings.[3] Deriving principally from Jacques Derrida's view of western thinking as fundamentally "logocentric" or dualistic, that is, thinking in terms of such polarities as mind-body, thought-feeling, presence-absence, Deconstruction, with its concomitant linguistic antihumanism, views any idea of "presence," an experience or meaning being experienced in itself, with a characteristic sense of suspicion. Increasingly, Beckett has come to be seen as a "messiah" of postmodernism, rejecting the absolute, transcendent values still aspired to by even the last modernists. I will briefly dwell on some of these critics whose work I have found germane to my subject.

In fact, the notion of the postmodernist Beckett may be a plausible explanation for Beckett's obsession, two hundred years or more after Descartes, to preoccupy himself for more than fifty odd years of his writing career trying to analyze the Cartesian philosophical position that has had such a tremendous impact on the worldview. Surely and quite evidently, Beckett was part of a zeitgeist, a cultural phenomenon where he found himself trapped within a problematic from which there could be no real escape. To be sure, Beckett found himself at that particular historical juncture, that accidental moment in history and place when there was a collective and willed 'intentionality' to renew and see from a modern perspective, the fusional metaphysic into which the Cartesian paradigm had introduced a fissure, an erosion. By abolishing the world of essences, by replacing the primacy of identity and representation with difference and repetition, the anti-Hegelian characteristic of modern philosophy destabilizes and subverts the traditional order of truth and knowledge. Poised on that vantage point between and after the two world wars of the twentieth century, between the Modern and the Postmodern, if such periodizing be permitted, Beckett, like many others, found himself caught between the past and the future in an immense fusional sense.

Beckett prefigures crucial elements of poststructuralist thought, foregrounding the centrality of language as well as the shifting, changing assumptions of literary modernism. Beckett's phenomenalism received its impetus from the general crisis in European culture, from the contemporary cultural paradigm or 'episteme,' all of which effected the transition from modern to postmodern literature. The turning point is the conceptual fulcrum upon which Beckett's writings rest. His breaking away from the Joycean influence, and not just his decision to settle in Paris, paradoxically also signalled his break with modernist configurations. It is a critical commonplace that the theoretical conceptualizations of writers like the later Wittgenstein, Martin Heidegger, Derrida and others, are homologous with contemporary writers who attacked the metaphysical underpinnings of modernism, particularly the epistemological tradition running from Descartes through Kant and Hegel and onto Edmund Husserl. In this sense, Virginia Woolf's lament in *To the Lighthouse* that the mirror of nature had cracked, was another way of describing the subject-object dichotomy.

Among postmodern writings, Thomas Trezise's *Into The Breach: Samuel Beckett and the Ends of Literature* argues that until postmodernism dismantled the phenomenology of the Sartre and Husserl tradition, Beckett's writings could hardly have been appreciated. This is, of course, an overstatement, and as an overstatement, offers me a valuable perspective to validate the middle ground that my own argument values. Trezise believes that the idea of the human subject in Beckett's works has not been properly explored because the critical endeavours devoted to him have largely been ideological exercises. This problem largely arose, according to Trezise, because Beckett wrote at a time when the intellectual life in France was besieged by existential phenomenology with which Beckett's work has always been linked. Trezise explicitly offers a sustained challenge to existential humanism, and "in so doing [challenges] the assumptions underlying virtually the entire corpus of

Beckett's criticism" (ix). Associating Beckett's work with Gilles Deleuze, Jacques Derrida, Georges Bataille, and Maurice Blanchot, and hence another brand of "ideology" (he spends as much time on them as he does on Beckett's trilogy), Trezise cuts through the intertextual force of Beckett's trilogy, to reveal, in the spectacle of the dispossession of the self, a poststructuralist's delight in Beckett. Trezise powerfully demonstrates how the constituent works of the trilogy posit the autonomous speaking self as prior to and distinct from the supplementary structures of temporality—the resultant breach between the subject and its outside is seen in Beckett's writings as a breach within the subject. It is, Trezise observes, "into this breach that Beckett writes" (33). Using Bataille's concept of a general economy of excess and transgression, he establishes a context for analyzing the nature of the "subject that compulsively exceeds itself" (115), for analyzing, in sum, the nature of intersubjectivity found in Beckett. Trezise argues that, in each instance of bodily reduction in Beckett's metaphysics,

> this paralyzed mobility or mobile paralysis describes an ambivalence or ambiguity intrinsic to the body, as that which is, literally speaking, the differential embodiment or incorporation of an economy that exceeds it. . . . (140)

Beckett, however, remains a rift case. The opposition to the humanist paradigm notwithstanding, I believe that there are significant moments in all the poststructuralist readings when the denunciation of presence and logocentric certainty does not seem very convincing, and often goes unexamined. Stanton Garner has exposed the lack of conviction in Derrida's own conceptualization while stating clearly his intention not to dispute the deconstructive readings of Beckett. Rather, he wishes to challenge the repudiation of phenomenology which is the guiding premise of deconstruction. Garner's essay, "Still Living Flesh: Beckett, Merleau-Ponty, and the Phenomenological Body," now an essential part of his book, *Bodied Spaces*, has given me that middle ground I seek in placing my own argument.

Stanton Garner's interest in Beckett primarily stems from his directorial experiences and focuses on the theatrical phenomena of audience-stage dynamic. His exploration of the phenomenological body is overdone when he perceives the "fetishizing of the flesh" in a "post-modern primitivism" on Beckett's stage. To that extent, the development of my argument does not partake of Garner's preoccupations. However, some of his insights into the phenomenological aspect of Beckett coincide with my critical stance.

Garner questions Trezise's critique of the Husserlian formulation of phenomenology as "a polemical construction" (446), one which denies it its historical contingencies, its developmental changes and revisions. Garner also traces the theoretical affinities between phenomenology and deconstruction, affinities which bear out the idea that Derrida's hostility to Husserlian theory concealed his admiration as well as his links with the latter. In this way, Garner shows how the validity of such concepts as "absence" and "decentering" can be appropriated by both deconstruction and phenomenology. With this basic kinship in mind, Garner demonstrates that:

> Like the history of phenomenology itself, Beckett's work represents an evolving and increasingly complex response to a set of essentially phenomenological questions concerning subjectivity, embodiedness, and perception. (447)

In a bid to relocate Beckett, Garner believes that Maurice Merleau-Ponty's postulations on the "embodiedness" of consciousness in *The Phenomenology of Perception* provide the best frame of reference for examining Beckett's radicalized treatment of the body. While Husserl's pursuit of phenomenological "essences" made him "bracket" the body in its material facticity, Merleau-Ponty could conceive of a consciousness inflected with an inescapable corporeality. Beckett's "intensely embodied theatre" can be best studied and understood, according to Garner, in light of Merleau-Ponty's concept of "lived bodiliness." Further, the preponderance of theatrical metaphors in Merleau-Ponty's writings correspond with, and shed light on, the play of corporeal problematics in Beckett's drama, a field of inquiry neglected by the deconstructionist fetishizing of prose texts. In this respect, Garner believes that "Phenomenology offers a way of re-embodying the discourse of theatre" (448), through not only the dynamics of vision, but also the absent presence of the body as staged in Beckett's theatre. He thus argues the need for a phenomenological reading of Beckett, more particularly, as seen through the contours of theatrical performance. My own critical project shares Garner's guiding premise of resurrecting the phenomenological aspect of Beckett's writings, although I aim to comprehend many more aspects of the concept of the body in Beckett.

"The body" has a very particular urgency as it is represented, or rather as it is present on stage, in drama. The seminal essay which depicts the "presence" of the body in Beckett's writings is a short article by Pierre Chabert "The Body in Beckett's Theatre." In his essay, Chabert distinguishes the stock, typical use, of the actor's body by dramatists to reveal psychological states. Against the use of the body as a defensive mechanism, Beckett presents the body as being

> worked, violated even, much as the raw materials of the painter or sculptor, in the service of a systematic exploration of all possible relationships between the body and movement, the body and space, the body and objects . . . and the body and words. (23)

Focusing on the facticity of the body as reviled and abused, Chabert sees the body in Beckett as defined by "lack." The situatedness of Beckett's character shows them as "always exist[ing] in a state of lack or negativity" (24). Being unable to see or be seen, their condition adds to the dramatic force of their body's presence on stage. Chabert argues that "it is the distinction of the Beckettian stage to translate everything into specific physical terms" (26), and that, "in Beckett's theatre, the body is the object of an exploration and a dramatization unprecedented in theatrical history" (28). Pierre Chabert's own concerns seem to do with realism on stage, but in effect, he has highlighted an astute point about Beckett's theatre.

In Beckett's plays, there is no definable meaning located within the text as there is no physical space within which the contents of the drama are played out. It is only the body of the actors that forms the physical space within which the narrative is enacted. In the theatre itself, the performing bodies of the artists foreground the physical presence of the characters. Despite the epistemological lie of the fictional character of theatre, the continuing presence of the artists grounds the experience of the audience in the concrete particularity of the bodily. Alain Robbe-Grillet's concept of "thereness," of "being-there" or "realism of presence," was meant to demonstrate the intensely embodied nature of Beckett's theatre. Pierre Chabert's very illuminating critical piece—growing in great part out of his association with Beckett as a director of his plays—aligns him with Robbe-Grillet and others who have commented insightfully on embodiment in Beckett's theatre.

Pierre Chabert's representation of violence carried out upon the body leads to an important consideration of Beckett's drama as political play, a feature commented on by Beckett scholars who take recourse to current theoretical discourses of performativity to describe Beckett's politicization of the body.[4] This significant dimension of Beckett's plays has been discussed in an excellent article, "Beckett's Actor," by W.B. Worthen who has focused attention on the actual forms of performance. In so doing, Worthen demonstrates how Beckett "literalizes" the predicament of his characters in the tangibly straitened conditions in which they perform on stage, thus "dramatizing the essential dynamics of stage performance" (420). Through the medium of the actor's body, theatre is able to achieve the necessary "counterpoise between self and role, presence and absence" (420), even as Beckett reduces the audience to a role, and the characters to a mouthpiece. Worthen's incisive analysis of the political manipulation of the body reveals the post-Cartesian theatre as disrupting the very notion of a self in the tension between the discursively-defined, disembodied self in the text, and the insistent bodily presence in the theatre. A representative case of bodily politics is Beckett's *Catastrophe* with its confrontation between the private, textualized, Cartesian self and the subversive nature of the body repressed and censored. I disagree with the deployment of dualistic terminologies in both Pierre Chabert and William Worthen's arguments as restraining the full play of the material body in Beckett's theatre. Nonetheless, I have found W.B. Worthen's essay useful for my third chapter, where I have tried to show how the traditional structures of identity offered by the dominant forms of representation and authority are assaulted and undermined through the dynamic of the body.

The body as it configures in Beckett has been, as I have shown, investigated by some scholars, but readings supported by a theoretical or methodological framework encompassing his entire corpus have yet to be systematically attempted. Without espousing faith in any particular critical theory or creed, without privileging the need for any particular "political" valence, marxist, feminist, postcolonial, or otherwise, I only wish to use the opportunities offered by current theoretical practices to bridge the gaps between them in an eclectic way. I find most attractive—because most usable and revealing—an alliance of the traditional existentialist reading of Beckett with the more recent, postmodern position within the conceptual apparatus of phenomenological embodiment.

My project is an attempt to engage with the critical interpretations that perceive Beckett's presentation of the body as either rooted within a Cartesian self, which is still a modernist conception of the self, or as a surface without depth, a postmodern configuration. I aim to negotiate a via media which will accommodate that which seems to me the most legitimate way of perceiving Beckett, the "last Modernist" as well as the "first Postmodernist" (John Fletcher calls him "postmodernly modern to the last"). Postmodernist writers, working on the bodily inscription of social markers such as gender, sexuality, class, race, ethnicity, and age, are exploring the reconceptualization of the body under the influence of information technologies. For the postmodernists, the body is not only part of or "in" their texts, but is also inscribed by the social practices and markers they explore. There is no "grand narrative" of the body as exists in the Cartesian project. Nevertheless, the disparate sources of postmodernist interest in the theorization of the body lead to the breakdown of older notions of the body as a coherent and unified entity, defined and regulated by dualisms such as mind/body, male/female, human/animal. The fluid nature of the social reality in which the polymorphous body is positioned remakes the body in new and different ways. This becomes an important concern of my study.

Again to a large extent, my reading of "the body in Beckett" is postmodernist in the sense I read and understand postmodernism: as a thrusting forth of possibilities minus all element of political tendentiousness. But if it is true that there are no fixed relationships, and no fixed meanings, then I too could change relationships from within relationships, meanings from within meanings. Derrida argues that language has two dimensions: "presence," in which meaning is stable and fixed, and "difference" where within an infinite form of difference, there can be no possibility of any individual meaning. With this lead given by Derrida, I hope to argue a case for bodily "presence" in Beckett's works. I believe that if the concern of the protagonists in Beckett with the "ideal core" of mental reality leads them to impatience with physical reality, then there are many more layers to be unfolded before the "ideal core" can be reached.

While ideas about the subject and subjectivity have been linked to particular forms of representation at least since Descartes, the emerging forms of postmodernism point toward the radical dissolution of the subject as it has been known to be represented. Subjectivity is no longer understood as a phenomenon of an essential interiority containing a mind or a soul. Beckett's writings participate in this postmodernist notion of the subject by giving free play to the representation of the body from both within and without. In postmodernist writings, the concept of "self," "character," or "identity" is subverted by a textual play of repetitions and displacements. The complex relational structure between what can be called "character" in the older modernist sense, and the recognizable postmodern disjunction with realistic modes of fiction becomes pronounced, in the entropic, decaying and disordered, rather surreal landscapes of the Beckettian kind of writing. The concomitant rejection of humanism is a rejection, not so much of abstract ideas of "man" as the set of assumptions, of meaning, of value, that go into the making of a literary work.

What the classic modernist writers like Lawrence, Joyce, Woolf, or Pound had to suggest as an alternative to the shattering of the ego, the atomizing of the subject, was the apprehension of a more integrated self, of new modes of being and perception. They could never completely give up the idea, or the desirability, of identity altogether: they could only hope to expand its frame of reference. As against the modernist possibility of a larger sense of identity, the postmodernist conception is one of a decentered structure with the individual as the site of transindividual singularities. Beckett is arguably the central European writer in that transition from modernism to postmodernism, that paradigm shift between the first signs of breakdown and the eventual complete dissolution of ego boundaries. If I can state the case as baldly as that, I would locate Beckett's retention of at least one major character if not more, struggling with the boundaries of his identity, even at the risk of his sanity as the locus point of that imminent change. The narrators of Beckett's writings cannot be acccepted as mere fictional voices. They do seem distinct individuals in their own right. Even the disembodied figures of Beckett's last works are in some sense, full-blown. The obsessive persistence of the same character and voice recycled through so many texts is an indication that the idea of "character" of naturalistic practice can still be traced in Beckett. It seems to me that Beckett is still constrained by the exigencies of representation to be able to abstract out a complete personality breakdown. It is this concern and persistence of character (in fact, if anything represents Beckett best, it is the names of his most well-known characters) that distinguishes him from the linguistic and tropological subversions of his postmodern contemporaries.

In handling such a vast subject, I am aware that I will be forced to overlook and brush aside many complexities. I am also aware that this vast subject compels me to reduce the career and writings of Beckett to, as it were, a single thematic reading. As a proleptic defense against that anticipated critique, I would argue that despite the length and variety of Beckett's career, spanning more than a half-century, there is a quality of deep, relentless consistency about all his writings. This is perceived in the carefully structured repetitions and reiterations of themes and ideas, action and episode, style and phrase, which bind together the diversity, generic, linguistic or thematic, of his work. From his early *Whoroscope* written by a young man in his twenties, and in the twenties, to his late *Worstward Ho* written by an old man approaching his eighties, and in the eighties, is a broad span. Nonetheless, there are connections and links which I am not the first or only one to observe. In Beckett's own words, his characters reenact "over and over again" what has gone before. Among these links and connections, among the plenitude of repetitions and resonances, is the persistent presence of the body which runs through all of Beckett's writings, the primacy of the phenomenological body whose varied manifestations and aspects form the subject of my book. And if "The Body in Beckett" seems such a large and overriding term, I have consciously made it so, in order to prove, over and over again, the preeminent sense of the body dominating Beckett's writings.

NOTES

1. The critical response to the issue of Beckett and Cartesianism, registered in the Sixties, primarily by Ruby Cohn, John Fletcher, Richard

Coe, Robert Harrison, and Michael Robinson, and in the Seventies, by Edouard Morot-Sir, Lawrence Harvey and David Hesla, among many others, was largely inspired by Hugh Kenner.

2. Beckett the phenomenologist, has many subscribers, most notably Lance St John Butler, David Hesla, Alain Robbe-Grillet, Andrew Kennedy, Sidney Homan, and Thomas Whitaker.

3. Ihab Hassan was among the first Beckett scholars to encode Beckett within a postmodernist paradigm. Programmatically committed to a poststructuralist reading of Beckett's works, Steven Connor, Herbert Blau, Paul Bove, Angela Moorjani, Stephen Barker, Leslie Hill, David Watson, Carla Locatelli, Iain Wright, Theodor Adorno, Peter Gidal, Stanley Cavell, Sylvie Debevec Henning, Paul Davies, and Richard Begam have also, indirectly, offered perspectives on the "body" theme.

4. Sheila Rabillard and Anna Mcmullan have persuasively shown how the theatrical undermining of the body in Beckett's plays, as an object to be manipulated through the mechanisms of control and discipline, extends to the challenging of the repressive mechanisms of logocentric representation.

CHAPTER ONE

The Body-Mind Connection and the World of *Murphy*, *Watt* and *Molloy*

"*The essence of Dasein lies in its existence*"
Martin Heidegger, *Being and Time*

The problematic of the human body generates a powerful discourse in the writings of Samuel Beckett. The foregrounding of the "inscribed" body in Beckett not only offers a radical challenge to, and a subtle critique of, Cartesianism, but is also a rewriting and a reconfiguration of the psychosocial dynamics of human identity. Within the framework of the body's materiality, Beckett takes up the problem of dualism that Descartes explored in the seventeenth century. As his canon expands, Beckett establishes the theme of duality as an integral part of the structure of his works. I plan to show this by focusing primarily on *Murphy, Watt,* and *Molloy* in developing the argument of this chapter.

By explicitly grounding his writings in the human body, by rendering his characters incapable of total separation from the body and the purification of the mind that Descartes recommended, Beckett evolves a post-Cartesian universe in which binary oppositions are deconstructed. Beckett demystifies many metaphysical issues concerning the meaning of the word "I," the relation of the physical and the mental, and ultimately the nature of reality in formulating the concept of human identity. In my view, Beckett argues that if the mind is epistemologically primary to the body, its primacy is recognized only through the mediation of the body, and thus presupposes the recognition of the body.

In this sense, Beckett breaks down the traditional conceptual machinery of thinking in terms of binaries as inadequate terminologies that fail: he uses the binaries that are so ubiquitous a feature of his writings to deconstruct binaries. He uses the pervasive presence of sensory data in his writings to show that the existence of anything or anybody has to be inferred from the existence of directly experienced physicality. Beckett's crucial first premise then, would be that if the exercise of the mind is possible only when constructed out of physical perceptions and sensations, the body is as much a necessary condition for identity as the mind. Beckett's scepticism about any theory of identity which reduces the concept of identity to a set of absolute psychological or mental criteria is apparent in his critical pronouncements as well as his works. As he believes that certainty requires a mythology and a discourse to promote the romantic nature of all mythologies, he would rather do away with all certainties in his skepticism of the very basis of identity.

Although Beckett also questions the ultimate nature of the empirical evidence of personal identity, he knows that there is no escape from the pervasiveness of the bodily. In combating the mind-body dualism, Beckett concentrates on how it is impossible to erase the outline of the body, how it becomes a heresy to claim that the world is only a reflex of one's emotional self or a reduction of the ego.

By focusing intensely on physical facts, Beckett concretizes and makes more real the reality of bodily existence. I quite support the reading of Lance St John Butler who perceives the literary evocation of Heidegger's philosophical concept of "being-there" or "Dasein" in Beckett's writings, and believes that "the characters of the novels share this kind of contingent Being-Thereness, this presence" (11). Thus Molloy and Malone are "there" in their mothers' rooms, and the Unnamable is "there" in his immobile, static form. Watt, Murphy, Molloy, Moran, and Belacqua are all there, whether maimed or fixated in mud, dustbins, sand, jars, or wheelchairs. It is the restless energy and the resilient resourcefulness of their corporeal life that comes through, and not simply the vulnerability and fragility of the mental. Though these characters are literary creations, artifacts first and last, it is the sharp bodily feel of them that is their most outstanding aspect. Beckett exposes the difference between metaphysics and materialism in that the former starts from an assumption of judging the reality of things by a standard, while the latter insists upon concrete phenomena based on empirical knowledge. Beckett insists that to penetrate the unknown, one must follow the way already known, and the unknown, if it really exists, must be only a prolongation of the known. The cardinal principle of materialism is that sense perception is the foundation, although not the ultimate truth, of all knowledge. In one of his rare miscellaneous pronouncements published in *Disjecta*, Beckett has deemed intellection a "sensuous untidy art" (27). While the Western philosophical tradition, then, has tended to privilege the concept much more than the sensation, Beckett challenges one to rethink one's intellectual responses about the bodily sensations which the mental faculties convert into abstract ideas.

The extent to which the body authenticates identity is an issue Beckett addresses insistently in his writings. The keenness of sense reaction in Beckett is underscored by the intensity with which he focuses on human corporeality—the grotesque caricaturing of the human body, the physically decrepit, maimed, denatured and dismembered characters that proliferate in all his writings. Physically and emotionally homeless, moving like machines, "their great balls and sockets rattling and clacking," they are ageing characters, inhibited by sensory confusions and impediments, and shut up in dustbins, urns, jars, piles of sand, or bone of skull. Beckett's early characters find themselves fastened to cells and trash cans, and often eat and excrete into pots that are delivered and removed as required. Murphy is discovered tied to his rocking chair by seven scarves, Watt is caged in by wounds that never heal, Molloy and Malone are rendered immobile in their rooms, while the Unnamable gradually disintegrates physically. Molloy and Moran become crippled, Malone cannot even crawl, Mahood is barely head and torso, and the Unnamable is left a voice drifting in the void. In his later and subsequent writings, we shall observe the phenomena of bodily absence and refusal, of characters who often emerge beyond their graves to relive their bodily selves in a curious foregrounding and reinforcing of the presence of the body.

If, as the ontological argument goes, all realist constructs must necessarily be reductionist, the integrity and stability of the body can never be more than an ideal. Beckett sets upon himself to challenge such a construct in the dual rupture of the body's spaces, as well as the connection between body and mind. The fragile connection of body and mind is reinforced, as if by negation, by showing the loss of an integrated comprehensible structure that relates the body to the world outside.

The rooms and houses pervading Beckett's writings become

metaphors for the head: Murphy's garret, Molloy's mother's room, Malone's room with six planes of solid bone, the interiorized world of the Unnamable, Watt's thinking of himself "as a box, or an urn" (83). Beckettian creatures are often torn apart as they, Murphy-like, struggle to free themselves of the bodily "cage" of this phenomenal world. There are repeated and, of course, critically significant references to what the narrator of *The Unnamable* calls "the inside of my distant skull where once I wandered" (20). The hero of "The Calmative" more baldly states: "We are needless to say in a skull" (43). The skull is perceived often as a confined place, the "ivory dungeon" in *Texts for Nothing*, and in *Malone Dies*, the "foul little den all dirty white and vaulted, as though hollowed out of ivory" (63). In *That Time*, the examination of the mind becomes a search for one's identity: "not knowing who you were from Adam no notion who it was saying what you were saying whose skull you were clapped up in. . . " (231). But even this attempted withdrawal into the mental is inescapably imbued with the physical; for, if the head figures and contains the mind, it is also true that the head is part of the body to which everything and everyone eventually returns.

The turning inward of the mind upon itself is perhaps the most characteristic feature of Descartes's thinking, and its true manifestation is, of course, the "cogito"—the mind's initial apprehension of its own existence. What one believes about one's mind cannot be false, according to Descartes, though even the belief that one has a body could be false. The conviction that one is essentially a conscious, mental thing, a "thinking substance" leads to the Cartesian insistence upon the independence of the mind from the body. This has also driven a wedge in western culture between subject and object, self and other, reason and emotion, mind and body, at the same time that it has implicitly polarized gender relations.

Many of Beckett's characters hold that one's knowledge of oneself as thinking being is primary and non-sensory. Consequently, they attempt to withdraw from their physicality. Strongly grounded as they are in their Cartesian beliefs, they believe their non-sensory awareness of the nature of the body itself is superior to the knowledge gained by direct sensory apprehension. The Cartesian-minded Murphy strives to exclude all perceptions of "the vicissitudes of the body" (109) as he seeks sanctuary within his mind, "a large hollow sphere, hermetically closed to the universe without" (107) which he naively supposes to be a source of "unique delight." He perceives himself as a creature composed of the apparently contradictory elements of mind and body, and he decides that his only freedom is in the mind, which is also the only area he can control. The story of Murphy's retreat from the physical realm into the inner recesses of the mind is, in a sense, the story of Beckett's quarrel with Cartesian dualism. In *Murphy*, the image of mind "not as instrument but as place" is described from the outside, by a third-person narrative voice who describes the after-effects of venturing into these "pleasure-zones."

Written at an early stage of Beckett's literary career, *Murphy* can be said to contain the essence and embryo of virtually everything that Beckett's subsequent protagonists discover in their flight from their physical selves. Murphy is eager to escape the bodily "cage " or the "big world" to which he believes he does not belong—or so "he fondly hopes" (2). Fundamentally indifferent to the whole system of "pensums and prizes," he refuses not only to earn a living, but also to associate in any meaningful manner with the outer world. He endeavours to sit "out of it"—that is, "the big, blooming buzzing confusion" (4) of the phenomenal world—by annihilating the physical part of himself, "which he hated" (8). In his younger years, Murphy had been a student of theology, and he still tries to impose explanations on the world. The narrator of *Murphy*, however, makes a significant distinction between "the world" and Murphy's conceptualization of it:

> Happily we need not concern ourselves with this apparatus as it really was—that would be an extravagance and an impertinence—but solely with what it felt and pictured itself to be. (107)

Descartes theorizes that the connection between body and mind is at the site of the pineal gland. Murphy exhibits an anxiety only to escape one for the other, from the confusion of the macrocosm without to the sacrosanct microcosm of his mind within. "Clothed" only in his thoughts, he envisions life in the phenomenal world as simply a "passing through," even as his pineal gland has been reduced to "nothing" as a result of Murphy's battle against the "physical fact" of his body. As Neary states, Murphy's "conarium [the pineal gland] has shrunk to nothing" (6). To Murphy, the body is the mind's curse, from which he struggles to get freedom in order to achieve the impossible ecstasy in the mind which offers "such pleasure that pleasure was not the word" (2). Although Murphy feels that his body can "think and know after a fashion sufficient for his parody of rational behaviour" (110), physical motion must be performed "carefully" and with an awareness that the necessary energy might dissipate "before he had half ended" (138). For Murphy, a true sense of freedom can exist only when the body is still and the mind can move freely through its various zones. Murphy believes that his freedom is in the mind, and that he should therefore focus only on the mental sphere and ignore the parameters of the external world which includes the body, and which is impossible to control. Increasingly disenchanted with even astrological predictions as determined by bodily changes, he distances himself from all physical phenomena, calling them "a murk of irritation" (105).

Murphy's mind imagines itself to be "a large hollow sphere, hermetically closed to the universe without" (107). Murphy believes

> that his mind was a closed system, subject to no principle of change but its own, self-sufficient and impermeable to the vicissitudes of the body. (109)

Like his mind, his clothing is "hermetically closed," and the non-porous suit "admitted no air from the outer world, it allowed none of Murphy's own vapours to escape" (72). Seeking complete self-enclosure, Murphy has trained himself to acquire a state that lies beyond desire—the absence of the will, that "nothing, that colourlessness which is such a rare post-natal treat" (246). He believes himself to be aware of the actual structure of his mind, or of "what he liked to call his mind." By transferring the structure of his mind into symbols, he hopes to connect the negative or void of his inner self, with the rational world outside. And by relying on the supreme virtue of silence, he is able to abandon the entrapment of the intellect within the straitjacket of words.

Murphy is first presented to the reader as a prisoner of his body, lying face down in his rocking chair:

> Part by part he subsided, as the bonds that held him fell away, until he lay fully prostrate in the crucified position. . . . (28)

Like Belacqua, Murphy strives to sever all connections with the world of sense and outer meaning, since "Murphy believed there was no dark quite like his own dark." Keen to retire into the calm of his mind, he initially seeks external aids in reaching his goal of "checking the starry concave" (21), of releasing himself from his bodily self. His rocking chair is one such mechanical device; he ties himself to it with the help of scarves in order to rock himself to oblivion. The rocker lets his mind spin away from his body to "the freedom of that light and dark that did not clash, nor alternate, nor fade nor lighten except to their communion" (9).

At other times, Murphy, lies supine on the grass of Hyde Park for hours. He also looks for alternate methods of dulling his senses, such as walking "round and round Pentonville prison," or "round and round cathedrals that it was too late to enter" (54). Murphy's friends likewise engage in verbal or physical gestures to escape the "mess." There are the "alcoholic depressant" (41) preferred by Cooper, the "dingy stingy repose" (21) relished by Mr Kelly, or Celia's "clockwise" walks about the Round Pond in London. Murphy's former instructor, Neary, has tried to teach Murphy how to stop his irrational heart "in situations irksome beyond endurance," but "like Petrouchka in his box" (3), Murphy's heart fails to achieve what Neary calls "Apmonia" or "Isonomy" (4). Celia learns to distinguish Murphy from "a merely indolent man" since it is not "the frenzied justification of life as an end to means" (67) that he seeks. Like Belacqua, who can possess his beloved "truly and totally" only when she "fidget[s] in the catacombs of his spirit," Murphy reckons with his mind "not as an instrument but as a place" (178). Just as Belacqua's hunger is "more of mind," his "four-penny lunch was a ritual vitiated by no base thoughts of nutrition" (80). He is a dualist who evidently seems "ashamed of being in a body" which can, according to him, never work in tandem with his mind. He persistently attempts, therefore, to elude the habitual world of phenomena which resembles "a well with two buckets . . . one going down to be filled, the other coming up to be emptied" (58).

Murphy himself echoes, and is philosophically influenced by Arnold Geulincx, a seventeenth-century Belgian Cartesian who believed that every bodily act is "occasioned" by God's intervention between mind and body, that we do not possess the ability to initiate bodily action, but are free to imagine whatever we wish to. Using the analogy of two buffer clocks representing matter and spirit within synchronous but unconnected systems, the "Occasionalist" philosophy of Geulincx separated the two even more radically than did the philosophy of Descartes. Murphy, "that schizoidal spasmophile" (49), admits "partial congruence . . . as due to some process of supernatural determination" (109)—the stars. Closer to Geulincx than to Descartes, Murphy places the physical hierarchically below the mental where, he thinks, the inner self and its true reality are to be discovered. The calculated indifference of Murphy to the events of the external world is in the direct tradition of Geulincx's proposition that, in view of external impotence, one can achieve autonomy only in the mind.

Murphy is acutely aware of the distinction between what he calls "the big world" and "the little world" (178) of his mind where he wishes to enjoy his freedom. But the "mental Murphy" cannot make his escape until the "physical Murphy" is appeased. Hence, he repeatedly experiments in transcending his physical confines, the unenchanting "underground of his habitation" (38). He therefore flees from his former mistresses as well as his confidants. But, comically, the corporeal demands of Murphy's body, "his deplorable susceptibility to Celia, ginger, and so on" (179), tempt him back into "the big world," and he consequently "[feels] himself split in two, a body and a mind" (109). The former prostitute Celia, of course, seems to remind him all too tangibly of the existence of his body. Murphy cannot reconcile his need for "self-immersed indifference to the contingencies of the contingent world" (168) with his craving for Celia. According to Celia, the reason she wants Murphy is that he alone is not "defiled" by "the crass and unharmonious unison, the mind at the cart-tail of the body, the body at the chariot-wheels of the mind" (218).

Celia is, of course, an aspect of the external world from which Murphy endeavours to escape. He knows he repulses her from that mental aspect of himself that he loves, yet nonetheless, he loves her from that physical aspect of himself he is repulsed by. Caught in this bind, his mind functions independently of the "ethical yoyo" (76), and "could not be disposed according to a principle of worth" (77). Murphy constantly falls back into the world of the senses: the mere ring of the telephone takes him back to Celia. Murphy's emphasis is not on the mind "as it really was . . . but solely with what it felt and pictured itself to be" (76). Of a subjective cast thus, it is subject to his individual perception of reality. "Nothing," Murphy is convinced,

> ever had been, was or would be in the universe outside [the mind] but was already present as virtual, or actual, or virtual rising into actual, or actual falling into virtual, in the universe inside it. (76)

The narrator describes Murphy's mind in Chapter Six, which most compellingly brings alive the Cartesian construct. Murphy's mind imagines itself to be a hollow sphere where there are "three zones, light, half light, dark, each with its speciality" (111). The elaborate description of the self-contained universe of the mind of Murphy has this epigraph: "amor intellectualis quo Murphy se ipsum amat," that is, the intellectual love with which Murphy loves himself. Finding himself a Nothing in the outer world, Murphy withdraws into the inner, "where he could love himself" (7). Murphy's binding himself to a chair to make his body quiescent and thus sustaining himself unshackled in his mind is a comic distortion of Descartes's cocooning himself in his stove in order to navigate his mind toward the truth of his own existence.

There are three zones in Murphy's mind. The first zone, the zone of light, is that mode where mental experience is "parallel" with physical experience. Murphy regards it as merely "a radiant abstract of the dog's life. . . . Here the whole physical fiasco became a howling success" (111). This is because here he can enjoy complete sovereignty in reconstituting his world according to his own imaginative wishes. This region contains "the world of the body broken up into the pieces of a toy" (112), as well as the potential for revenge. The pleasure experienced here is that of reprisal, the pleasure of reversing experience when the kick the physical Murphy received the mental Murphy returns. Here he can, with smugness, exact revenge for the blows of this cruel world, even exposing "Miss Carridge for rape by Ticklepenny, and so on" (111).

In the second zone are "the forms without parallel," where the pleasure is that of "contemplation," "the Belacqua bliss" (111). The sense of contemplation and beatitude is akin to Blake's "Beulah" state when even thought ceases though disconnected visual images float before the eyes. Here Murphy indulges his "Belacqua fantasy" of believing himself in Antepurgatory. Murphy dreams of being released by death into the inaction of Antepurgatory where he will sit in "embryonal repose, looking down at dawn across the reeds to the trembling of the austral sea" (56). Several of Beckett's other protagonists also experience the infinite peace discovered at the seashore: Beckett the poet in the four Dieppe poems, Henry in *Embers*, and, most famously of course, Molloy who recalls that "Much of my life has ebbed away before this shivering expanse" (92).

Murphy, however, is not content with the first two zones of his mind. It is the last zone, of the dark, to which he aspires, where in a perfectly beatific sense, Murphy believes he will become "a point in the ceaseless unconditioned generation and passing away of line" (112). In other words, he will lose all sense of identity here, and even cease to be Murphy. Here the virtual will rise into actual and actual fall into virtual in "a perpetual coming together and falling asunder of forms" (112). The dark here is characterized by "a flux of forms" (112). Here he believes he will be able to become "a mote in the dark of absolute freedom" (113). Murphy wishes to "enter the landscape" where he would be "improved out of knowledge" and where his will would be "dust in the dust of its object" (105). In this dark, will-less zone, Murphy thinks of becoming a part of nothingness. Hence, this third, dark zone grows more and more attractive to him, and he spends less time in revengeful daydreams in the light or in blissful contemplation in the half-light.

In the dark of the third zone, Murphy hopes to achieve an "immunity" that goes beyond all forms of experientia that Belacqua in *Dream of Fair to Middling Women* (107) conceptualizes as "the apex of ecstasy" (165). Beckett's later characters, Molloy, Malone and the Unnamable, also occupy themselves in reaching this non-personal self which is simultaneously nothingness and infinite. Whereas the first zone of light contains figures, "the world of the body broken up" into pieces, and the second zone of half-light contains "states of peace," the dark zone contains neither subject nor object, only the "absolute freedom" attained when there is no freedom at all and no subjective being. To Murphy, the third zone is akin to "the sensation of being a missile without provenance or target, caught up in a tumult of non-Newtonian motion" (112-13).

This third state or zone of complete will-lessness and desirelessness has many variants. It has been perceived by some Beckett scholars as corresponding to the "Nirvana" stage in Buddhist philosophy which Schopenhauer popularized in the West. Posing as a kind of acme, all conflict between self and other is completely resolved here. In the first two zones, Murphy feels "sovereign and free, in the one to requite himself, in the other to move as he pleased. . . ." (112). However, in the third zone, he is motionless, and contrary to his expectations, not really free as he is caught up in the actual/virtual flux. Whereas the first two zones occur on the surface of the mind, the light becomes increasingly dim as he submerges into what he believes is the oblivion of the third zone:

> Thus as his body set him free more and more in his mind, he took to spending less time in the light, sitting at the breakers of the world. . . . (113)

He is quite sure that the dark zone offers the greatest possible autonomy from all desire, the greatest possible release from phenomenal reality.

Later in the novel, Murphy believes he has gained his opportunity to enter the dark zone permanently when he finds employment at the Magdalen Mental Mercyseat. At the head of Chapter Nine, in which Murphy starts his work as a nurse in the mental asylum, Beckett places an epigraph: "It is difficult for one who lives outside of the world not to seek his own kind" (156). For Murphy, "his own kind" are the mental patients whom he assumes "one and all to be having a glorious time" as he perceives them with their "self-immersed indifference to the contingencies of the contingent world" and confined to their "indoor bowers of bliss" (168). While he is among the patients, Murphy recalls the words of Geulincx: "Ubu nihil velis, ibi nihil velis"—where you are worth nothing, there you should want nothing. It is in order to achieve a state of nothingness beyond physical desire and want that Murphy seeks to enter the world of these inmates of the mental asylum. He must bridge the "unintelligible gulf" that he feels exists between himself and them. He also needs a key to gain access to the dark zone: "It was as though the microcosmopolitans had locked him out." Here, among the "higher schizoids" (180), he finally meets exemplars of what seems to him to be a state of mind in which one is totally disconnected from the world of time, space, and desire.

At the mental asylum, Murphy resists the scientific donnee according to which contact with outer reality is a symptom of mental well-being. He is reluctant to bridge the gulf between the inner and the outer which the patients themselves are unable to synchronize:

> His experience as a physical and rational being obliged him to call sanctuary what the psychiatrists called exile and to think of the patients not as banished from a system of benefits but as escaped from a colossal fiasco. (177-78)

The asylum's padded cells stand for that part of the mind Murphy is eager to retreat into when he succumbs to the forces of the mind:

> Within the narrow limits of domestic architecture he had never been able to imagine a more creditable representation of what he kept on calling, indefatigably, the little world. (181)

Although Beckett has written sympathetically of mental illness, especially in his essay on *Proust*, Murphy's admiration for the mental patients of MMM is not shared by Beckett who gives an ironic treatment of Murphy's enthusiastic association with them as "vicarious autology" (189). Even Murphy himself must acknowledge that the inmates of the asylum are as much prone to "outbursts," to "frequent expressions . . . of pain, rage, despair, and in fact all the usual" (179) as those outside it. More importantly, he cannot determine whether they really have been able to attain their mental paradise, or offer mere automated responses to their sorry condition. But Murphy tries to perpetuate his illusion of the happiness of the insane in order that, "stimulated by all those lives immured in mind, as he insisted on supposing," he might labor "at his own little dungeon in Spain" (180).

The inmates cannot admit him into their kind of mental peace although they do manage to differentiate him as belonging to their tribe. As against the "therapeutic vexations" they suffer at the hands of the tormenting medical staff of MMM, they have the perception to see him as a sympathizer but not as an insider. Reminiscent of Ibsen's *Peer Gynt*, the inmates are also subject to the "pain, rage, despair and in fact all the usual" (124) which memory evokes, and the "inner voices" which produce "the mental belch" (158). Troubled by what the narrator refers to now as "a fly somewhere in the ointment of Microcosmos" (124), Murphy gradually reaches a point where he actually desires abandoning "the little world" (125).

Murphy's responsibilities as the custodian of the asylum enable him to meet Mr. Endon whose name implies "within," a man with a "tiny body" and a "skull, large for any body, immense for this" (186). Dressed in a scarlet dressing gown, with rings on his fingers, Mr. Endon appears to Murphy as the embodiment of the dark zone. Murphy is drawn to Mr. Endon as "Narcissus to his fountain." With this "schizophrenic of the most amiable variety," Murphy plays a chess game in which he tries to engage Mr. Endon's attention, but in which the totally self-absorbed Mr. Endon takes no notice of the positions of his opponent. The game is started in the morning, and "evening found it almost as level as when begun" (187). Since neither player engages his pieces in conflict, there is never an endgame, and nothing is decided. The game removes Murphy to the nearly timeless realm he has dreamed of: "Time did not cease, that would be asking too much, but the wheel of rounds and pauses did." After this chess-game without victory, Murphy looks deep into the eyes of his presumed double. Gazing into Mr. Endon's eyes, Murphy sees, "in the cornea, horribly reduced, obscured and distorted, his own image" (249). Murphy sees Murphy, but Mr. Endon does not. Again, he tries to establish contact, but he is forced to the recognition that he is a mere "speck in Mr. Endon's unseen" (250). He realizes that no contact can be made, nor can he ever will himself to be Mr. Endon: "The last Mr. Murphy saw of Mr. Endon was Mr. Murphy unseen by Mr. Endon. This was also the last Murphy saw of Murphy" (250).

Murphy's despair after this gaze stems from the recognition of his inability ever to reach the Endon state. The experience with Mr. Endon destroys Murphy's illusion about being able to "disconnect his mind from the gross importunities of sensation and reflection" (105). In Mr. Endon, he finds the "ground . . . free of figure," pure ground without figure, objectivity without subject, and this becomes an extraordinarily shattering experience for him. Murphy is led to ponder that although it may be possible for him to come alive in his mind, it is not possible to break off completely from the body. Indeed, the very desire to make contact with the "mental" Mr. Endon is, paradoxically, a sign of Murphy's continuing physical needs. In alternate terms, Murphy realizes that those "immured in the mind" (125) do not simply have "a glorious time" (124) fathoming its "unique delights" (123). Unable to plumb the "inner coils," all he can perceive is a vista Murphy envisages as "Scraps of bodies, of landscapes, hands, eyes, lines and colours evoking nothing" (172).

They rise before him "as though reeled upward off a spool level with his throat." And "it was his experience that this should be stopped, whenever possible, before the deeper coils were reached" (172). Murphy cannot establish any interdependency with Endon who is prone to "lay back and [fix] his eyes on some object immeasurably remote, perhaps the famous ant on the sky of an airless world" (248). The pupil and the white of Endon's eyes are sutured by the "spawn-like" iris in order to make the eye have three parts: dark, light, and neither. Endon's iris is reduced

> so like a ballrace between the black and white that these could have started to rotate in opposite directions, or better still the same direction, without causing Murphy the least surprise. (249)

In following through this movement, Murphy has arrived at the experience of nothingness, that is, the absence of being perceived. Then when he makes himself appear and disappear in Endon's eyes, he does see his own distorted reflection in the cornea, but also that he was unperceived by Endon, who could only see himself. As Murphy collapses, and as he alerts himself to the truth of his own "yellow spot," Endon is free to play a precise "amental pattern" on another cell's light switch. As yet a "prisoner of air," Murphy looks into Endon's eyes "across a narrow gulf of air" and withers.

When Murphy looks into Endon's schizophrenic eyes, "across a narrow gulf of air," he realizes that he is unbeheld by Endon who can see only himself. This is what Murphy had imagined for himself in the third zone, but being replicated in the mirror-image of Endon, he is filled with despair. His despair stems from the fact that he cannot will himself into Mr. Endon's state, and that the latter always remains a stranger for him. It is also his one moment of recognition when he realizes that he had willed himself into a state of mental alienation so complete that it had closed the gap he had always sought between his mind and his body. The belief in indifference which Murphy has assumed would lead to oneness with Endon is another kind of immoderation from which he has all along been fleeing. Intensely dejected by "seeing himself stigmatized in those eyes that did not see him" (170-71) and failing to make contact, Murphy withdraws from Endon "without reluctance and without relief" (171). His acute "torment of mind" has led to the experience of "Nothing":

> His . . . senses . . . found themselves at peace, an unexpected pleasure. Not the numb peace of their own suspension, but the positive peace that comes when the somethings give way, or simply add up, to Nothing. (168)

Even though Murphy has achieved the power of "Nothing," he has also simultaneously realized that "seeing" with his mind's eye cannot procure for him pure or a complete sense of freedom, that it isn't really any kind of Cartesian celebration of the mind. He is sensitive to the fact that his imagination is not absolutely within his control, just as he is aware that in the third zone of his mind, he has not been able to attain any true freedom. He cannot get rid of "the mortal mange." "The fire will not depart from his eye, nor the water from his mouth, as he scratches himself out of one itch into the exit" (201-2). As he begins to accommodate himself to the loss of his illusion, "Murphy felt incandescent." The phenomena of light and colour is associated with moments of release which Beckett has explained in *Proust* as "explosive, 'an immediate, total and delicious deflagration'" (20). Murphy's effort to shed his clothes, to lie on the hospital grounds after leaving Endon, evidences his belief in the spurious freedom his search for an inner self has helped him attain.

Just before his death by asphyxiation, Murphy discovers that he could not get a picture in his mind of any creature he had met, animal or human. He is closer now to the ground of things where there is neither self nor world, only genuine figurelessness. Seeking perfect detachment from the outer world of things, he has tried to immure himself within his own mind, but he discovers, in this closing moment, a powerful nostalgia for that outer world. The fiction of his sovereign mind has collapsed, scattered, just as the kite snaps its string and flies out of sight at the end of *Murphy*, a parodic version of the soul's escape. Murphy's experiment in self-isolation—his retreat into the Magdalen Mental Mercyseat—ends in a gruesome death by explosion when he pulls the wrong lavatory chain, resulting in the release of gas instead of water. He blows up in an explosion of dust, gas, charcoal, "superfine chaos."

Following this exposition of the Cartesian dilemma in *Murphy*, I will only briefly discuss my views on Beckett's *Watt* where the writer parodies and caricatures the logical exercises of sanity.

Through a facetiously philosophical style, Beckett here exposes the hollowness of any pretense at certainty and simultaneously offers to Watt as well as to the reader a field of unlimited possibilities in which many alternatives are equally available.

While Murphy quests for escape into the world of the mind, Watt searches for meaning. Watt is about ten years older than Murphy, and is also "probably a University man" like Murphy. Watt has a grotesque exterior and his ridiculously precise gait, a "funambulistic stagger" (31), and his slow-healing skin, starkly contrast with that which happen outside the habits of his mind. A rationalist, Watt is painfully aware of all that takes place around him: what he sees, hears, smells and feels. But the results of his close observations lead to no explanation of "meaning" in spite of the systematic manner in which he tries to explain and give shape to the phenomena he observes. Watt observes reality, but only to deny it as existing except in terms of his "system." Believing in reason, Watt tries to explain the order in which he involves himself, but the explanation remains elusive. He attempts to impose rational patterns even in the mundane situation of a locked backdoor or a bell ringing, but his ratiocinations collapse under the stress of their own pseudo-syllogistic twists and turns. This results in the "dianoetic laugh . . . the laugh of laughs, the risus purus" (48), described by Arsene, Watt's predecessor at Mr. Knott's house. While the ethical and intellectual laughs point towards that which is not good and not true, the dianoetic laugh is directed at the "excoriations of the understanding" (48). Arsene, who is just completing his stay at Mr Knott's house as Watt arrives there, warns Watt of his "quite useless wisdom so dearly won." Arsene's farewell speech relates to the unreliability of conventional meanings:

> What we know partakes in no small measure of the nature of what has so happily been called the unutterable or ineffable, so that any atttempt to utter or eff it is doomed to fail, doomed, doomed to fail. (62)

Arsene correctly guesses that Watt is a compulsive speculator in the tradition of Descartes's "cogito ergo sum."

At Mr. Knott's house, all of Watt's expectations to define the meaning of things come to naught. His desire that things conform to those neat concepts that reason brings with its presumed ordering of the world fails to "foist a meaning there where no meaning exists" (74). The need experienced by Watt for a meaning is so acute that he attempts various names for things "almost as a woman hats" (90). However, Watt's reason does not allow him to go beyond surface appearances, as happens in the case of the piano tuners: "The most meagre, the least plausible, would have satisfied Watt, . . . who had lived, miserably it is true, among face values all his adult life, face values at least for him" (70). There are other parallel episodes in the novel which reveal how Watt's reason leads him nowhere. Thus the steps of Mr. Knott's house, "now long, and now short, and now broad, and now narrow" (126) keep changing. Even the appearance of Mr. Knott changes: "For one day Mr. Knott would be tall, fat, pale and dark, and the next thin, small, flushed and fair. . . " (230). Since Watt's reasoning is the ground of his existence, Watt eventually learns that his existence which is completely enclosed within his mind, breaks down with the breakdown of the rational structures of his mind. Even a pot stops being a pot for Watt, the longer he contemplates it: "It resembled a pot, it was almost a pot, but it was not a pot of which one could say, Pot, pot, and be comforted" (89). His efforts to superimpose the rational constructions of his mind on the irrational world prove futile, and he fails to "penetrate the forces at play . . . or even perceive the forms they upheaved, or obtain the least useful information concerning himself, or Mr Knott" (117).

Watt's need for certainty is a need to chalk out the boundaries of the mind and of the world. In the arbitrarily unpredictable structuring of *Watt*, Watt's assumptions are repeatedly undercut, no matter how many hypotheses he formulates or how many generations of "needy local men" he hypothesizes to guarantee the feeding of "two famished dogs." His indefatigable search for explanations—"For to explain had always been to exorcise, for Watt" (85)—gives a characteristic distinction to his thoughts. Watt undergoes an experience where he can no more make "a pillow of old words, for a head" (128), where the space between word and world widens. The more words Watt accumulates the less meaning he obtains. He finds himself in a situation in which matching words with objects becomes a meaningless exercise. The differences that individuate characters are described so meticulously and for so long that the differences become blurred and confused, and the result is grotesquely comic. The similarities among the characters and the mixup of names play on the issue of what constitutes identity. Watt's world is a defamiliarized one, and the defamiliarization extends to Watt himself, who must from time to time reassure himself of his own generic identity: "he found it a help, from time to time, to be able to say, with some appearance of reason, Watt is a man. . . " (89).

Watt's faith in Mr Knott as a demigod is exploded when the latter shows himself as irrationality incarnate, and his house, far from offering sustenance and security, mocks any systematic explanation of domesticity. Mr. Knott serves in many ways, the function for Watt that Mr Endon served for Murphy, and neither Murphy nor Watt ever recovers from the shaking effects of his experience. Increasingly, the "fragility of the outer meaning had a bad effect on Watt" (79), and he finds himself, as in the case of the pots, "in the midst of things which, if they consented to be named, did so as it were with reluctance" (89). Watt is then completely ground down by his experiences at Mr. Knott's house. He discovers that his self has insistently been subjected to reduction:

> He saw himself then, so little, so poor. And now, littler, poorer. Was not that something? . . . As the comparative is something. Whether more than its positive or less. Whether less than its superlative or more. (147)

Watt loses all knowledge about himself with the consequence that he appears as a total stranger to himself, "the laurel into Daphne", as Arsene puts it. Watt's scrupulous though piteously humble search for identity through rational methods results in acute anxiety and finally mental breakdown. But his confrontation and efforts at explication of events "of great formal brilliance and indeterminable support" (74) do not fail because of inherent inconsistencies in his system of logic. Rather, they fail because that system is irrevocably separated from the world of phenomena it is meant to describe. The contradictions in Watt's rationalizing quest are effectively placed by Arsene who knows that "[t]he glutton castaway, the drunkard in the desert, the lecher in prison, they are the happy ones" (48). Arsene's examples are reminders of the pure sense of being, of not finding meanings and significances where no meanings and significances exist. In this way, the anatomy of Watt's thoughts is gradually corroded and his hunger for the explaining formula is undermined.

Concerned about attaining "semantic succour" not with what events and figures are in reality, but only with what they appear to be, Watt's logic develops cracks. The divisions between inner and outer, between word and world, begin to disappear. The structures of logic are rendered useless in a hypothetical world divorced from empirical evidence. When the system of discrete identities collapse, Watt begins to feel the deprivations of the empirical truths of the objects he had tried to label and name in his nonrelational world.

Watt's regressive reasoning mirrors to him the truth that there is no source of ultimate meaning. Watt's schizoid flirting with the logical possibilities of the mind brings him back to his real self. He has allowed his desires, his thoughts, his everything to be translated by what is other than being. And in doing so, he was alienating himself from his own being. Like Descartes, Watt has taken refuge from the contingencies of temporality, experience, and the material character of the self. The escape Watt eventually realizes can never be complete. For in the very attempt to exclude all these things via a logical schema, Watt, Descartes-like, cannot help but include his exclusions. The Cartesian subject that Watt has become has cut him off from all empirical possibilities to a mere grammatical position, a pronoun, "Je pense" or "I think." It has blunted him to his own material, empirical, physical self. He must ultimately reject it for having failed to let him realize the possibilities of his self:

> He lay on the seat, without thought or sensation, except for a slight feeling of chill in one foot. In his skull the voices whispering their canon were like a patter of mice, a flurry of little grey paws in the dust. (232)

The formal order of rationalistic logic is only a schematic diagram that Watt's Cartesian subjectivity must project onto a space "within." The internal axiomatic of the self has never been reckoned with as a simulacrum of the self without. Watt's self thus emerges not as a unitary, locatable entity or identity, but as an aggregate or multiple of discursively elaborated locutionary positions. In eliminating outer reality by labelling it, he is condemned to being, in the last analysis, an unmediated being. As Watt tells Mercier and Camier, "I too have . . . sought all on my own, only I thought I knew what" (*Mercier and Camier*, 113-14).

Turning to *Molloy* now, the first novel of Beckett's trilogy, I wish to discuss Moran as a representative instance of Cartesianism, searching for his identity within. The reason why I choose not to discuss Molloy here is that Molloy never reveals any intense anxiety about escaping into the inner realm of thought. Moreover, Molloy's narrative, is a state of journeying in physical being. This is certainly not true of Moran who is perhaps the best example of the struggle in some of Beckett's characters, to assert the superiority of mind to body, only to end in some state of awareness of the impossibility of severing the two.

Moran's mind offers him a refuge from the contingencies and disasters of his body. Like Molloy, Moran is subject to "drown in the spray of phenomena" (151) when, "each pin-point of skin screams a different message." But unlike Molloy, Moran early in his narrative believes in a carefully reasoned, well-ordered system, and projects a compulsively neurotic need for causal explanations. Moran strives in his own narrative to obliterate anything that is random or inconceivable to a teleological imperative. His writing, unlike the narrative of Molloy, is orderly and precise and is in keeping with his claim, "I like punctuality" (133). Even amid the confusion of preparing to depart on his mission to find Molloy, Moran goes up to his room, stretches out on the bed, and takes a sensuous delight in the pleasures of the mind:

> I wandered in my mind, slowly noting every detail of the labyrinth, its paths as familiar as those of my garden and yet ever new, as empty as the heart could wish or alive with strange encounters. (144-45)

Like Murphy for whom the mind functions "not as an instrument but as a place," Moran retires far from the world, its clamours, frenzies, "bitterness and dingy light, . . . There somewhere man is too, vast conglomerate of all of nature's kingdoms, as lonely and as bound" (151). Self-sufficiently resting within his mind "where all I need is to be found," Moran thinks of his body "as a being apart," but is gradually compelled to review and revise his thoughts about that for which "his life has been nothing but a waiting." But while his character centers on certainty, Moran is profoundly ignorant of the uncertainties of his phenomenological self.

Prior to his receiving Youdi's message to search for Molloy,

Moran lives smugly among his possessions in a world that is so sensibly organized, ordered and arranged that it strikes one as a comic caricature and a beautiful parody of the entire Cartesian framework, psychologised and socialized. Faithfully adhering to his habits and duties, Moran insists that others, in particular his son and his housekeeper, must be meticulous in fulfilling their own duties. Moran's housekeeper looks after his house scrupulously by the clock, and his life is governed by a willed sense of reason and discipline in which institutionalized religion has a central place. In a parodic instance of his pride in his rationality, Moran declares: "I had a methodical mind and never set out on a mission without prolonged reflection as to the best way of setting out" (134). He certainly does not seem taken up by the Molloy-like sense of indifference to living and procreating, and, unlike Molloy, is fussy and conceited. His obsession with duty, profession and external appearance shows him to be a compulsive respecter of status, duty, and manners. He judges Father Ambrose severely for flattering himself "with being a man of the world and knowing its ways." By implication, Moran knows these ways better. Strict with his son and servant, Moran uses a moral vocabulary, perhaps, to reassure himself of his faith in the "falsetto of reason." Moran is inclined to emphasize his rationality in order to comfort himself of its firm guidance. For Moran, an individual is most reconciled with the social order when one is evidently subordinate to it. He dismisses self-doubt by means of his devotion to moral principles and order, of himself as "so meticulous and calm in the main." Narrow-mindedly exacting towards all, he is attached to his son, his house and garden in a precise manner. That he evades all that is fanciful is emphasized by Moran himself in one of his fatuous self-descriptions that borders on self-mockery: "a man like me, so meticulous and calm in the main . . . reining back his thoughts within the limits of the calculable so great is his horror of fancy" (156). A thoroughgoing petit bourgeois, he lives within the realm of certain experiences and ignores anything that lies outside or beyond them. Moran thus typifies "mass man."

Moran receives unexpectedly on a quiet Sunday the order to embark on a search for Molloy. Gaber appears bearing orders from Youdi for Moran to depart in search of Molloy whose spectre has long haunted Moran, and whom Moran describes as "Just the opposite of myself in fact." He soon begins, however, to identify with Molloy, and even to take on his traits: we are already headed for the moment at which Moran's familiar and secure self, which is a close portrait of the petit-bourgeois described by Kierkegaard in *Sickness unto Death*, appears as a stranger to him. His identity develops cracks, and starts assuming new, unknown possibilities. He starts experiencing dread:

> I stirred restlessly in my arm-chair, ran my hands over my face, crossed and uncrossed my legs, and so on. The colour and weight of the world were changing already. I would have to admit I was anxious. (132)

Becoming conscious of new possibilities represented by Molloy, Moran admits: "I could not understand what was happening to me" (139). The resultant "uproar, bulk, rage, suffocation . . . frenzied and vain" (155) leads to "a great confusion." Having made preparations for his journey, and "making ready to go without knowing where [he] was going" (169), Moran turns, unlike Molloy who cannot bear to see anything receding behind him, "a last time towards my little all, before I left it, in the hope of keeping it." Moran's departure effectively strips him of his possessions and of his early self-definition. Entirely devoted to "my trees, my bushes, my flower-beds, my tiny lawns" (181), he is aghast at the idea of the "long anguish of vagrancy and freedom" without them. The hermetic enclosure of his inner self, bound within the "black mass of vegetation that was mine and with which I could do as I pleased and never be gainsaid," can no longer be predicated on the economy of his belongings. What thwarts his rational instincts is that he, a Cartesian creature, should of all men be thrust into an irrational world and undergo not just bodily degeneration, but mental dispossession as well.

As he is plunged into a series of irrational encounters, Moran's narrative, the recording of external events, exposes his internal depths. Although Moran begins in complete command of his rational faculties, his firm confidence nevertheless has the seed of doubt, in that he has always imagined himself to be "beset by enemies." Moran's confident notion of his own identity is terribly undermined in the course of his pursuit of Molloy. Eventually he will win through to "a sharper and clearer sense of [his] identity than ever before, in spite of its deep lesions and the wounds with which it was covered" (233), an identity his world of reason would have been incapable of discovering for him.

Soon after Moran sets out, his leg begins to stiffen, and the condition subsequently worsens. The sharp pain, reminiscent of Descartes's pain in the knee (a subject I have referred to, in the Introduction, as something which directly contradicts the Cartesian neglect of the body), had first struck him in the knee while he was giving an enema to his son. As he travels in search of Molloy, the gradual, calamitous deterioration of his body leaves him decidedly a creature of the physical world. Like Molloy, Moran tries to compensate for his physical limitations with the help of the bicycle for which he shares an unexplained enthusiasm. Just as Molloy finds it "a pleasure" to describe it, so does Moran comment: "I would gladly describe it, I would gladly write four thousand words on it alone" (213). As Hugh Kenner has suggested, the bicycle represents an ideal body which both Molloy and Moran desire to appropriate (134). However, as in the case of Molloy, Moran's riding the bicycle involves bodily peril, as he expresses concern for "my testicles which swing a little low" (215). Responding keenly to his "extremely sensitive ear," his toothless chaps, and his eventual immobility, Moran seems far from his original Cartesian certainties. Both Molloy and Moran endure the same painful decline of body and mind. Like Molloy, Moran soon realizes the limited utilitarian value of the cycle and abandons it for the crutches, which suffer a similar fate. The signs of his regression include Moran's greatly weakened intellect and his body's collapse as he evokes the image of life as "a turd waiting to be flushed" (223). His increasing physical deterioration and lapses of memory render irrelevant his goal as he perceives himself ageing "as swiftly as a day-fly."

Moran's former world had been predicated on neat categories through what he believed were the rational operations of his mind. His present reality, unintelligible and amorphous, has blurred those neat categories and shown them for what they are. After the departure of his son, Moran's encounter with the two strangers (avatars, perhaps, of the two travellers, A and C, Molloy had earlier sighted), the feverish cutting of a branch of a tree, and the gazing at his own reflection in the pool of water all lead to an inner metamorphosis. To Moran, the "frenzied collapsing . . . was like a kind of clawing towards a light and countenance I could not name" (203). The "crumbling" that takes place leaves him prey to a world without mental categories. He experiences visions of an "intruder self" which is at once Molloy and himself. In these expanding moments, Moran realizes that he has undergone a tremendous transformation within himself, and he reflects deeply "on me so changed from what I was."

Moran returns to an empty home, with the hens dead, the bees only a ball of dust, and Martha gone. We are back to square one: the Beckett protagonist tries to escape the hollowness of his own selfhood by deadening the body and escaping into the mind, only to discover, like Moran, that the collapsing of the bodily self only leads to a sharpened awareness of it. In the end, there is only a sense of doubt in Moran. The theological questions with which he tries to engage himself are a parodic version of the Cartesian order of statements and answers. Shaken out of his "complacent solidities " he is compensated with the freedom of dispossessed reason. The dispossession is most explicitly communicated in the last lines of the novel which in effect constitute a denial: "It was not midnight. It was not raining" (241).

What makes Beckett's writings distinctively anti-Cartesian, in this sense at least, is his conviction that the experiential field cannot be bifurcated in terms of the subjective and objective poles of consciousness. The dynamics of body and mind are subsequently expanded on not only in the trilogy, but also become a major and persisting "bodily" concern of Beckett's later prose and dramatic writings. The leap from the body to the mind, what Beckett in the *Dream of Fair to Middling Women* calls, "the circular movement of the mind flowering up and up through darkness" (14), is also evident in the fictionalizing and fantasizing that preoccupies so many of Beckett's characters, notably of course, Molloy, Malone and the Unnamable. The escape from physical limitation is enabled by the endless stories that the amputated, blind, paralyzed beings invent in order to delimit their physical environment. As in a powerfully suggestive sentence in *Molloy*, Moran strips off the unknowable nature of the "unfathomable mind, now beacon now sea" (145). The Beckett protagonists must realize that the identity within and the identity without, is intricately enmeshed since the concept of human identity cannot be predicated in terms that do not include the terms of the body.

Whereas in the Cartesian tradition, the experiential framework is understood in terms of inner and outer, or mind and matter, Beckett moves away from such mutually exclusive realms of thought. In an overwhelming number of his writings, Beckett tends to resolve the schism between the cognitive and corporeal aspects of human identity set up by Cartesian philosophy. The gap between philosophical discourse and the individual experience is curiously played out in all of Beckett's works. It is a calculated response to the mind-body opposition privileged by Descartes who frowned on the deceptive nature of sensory experience.

In longing to retreat from the confines of their sensory apparatus, Beckett's protagonists turn away from the impermeability of the phenomenal world to locate a center of subjective mental reality. As we see, they all discover that retreating into the inner world can be equally frustrating. Their optimism evaporates as they find the mental world confusing and even perilous. They long to escape the burden of the flesh, to keep the "mind a blank" with "all the candles quenched but one" (76) as Beckett phrases it in *Dream of Fair to Middling Women*. However, even the Belacqua of *More Pricks Than Kicks* knows that the way out is not the way in, the retreat from both the external world and from the internal "last ditch" is no "ideal core of the onion." Moran may be repulsed by "the horror of the body and its functions" (161). And Malone in *Malone Dies* may claim: "If I had the use of my body I would throw it out of the window" (44). Nonetheless, the retreat into mental reality will always prove insufficient. Beckett's narrators experience the close interdependence of the two levels of reality, mental and physical, and in their difficulty in escaping from the physical into the mental, comprehend how closely conjoined the two are. Instead of rejecting the primacy of sense data as Descartes did, Beckett makes it the central focus of his epistemological argument, as my second chapter will further demonstrate.

CHAPTER TWO

The Body's Presence in *Molloy*

A terrible doubt racked his brain: should he weep over the death of his wife or rejoice over the birth of his son? . . . As he spoke, he cried like a cow. But suddenly, struck by the thought of Pantagruel, he began to laugh like a calf.

Francois Rabelais, *Gargantua and Pantagruel*

My argument about Beckett's subversion of the Cartesian body-mind divide logically leads to the theme of the pervasiveness of the corporeal element in Beckett's exploration of identity. In this chapter, I wish to examine the complex issues involving Beckett's perception of a large term that is variously known as self or identity and its relationship to the keen intensity of bodily sense so preponderantly there in Beckett's writings. The theoretical traditions relating to being "enselved" are really analytical cul-de-sacs for Beckett. But within the debates emerging from his writings, the issue does assume interesting dimensions. What constitutes the self of an individual is the predominant query in Beckett's "bodily" theme. If self has anything to do with body and the bodily sensation of being, then self must have certain typical attributes relating to the construction of the body, that is, one's sense of being as an embodied person. This is what I shall explore in my second chapter where I focus on the body's "presence" in Beckett's *Molloy*. I draw upon Mikhail Bakhtin's theoretical conceptualizations on the body to throw light on my discussion of the narrative of Molloy. It is my endeavour here to show Molloy as a very Bakhtinian kind of figure. I believe that Molloy's acceptance of his body liberates him from it. It is in this attitude of easy acceptance and affirmation of his body that I find an analogue to the carnivalesque in Beckett.

Mikhail Bakhtin's conception of the "lower body stratum" is extremely relevant to Beckett's idea of the body. In some ways, of all the theorists I have found useful for my argument, Bakhtin's postulations are most germane to my substantiation of what constitutes the self in Beckett. The keen intensity of bodily sense in Beckett's writings shares some affinities, in my opinion, with the intensity with which Bakhtin privileges every transgression of limits, beginning with *Rabelais and His World* where he sets forth his concepts of the "classical" and the "grotesque" body. Bakhtin's distinction between what he terms "grotesque realism" and the "classic canon" or the "new bodily canon" relates in a significant manner to his spurning of essential selfhood or individualism. While the "classical body" is the locus of humanist ideas of selfhood, Bakhtin privileges the "grotesque body" as rendering irrelevant all notions of selfhood. Inspired by the work of the Russian physiologist, Aleksey Ukhtomsky, Bakhtin conceives of the relation of the body to the physical environment as a dialogic continuum. While the "classical" body is unchanging, closed and complete, the concept of the "grotesque body" links human physiology with the natural environment.

While the classical body effaces orifices, the grotesque model emphasizes those parts of the body "that are open to the outside world," "the open mouth, the genital organs, the breasts, the phallus, the pot belly, the nose" (26). The prime organs here are the orifices and the apertures of the body, while the prime processes are eating and evacuating in any manner possible. According to Bakhtin, the classical is in many ways interrogated and subverted by the grotesque, unfinished body, elastic and malleable, with all its "base" products and secretions—the farting, sweating, lubricating, defecating body. But this does not imply that the grotesque frees and liberates the selfhood that finds embodiment within the "classical": for the excessive and unfinished energies of the "grotesque" body render irrelevant the very concept of the self. The "grotesque" body has celebration as its chief characteristic and is associated with the carnivalesque in the fetishization of "the material bodily lower stratum." For Bakhtin, the body is not a closed system but a perpetual dynamic. In this sense, Bakhtin eschews all forms of hierarchies or categories. According to him, this simultaneity "seeks to grasp in its imagery the very act of becoming and growth, the eternal incomplete unfinished nature of being." Its image presents simultaneously the two poles of becoming: "that which is receding and dying, and that which is being born" (52).

Like Bakhtin's Rabelais, Beckett underscores life in corporeal terms: the body's apertures, orifices, and functions, with the various ramifications and offshoots, the vulgar senses of smell and taste, the excretory functions, the endless gluttony, and the indefatigable sexuality of the "lower bodily stratum" transfer all that is spiritual, ideal, and abstract to the material level, to the sphere of the body as a site for the life cycle. Beckett foregrounds the organicity of life's processes, of eating, defecating, and of what Molloy refers to as "certain habits such as the finger in the nose, the scratching of the balls, digital emunction and the peripatetic piss" as "the first rules of a reasoned theory" (32). Beckett's characters with their disproportionate, often dismembered and fragmented bodies bring to mind both the physically transgressive state of the "grotesque" in Bakhtin's semantics of the body and the "classical" body they keep fighting against, an issue I shall explore in my next chapter.

In his preoccupation with physicality, Beckett's "material" imagination also plays on the issue of human beings as mere biological organisms with only a veneer of social polish. Beckett's focus leads him to close inspection of the naturalistic details of the body, not only of its reproductive and sexual aspects, but also the digestive and excremental ones. Norbert Elias has written extensively on the civilizing process, which has entailed, as a natural corollary, the taming and quieting of the body on which the social processes of differentiation and hierarchizing are historically inscribed. What I want to argue here is that Beckett emphasizes the biological against the social which, as he reveals, is merely an accretion, a carapace.

Beckett's strategies of representation and emplotment are designed to show how the biological constantly wrestles with the social, and fights back with bodily belches and sour cuds and hard stools. Akin to Bakhtin's concept of the "grotesque body," Beckett's idea of the physical is insistently concerned with bodily excreta, with the symptoms of organic corruption and discharges, with the flesh leaking, bleeding, sweating, drooling, spitting and vomiting, with wombs and tombs, with birth, expulsion, copulation, excrement—in short, with all that is reductively physical. Examples abound: Watt's "bianial equinoctial nocturnal emission in vacuo," Krapps' "Sour cud and the iron stool," Molloy's "first taste of the shit" as well as his frequent allusions to the chamberpot, Moran's masturbatory tendencies and fetishization of "a few fibrous shreds float[ing] in the yellow liquid," and Malone's conviction that "what matters is to eat and excrete" (7). The bleeding, spitting, vomiting, oozing and leaking body—that "throne of the faecal inlet" as it is called in *Whoroscope*—leads to the elimination of differences. In addition to the obsession with grotesque genital and scatological functions, there is also the preoccupation with birth and death. Thus if Malone in *Malone Dies* believes he is "an old foetus . . . hoar and impotent" (51), Winnie in *Happy Days* pines for "the happy day to come when flesh melts at so many degrees" (18).

By inverting norms, by unlocking orifices, Beckett comments on and critiques that which runs against the biological continuum. As Martin Pops points out,

> the civilizing process conceals but cannot erase the anal priority of human beings . . . [b]ecause shitting is the bodily archetype of spiritual rebirth insofar as it liberates the body from itself. ("The Metamorphosis of Shit," 27, 29)

Beckett's conception of the body interrogates boundary structures, the dividing lines and mechanisms deployed for social discipline as well as the social dimensions of the exits and entrances acting as guarantors of social as well as corporeal stability. To quote Mikhail Bakhtin again, the physical will always defeat the mental because the essence of life lies in "the lower stratum of the body," the life of the belly and the reproductive organs, that which "relates to acts of defecation and copulation, conception, pregnancy and birth" (21). Behind this idea is Bakhtin's very intense sense of the physical materiality of bodily being. What Mikhail Bakhtin calls the "materialistic concept of being" (52) is predominantly present in Beckett's privileging of the "lower bodily stratum" in his works—the faeces, urine, sperm, menstrual flow—in sum, all the shocking physicality of the body that has been banished from respectable representation.

Both Bakhtin and Beckett display an acute sense of the dense particularity of lived experience, the ambivalent, sensuous materiality of human existence. Their phenomenological concern is so intense that they decry the arid abstractions of philosophical idealism. While it is true that Bakhtin chose to consider more optimistic alternatives among the possibilities of life, such as the celebration of the carnival spirit, it is also true that the so-called "bleaker" aspects of Beckett's vision have their liberating tendencies. In Beckett as in Bakhtin, liberation is perceived in carnivalesque transgression as a flagrant defiance of bourgeois society; in high and low discourse and images of linguistic mutiplicity and materiality; in the polemical undermining of authority, religious, literary, or political; and the celebration of the physical realities of life, especially the privileging of excremental imagery and the subversive energies of sexuality. In many ways, Bakhtin (1895-1975) and Beckett (1906-1989) were near contemporaries. Like Beckett's writings, Bakhtin's *Rabelais* is both a kind of requiem and a carnival celebration of modern Angst. What Bakhtin has to say of Rabelais applies closely not only to himself, but to Beckett as well:

> He did not speak in the conceptual language but in the tongue of popular comic images. While breaking up false seriousness, a false historic pathos, he prepared the soil for a new seriousness and for a new historic pathos. (439)

To apply Bakhtin's theorization to this so-called bleak vision of Beckett's world is perhaps to risk running against the accepted habits of critical thought. Unlike James Joyce, whose work has been perceived to have close affinities with Bakhtin's theories of carnival and of dialogism, Beckett seems to many readers monologically "uncarnivalesque." There have, of course, been a few attempts, notably that of Sylvie Debevec Henning, to show how Bakhtin's theory of polyphony and dialogism can be effectively used to enrich our understanding of the multiplicity of voices and the polysemous nature of Beckett's language. The interchange or jostling of high and low forms is an important aspect of carnivalized literature. Bakhtin's stress on "polyglossia" is perceived in the purely linguistic nature of action in *Molloy*: the way in which themes and words are quoted and parodied in Molloy's erudition (he quotes Geulincx and Leibniz and is fluent in many languages) played off against his bawdy diction. Few statements are accorded final authority in the narrative of Molloy. This sense of "mixture" of styles is the model of Bakhtin's poetic. However, the carnivalesque aspects and images in Beckett and the essentially comic nature of the transgressive energies informing his writings have largely gone unnoticed. I contend that Beckett draws his power from what Bakhtin calls the "popular" and "carnivalesque" aspects of his work. In fact, I consider Molloy as a perfect demonstration of Bakhtin's conception of the "grotesque."

For Bakhtin, "novelization" is something distinct from the novel. Bakhtin finds "conversational" folk forms particularly keen sources of multivoiced and parodic discourse which he privileged. The art of the novel is paradoxically an art with its roots in artless form. The "unofficial" is not marginal or repressed but is an expressed part of the culture as a whole. In *Molloy*, this broad category brings together all three of Molloy's subversions—miscellaneous learning, mock-gravity, and healthy coarseness. Molloy distorts language's communicative function to his own purposes. In the self-presentation of Molloy's narrative, fictional instability and process are part of the spirit of transgression and subversion. The carnival "voices" are also suggested in an inversion of the usual order of things. The function of facetious mimesis, of goliardic and jongleuresque play that Bakhtin foregrounds in *Rabelais and His World* desublimates and exaggerates erotic or aggressive or other forbidden desires covertly expressed through the words and gestures of authoritative and often ritualized texts. Bakhtin's Rabelaisian vocabulary is generally understood to mean broad, coarse humor. While "official" culture is fixed, serious, and dogmatic, popular culture is changing, open, unstable, egalitarian. Carnival, the single greatest expression of this culture, is "organized on the basis of laughter" (8).

Molloy's happy state of uncertainty and aporetic bliss in his physical being makes him the perfect example for my discussion of the grotesque. Molloy is the alter ego and complement of Moran whom I have discussed in the preceding chapter. The relationship has parallels to the relationship of Marlow and Kurtz in Conrad's *Heart of Darkness*. The contrast between Molloy's acceptance of his failing body and Moran's obsession with duty or external appearance or manners is extreme. Happily and endlessly, Molloy can speak at length about his crippled legs, his aching knees, his low-hanging testicles, his anus. Moran, on the other hand, is a compulsive respecter of status, duty, and manners. Setting out in search of Molloy, Moran describes with precision the clothes his son must take: the school suit, his toilet articles, one shirt, one pair of socks, and seven pairs of drawers. The anxiety for anal cleanliness in Moran contrasts with the relaxed habits of Molloy. Molloy, lacking the philosophical certainty of Moran, is aporetic with a vengeance: he vegetates, is without "much will left," and, while he "formulates his thoughts," is devoid of any sense of arrogance about his imperative need to finish writing. In fact, I would argue that if Moran is defeated by his suppression of the grotesque body, Molloy is liberated by his acknowledgment of it.

In physical appearance, Molloy is a "sorry sight": he emits repugnant smells, wears a hat attached to his greatcoat by a string attached to his buttonhole, likes to sleep in the mornings, and is lame and uses crutches. However, in his indifference to self-consciousness, Molloy is equally indifferent to outer forms of social identity. Molloy's absent-mindedness is not lacking in comic characteristics. He does not have a profession or a place of residence. He remarks, moreover, that he forgets at times who he is. He confesses outright at one point: "My sense of identity was wrapped in a namelessness often hard to penetrate" (41). Moran's confident claim that he knew who he was contrasts significantly with Molloy's state of indifference. Remarking on the namelessness of his own identity, and "all the other things which made merry with my senses," Molloy says:

> there could be no things but nameless things, no names but thingless names. . . . And truly it little matters what I say . . . this or that or any other thing. (41)

External reality turns out to be nameless too as Molloy realizes that there are only "nameless things" and "thingless names." Molloy perceives his hand on his knee as an inseparable facet of the physical world, an external object "which my knee felt tremble and of which my eyes saw the wrist only, the heavily veined back, the pallid row of knuckles" (13). Checking his cigar, his shoes, and wondering about his own existence after A and C leave, he exclaims with perfect equanimity: "I am still alive then. That may come in useful" (16).

Molloy is remarkably at ease in his description and discussion of his own body. He seldom feels shackled by a crippled body. His acceptance of his body is so complete, so mature, that he is able to accept as well its disintegration. In the course of his journeying, Molloy's legs become paralyzed, but he says he has "got used to it, in a way, yes in a kind of way." By keeping him close to his own body and far from the rule-governed world, Molloy's invalid state makes him a more dignified character. Supremely indifferent as he is to his own body, its decay becomes a liberation. His expansive description of his paralyzed legs carries no real air of complaint. In fact, he speaks of his body in an affectionate kind of way. There is a sense of liberation in his suffering, in wrapping his head in his coat "to stifle the obscene noise of choking" (107), and in alluding to his anus as "the true portal of our being":

> Almost everything revolts it that comes from without and what comes from within does not seem to receive a very warm welcome either. (108)

Molloy distrusts the capabilities of language. He does not so much reject language as simply feel himself inadequate about it. There is a parallel here to Bakhtin's reservations about the reifications of a formalist approach to language. Like Bakhtin, Beckett believes that the observed object or character lives in the language of the observing subject, not in an essence that the writer gives a voice to. In foregrounding Molloy's discomfort with words as discursive, mental constructs, Beckett reflects his uncanny ambivalence about a medium that is powerless to reach objective truth and yet is also persuasive. Like Bakhtin, Beckett sees us trapped inside the language of our thoughts. Molloy's distrust of the enunciating subject can be understood better by referring here to Bakhtin's notion of the "blazon," which comprises lists of attributes remaining "outside the official system of straight and strict evaluations." While "a monotone character of thought and style almost always prevails in the official spheres," those who are not authorized to speak create a disruption effect by a free and ambiguous speech which "never wants to halt the spinning wheel, to find and outline the top and the bottom, the front and the back" (432-33).

Both Bakhtin and Beckett's writings exhibit many forms of ambivalence about the "truth" that language generates. We see it in Molloy's lack of anxiety about the validity of language as an instrument of truth. Molloy values the sentient perception of things rather than their verbal construction. At ease with his own sentient body, Molloy freely confesses to an inability to judge the accuracy of his own narrative. In fact, through Molloy's compulsion to write, Beckett explores the gap between language and objective reality. Referring to his own mother, Molloy says: "As to her address, I was in the dark, but knew how to get there, even in the dark" (22). Acknowledging the lack of veracity of words, Molloy seeks various ways for the arrangement of words to palliate his need. "Truth" is completely out the window; he even admits at one point that he may be "inventing a little, perhaps embellishing" (9).

Molloy discovers humor and irony in the disjunction between objective reality and human language. So wrapped up is he in his own sense of being that words become meaningless and an imposition: "truly it little matters what I say, this or that or any other thing" (41). To him, "the whole ghastly business looks like what it is, senseless, speechless, issueless misery." His problematic relationship with language is spelled out in his confession that "I always say either too much or too little, which is a terrible thing for a man with a passion for truth like mine" (45).

It is only within language that the split between mind and body is constructed, while in actual fact the two cannot be separated. The systematic deconstruction of language in Beckett and the move towards minimalism are clearly evident in Molloy's distrust of language. The problem with the nature of language is its inadequacy as a tool for communicating the nature of reality. He wonders why one should substitute a word for every object, and prefers "nameless things" to "thingless names" (41). Systems of knowledge lead to dispossession, "ruins," "a world collapsing endlessly" (53). He therefore hates the imperatives he is led by and would prefer to be "a fool who neither knows where he is going nor why he is going there" (86). He believes his aimless folly may arrive at wisdom, a wisdom that does not consist in the possession of a new "truth," but rather in a dispossession, a loss of claims to truth and knowledge. Molloy describes this dispossession in his account of his "ruins," the remains of the systems of knowledge that he has exhausted:

> Yes, I once took an interest in astronomy, I don't deny it. Then it was geology that killed a few years for me. The next pains in the balls was anthropology and the other disciplines, such as psychiatry. . . . (52)

Throughout Molloy's narrative, Beckett undermines the adaptation of reason to the rational world that he apprehends. The story of A and C is a typical instance of the rational order and its falsification of experience. Molloy attempts to give an objective account of the event he perceives: of two men, A and C, walking toward one another, meeting briefly, and continuing in their different directions. Molloy becomes alert to the probability of error in the subjective interpretation of his experience: "And I am perhaps confusing several different occasions, and different times . . . perhaps it was A one day at one place, then C another at another" (17). Urged by confusions "deep down," Molloy finds the dissolution of the story of A and C into disparate elements easily conceivable. It becomes impossible for Molloy to behave as a rational person, living in obedience to "the murmurs of my little world, its dutiful connotations" (15) and reporting on what he saw from his "observation post." In the case of C, the self draws "near" to an "other." In the case of A, the other defeats and cancels out the self in the accumulation of "things I didn't know, things I had craved to know" (13). Only when Molloy is apart from A can he feel "free, I don't know what that means, but it's the word I mean to use, free to do what, to do nothing, to know, but what . . ." (16).

Consequently, Molloy feels more secure with his body's needs than with those of his mind. Molloy carries on his person a sucking stone made round and smooth by the pounding of the sea. Surviving the forces of disintegration the way his body has not, the stone has a talismanic virtue about it: "A little pebble in your mouth, round and smooth, appeases, soothes, makes you forget your hunger, forget your thirst" (33). The freedom and joy that Molloy has always found in handling and sucking the stone is reemphasized in the episode of arranging and rearranging the stones in his pocket (of course, a mockery of human rationality, especially mathematical systems of quantifying) and sucking them with calm effectiveness. Edith Kern's argument in the article, "Black Humor: The Pockets of Lemuel Gulliver and Samuel Beckett," about the kinship between the repetitive reference to pockets in this passage and the human mind is pertinent to this elaborate anecdote which provides an instance of Beckett's critique and parody of reason (64). Pockets frame the smallness of the human mind and the rational structures that the mind erects. Molloy recognizes the illusory quality of rational principles and the futility of actions directed by rational principles.

Similarly, Beckett undermines the hegemonizing power of reason in apprehending the world, by making Molloy indulge in the ludicrous process of counting his farts: "One day I counted them. Three hundred and fifteen farts in nineteen hours, or an average of over sixteen farts an hour" (39). What Beckett, in one of his critical comments, has termed the "comedy of exhaustive enumeration" (*Disjecta*, 82) also appears in Watt's ratiocinations, and also in *Murphy* when the urge to order four biscuits in a particular ratiocinative configuration becomes, to use Molloy's phrase, "a bodily need" (99). Molloy's obsession with the arrangement of his sucking stones and counting of his farts suggests that the logic of reason will always be held in contradistinction to the pure physical sensation of sucking the stones or farting. The comic disproportion between the solemn occasion of these ratiocinations and the resultant mockery suggests that reason, in its imperative to order experience, perceives its own exercise as intrinsically futile.

There is a bizarre intermingling of highbrow vocabularies with the crudest billingsgate and many scatological details in Molloy's narration. In fact, the spirit of Bakhtin's world of polyglossia breathes over the vigour of the comedy in Molloy's undermining of reason. Bakhtin sees the carnivalesque as functioning to give back to those who are not authorized to speak some kind of articulate solidarity. According to Bakhtin, the attempt to control and ultimately to eliminate what does not conform to the totalitarian tendencies of the rationalist order has persisted in Western cultural heritage. The carnivalesque has, however, coexisted with the rationalist tradition in an open confrontation where the unofficial draws upon the traditions of folk culture to undermine official hegemony. The totalizing impetus of monovocality and rational orderliness is countered by the linguistic dissemination of the carnivalesque. As a discursive strategy of subversion and disruption in Bakhtin, the body of the people translates into speech of the body, as communal speech, and operates most forcefully in a culture where the body exists but does not speak. As such it is a significant means of liberating consciousness from a hierarchical perspective and also opening the possibility of an alternative social order against authoritarian control and repression.

Molloy's relationship with his society, or rather the gap between the two, is, of course, a ludicrous subversion of the social contract that binds us to rationality and responsibility. He wishes for a life spent "straying with no other company" than "the fellow-convict you long to stop, embrace, suck, suckle and whom you pass by, with hostile eyes, for fear of his familiarities" (12). He would rather become the simple object of another subject. He argues that if he has "always behaved like a pig" (32), it is owing to the "negative and empirical" guides to conduct that he has been given. He has never been given general principles that define and sanction social behavior. He is therefore outside a social organization that bases itself on "the rules of a reasoned theory." He experiences persecution when he becomes the object of society's charity. Social workers, Molloy observes, "will pursue you to the ends of the earth, the vomitory in their hands" (30). According to Molloy, the creed of the social worker is that "To him who has nothing it is forbidden not to relish filth" (31).

Molloy keeps away from social regimentation and instead seeks comfort with his natural body. This results in many humorous incidents. He gets into trouble with the police and the law. As a doddering wreck supported by a bicycle, "my feet obscenely resting on the earth, my arms on the handlebars and on my arms my head, rocking and abandoned" (31), he gaily calls himself "a deplorable sight." He is, however, viewed with suspicion by the policeman who takes him in. From the policeman he learns that in the threatening world of social abstractions, there is only one law "to which all must bow, rich and poor, young and old, happy and sad" (26). To this, Molloy responds "that I was not sad." When the representative of authority turns hostile and asks for his "papers," Molloy takes the word in its everyday sense as implying paper of any sort. Since "the only papers I carry with me are bits of newspapers to wipe myself, you understand, when I have a stool" (26), the notion of papers as referring to social identity, as a social abstraction, is completely undercut by Molloy's humble state of forgetfulness of anything except bodily worries. Molloy has a limited understanding of abstract terms, and has trouble perceiving himself, the real, tangible Molloy, as in any way representing abstract concepts.

The disproportion between the ratiocinations of the figures of authority and Molloy's innocent incomprehension is an instance of the particular comedy of Molloy's narrative. When Molloy is taken to the police station, he is unable to answer any questions he is asked: "I am so little used to being asked anything, that . . . I hasten to answer blindly, fearing perhaps lest my silence fan their anger to fury" (27). He is so distanced from rules, symbols, and concepts that he has no idea of even routine information like his own family name or his mother's address. His quick release surprises him. Completely outside the laws of society, he can only dimly apprehend that "To apply the letter of the law to a creature like me is no easy matter" (31). He unsuccessfully tries to cultivate a physical attitude and tone of voice to "make my little speech which I wished to seem spontaneous" (84). What comes easier to him than interacting as a social creature is to "hug the walls . . . hiding but not provocatively, ready to come out, to smile, to listen, to crawl, nauseating but not pestilent" (88).

The power establishment is able to impose its "official" culture by creating a language that reflects and embodies the principles of this culture. As long as there is only this language—Bakhtin's "monologic" language—in which to think, there can be no alternative conceptions for a rationalized order of existence. In Bakhtin's terms, a "monolingual" person cannot conceive of another ideology, or set of values other than those of the establishment. For Bakhtin, "languages are philosophies, not abstract but concrete, social philosophies, penetrated by a system of values inseparable from living practice" (*Dialogic Imagination*, 62). Molloy seems to me an embodiment of one who is able to throw off the intellectual shackles worn by those who have only the language of official culture at their disposal. Molloy's antagonism toward the establishment extends to his discontent with a language he feels is not his own. He experiences difficulty in asking the name of a town which is something he has to share with others and also confirm from others. Language has a social character which exacerbates the gap between experience and expression. "To restore silence is the role of objects," since words express "something gone wrong with the silence" (88). Language does not give him access to freedom, spontaneity, or genuine utterance. Towards the end of his narrative, he muses that he has not really told the reader what happened. His sentences are "deceitful figures" produced by "complying with the convention that demands you either lie or hold your peace" (119).

Molloy's aversion to the punitive nature of the imperatives of rationality is externalized in his dislike of all rational activity. Beckett and his characters are sceptical of reason, which, they suspect, erects rules it cannot validate. The ironical situations Molloy finds himself in suggest to him the futility of the aims that reason impels him toward.

Molloy's glimpse at what lies beyond the life of systematized action and knowledge suggests to him "a world collapsing endlessly, a frozen world, under a faint untroubled sky" (40). He has a vision of "a world at an end, in spite of appearances" where beginning and ending coincide "with neither plan nor bounds" (40). All time and task stop in this world and he finds peace and surcease when he cannot will himself to be but simply finds himself: "And I too am at an end, when I am there, my eyes close, my sufferings cease and I end, I wither as the living cannot" (40). One focus of this kind of experience is Molloy's devotion to the object—a knife-rest—that he steals from Lousse's house. Because he is ignorant of its utilitarian value, he is set free to enjoy its inexhaustible pleasures:

> I could not therefore puzzle over it endlessly without the least risk. For to know nothing is nothing, not to want to know anything likewise, but to be beyond knowing anything, to know you are beyond knowing anything, that is when peace enters in, to the soul of the incurious seeker. (86)

So much a man given to his bodily appetite and sensation; so much outside the impositions and persecutions he has to suffer because he is outside the rational laws of society, Molloy cannot just be an abstract biological organism. Despite being excluded from the civilized order, Molloy's ambivalent need for inclusion defines him within the paradigm of Bakhtin's "grotesque." His search for a form of integration and inclusion includes his elemental need for sexual love whose romantic nature he displaces as easily as he undermines the beauty of "the witless moon" he observes with his observation that "It must be her arse she shows us always" (52).

Beckett does not use sexuality as a locus of antirepressive energies in the manner in which Joyce does. He does not implicate either religious authority or excessive sensuality in the way it is foregrounded in Joyce's transgressive sexual imagery. Instead, Beckett represents sexuality in such a way as to deconstruct all romanticizing about love. Reduced to a grotesque series of physical postures, sometimes to animalistic exercises, physical love in Beckett creates a schism between the intellectualized understanding of love and its physical negotiations. Sexual relations have no metaphysical locus standi. Molloy's narrative locates the idealistic terms of true love and romantic tenderness in contexts that ridicule them.

There is nothing cerebral in the attitude to love which, to extrapolate again from Bakhtin, centers on the "material bodily lower stratum."

In his attitude to physical love, Molloy illustrates a composite picture of Bakhtin's fascinating account of the transgression of body limits. Bakhtin has, of course, insisted that the key elements of the grotesque body are those points at which the body is "in the act of becoming. It is never finished, never completed; it is continually built, created, and builds and creates another body." (*Rabelais and His World*, 226). Privileging the orifices of the body, Bakhtin would have it that to be grotesque is to be forever available for fundamental change. Hence divisions that would routinely segregate are blurred; sex and mouth, anus and belly exist in a fluid continuum, and to dismember is, paradoxically, to multiply.

Bakhtin's concrete perception of a human being's spatial and temporal situatedness also informs his concept of the "chronotope." The chronotopic concept offers a spatial and temporal envisioning of human existence in its manifest materiality. The grotesque body, celebrating physicality in gross and exaggerated form, is not to be equated, Bakhtin argues, with either the individual biological body or with bourgeois individualistic life. Rather it is the body of all the people, a communal body which celebrates a continually renewing process of generation. In this context, though Bakhtin here focuses on the perpetuation of the human race, though he erases altogether the individual woman who creates life, this is no blind spot in Bakhtin's conceptualization. Specifically, Bakhtin refers in his discussion to the Kersch terracotta figurines of senile, laughing, pregnant hags as representing "the inexhaustible vessel of conception" (240) of the ambiguously conceived body. However, if Bakhtin can be faulted on transcending sexual difference and not individualizing the female body, this is because his central focus is on liberating human consciousness and on opening up the possibility of change and generation.

As for Bakhtin, love, for Beckett's Molloy, is just another organic drive of the sensate body. Molloy's toiling and moiling, akin to Macmann's in *Malone Dies*, who struggles to "bundle his sex into his partner's like a pillow into a pillow-slip" (89), is an apt comment on sexuality as a stimulus-response mechanism. In Molloy's generalizing vision, all gender distinctions are capable of collapsing. His mother, "a poor old uniparous whore" (23), is described as sexless or anatomically undifferentiated. He considers his own presence the result of an arbitrary, biological process in which one is "whelped" rather than born. It is in this sense of being "whelped" that he can execrate his own birth as anal secretion.

For Molloy, the body as an object of erotic desire shows no specific character. He is very matter-of-fact in alluding to sexual intercourse with the old woman who had "a hole between her legs, oh not the bunghole I had always imagined, but a slit, and in this I put, or rather she put, my so-called virile member. . . " (76). He can also, with an innocent sense of curiosity, recount and reminisce about a romantic encounter in terms of a canine image to depict sexual intercourse. Molloy's sojourn at Lousse's reminds him of his other love affairs. He remembers Edith, an old hag, who accosted him on a garbage dump and with whom he copulated like a dog. Molloy enters Edith from the rear: "It seemed all right to me, for I had seen dogs, and I was astonished when she confided that you could go about it differently" (76). At the height of sexual passion, Molloy bites Edith: "And all I could see was her taut yellow nape which every now and then I set my teeth in, forgetting I had none, such is the power of instinct" (76). To a close reader, the scene mingles with Moran's fascination with the genitalia of his neighbour's dog, Zulu, "his little black penis ending in a thin wisp of wetted hair" (105). Human or animal, desire is no more than fornication, a play of sex organs. One merely likes to think of desire as a "grotesque" substitute for ontological security and comfort.

This sexual reminiscence of Ruth/Edith has been compared by Helene Baldwin to Dante's dream of the Siren in the *Purgatory* or to the scenes of concupiscence in T.S. Eliot's *The Waste Land* (42). It is difficult to agree with this harsh criticism of what seems such broad humor in the scene of physical sexuality. In my opinion, the scene does not bring out Beckett's religious or moral scruples, nor does it smell of misogynist contempt. Rather, it is a naked, unabashed representation of a physical response which Molloy experiences. I believe that Beckett means to valorize Molloy's elemental physicality as well as his sexual fantasizing.

Molloy's apprehension of the physical world has taught him that this life, with its Lousses, its Ruth/Ediths, is only a reckoning with "the body's long madness" (75). His sensual response to a massage, and the "instant of bliss" which ensues "when your frantic member casts about for a rubbing-place" (77), results in his confounded query, "is it true love, in the rectum?" (76). He is not quite certain, but, as always, he reasons with perfect irony. He believes that the nature and needs of true love are characterized by the acceptance of poor conditions, like cutting the beloved's toe-nails or flying "High above the tight fit and the loose." So overwhelming is his body's presence that "I gave myself up to that golden moment, as if I had been someone else" (27). Nonetheless, his explanation for refusing to repeat the experience is suspect. He says that he wants to keep the memory "pure of all pastiche" which seems more customary than the desire to preserve love's uniqueness. And in discussing his relationship with Ruth/Edith, he constantly and ironically uses the word "love." He is even uncertain about the name of his true love which is more than a frailty committed by a truly amorous memory. As Molloy heaps up details, some sordidly hilarious, others poignantly funny, he commits a travesty of romantic assumptions about love. All the exalted definitions and descriptions of love are here satirized and reduced to comic deflation. (In this connection, Deirdre Bair has also recounted how Beckett remarked to some of his friends: "This thing called love, there's none of it, it's only fucking. That's all there is—just fucking.") Molloy calls it a "mug's game . . . and tiring on top of that, in the long run," and cannot help making the comparison that "twixt finger and thumb tis heaven in comparison" (76). Thus by reducing love to pure physical sensation, Beckett also reduces all sentimental claims about love to pure windbaggery.

Grotesque as it is, Molloy narrates his sexual encounter with Ruth/Edith with a great deal of comic vigour. Molloy remembers how he would rub wintergreen on his mistress's "rump." Edith's old age and her infirmity, however, soon lead to her death. "She died taking a warm tub, as her custom was before receiving me. It limbered her up" (78). It is not as if Edith is Woman the temptress whose pliant flesh threatens to absorb Molloy. The easy eroticism he shares with her does not enslave his body and his desires. Besides, Edith was too old to bear children. This leads to his guilty memory of conceiving a son somewhere, the upshot of a liaison with a chambermaid. He prefers to forget this affair: "Don't talk to me about the chambermaid, I should never have mentioned her" (79). Not really given to anxiety, Molloy says he ultimately prefers the "pleasures" of masturbation.

Although Molloy says he does not make love with Lousse, her sexual status, too, becomes a preoccupation for him. He is not sure what to make of the hairy face and deep, perhaps masculine, voice of Lousse. He gives up and in a kind of reprimand, tells himself: "Don't be tormenting yourself, Molloy, man or woman, what does it matter?" (75). Ruth/Edith was also "an eminently flat woman," and he suspects, with perfectly blase nonchalance, that "[p]erhaps she too was a man, yet another of them" (76). There is still a sense of uncertainty for he reflects that their testicles would have collided in their sexual encounters. These physical confusions turn Molloy into the most concrete, fleshed-out character in Beckett. There is pure ribald humour here in this play with gender boundaries. There is no clear distinction in Molloy's memory between the rectum and the vagina and male and female merge into androgynous figures. The fact that Lousse or Ruth might be a man becomes a problem of logic and not of observation. Finally, Ruth/Edith and Lousse are identified with the image of "the one and same old hag, flattened and crazed by life" (79). And Molloy observes that "to tell you the horrible truth, my mother's image sometimes mingles with theirs" (79). The grotesque comedy of these sexual relations which Molloy indulges in, not only subverts all romantic notions of love, but also collapses all categories of gender division.

In *Rabelais and His World*, Bakhtin discovers ambivalence in everything, ambivalence that leads to disruption of all hierarchies, all categories and all establishments. What Bakhtin calls "the carnivalization of literature" is a transposition, an overturning of the hierarchical order. Bakhtin pays particular attention to the ritual of gender transformation. In carnival, there is an abundance of deliberately violated proportions and numerous images of the inside-out. Bakhtin's idea of gender inversion, sex reversal and other disruptive elements of the grotesque shows how these disruptive elements serve to keep alive the possibilities for alternative distributions of power. Gender inversions (particularly female to male) abound in Beckett, both explicitly and implicitly. In addition, there is a constant emphasis on inscriptions of feminine excess. Recurrent images of such excess are the grotesque mouth and the grotesque womb. The protean dimensions of the female body lose gender distinctions and ultimately remind Molloy of his own mother. All the women Molloy shares his experience with, ultimately merge in the figure of his mother. Like the earth mothers in Joyce, Anna Livia Plurabelle and Molly Bloom, Molloy's own mother accommodates the images of the women in Molloy's love-relationships.

I turn now to Molloy's annihilation of his own bodily identity, in terms close to Bakhtin's own, in a continuum with the natural environment around him. Bakhtin sets about discussing the self not in terms of a conception of consciousness derived from empirical experience, but in terms of a constant interchange between individual and totality. In the relation of individual and totality, the former is inconceivable without the latter, inseparable from it and continuous with it. For Bakhtin, human consciousness always exists in a dialectical relationship between self and other. A single consciousness could not generate a sense of its self. Only the awareness of another consciousness outside the self can produce that image.

This dialectical relationship is best seen in Beckett in Molloy's relationship with his environment. In physically merging with his environment, Molloy can achieve complete forgetfulness of all external structures. Lying in the ditch "at full stretch, with outspread arms," Molloy plays placidly with the grass and mingles with it as if he wished to become part of the vegetation: "the smell of the earth was in the grass that my hands wove round my face till I was blinded. I ate a little too, a little grass" (35). The soft soil of the ditch promises him a sense of oblivion: "How joyfully I would vanish there, sinking deeper and deeper under the rains" (35). (Compare this with Moran to whom soft snow is a hindrance). Further, Molloy goes to the extent of not opening his eyes at times, since there is a whole world "behind my closed lids the little night and its little lights" (36). His bodily definitions are as large as he can travel, a "region so vast [that he has] never left it and never shall" (88), and at the same time, so small as to be a "narrow region whose administrative limits he had never crossed and presumably never would." It is the exigency of his physical life which contains, subsumes, but is unable to supercede or surmount the senses.

Selfhood for Molloy is thus a liberation from time and space. It is depicted as a transformation into a dimensionless point in the void. Molloy's body dimensions shrink to nothing: "I wither as the living cannot" (40). His inner space is a void, a nothingness beyond or outside time-bound reality. His reflecting consciousness and reflected consciousness coincide: "[I] but see and am seen." The topography of Molloy's mind differs considerably from Moran's: to use Molloy's term, Moran's mind has a "plan." On the other hand,

Molloy's mind contains no recognizable forms. Wandering through unrecognizable landscapes, Molloy enjoys contemplating vast, unbroken spaces. He believes that "when the storm raged, I felt reasonably secure from the elements and mankind" (102). By locating his body within a vast space, Molloy is able to reduce himself to a "black speck in the great pale stretch of sand" (92). He is able to obliterate himself completely as is suggested by his dimensionless self lost on the vast expanse of the limitless sea. The experience of simultaneity significantly points to complete lack of consciousness about selfhood.

Precisely *because* of his comfort with his body, precisely *because* of the absence of any anxiety in maintaining Moran-like illusions, Molloy seems to have particularly easy access to Nirvana-like states such as he experiences in Lousse's garden. It is in that garden that Molloy begins to lose all sense of time and space. Here he experiences an intuition of oneness with created things. Molloy merges with the garden, with the whole cosmos; for a time, the barrier between subject and object mysteriously, even miraculously, disappears:

> And there was another noise, that of my life become the life of this garden as it rode the earth of deeps and wildernesses. Yes, there were times when I forgot not only who I was, but that I was, forgot to be. Then I was no longer that sealed jar to which I owed my being so well preserved. . . . (65)

The image of the self as the "sealed jar" foreshadows the I-self in *The Unnamable*, and brings a darker, sombre note to what Molloy otherwise experiences as serenity or the "silence of the self." Molloy is so much a part of the scene that he remains unaware of seasonal change. The peace of not knowing enters him:

> to know you are beyond knowing anything, that is when peace enters in, to the soul of the incurious seeker. (68)

Abandoning his being to the being of the universe in a Whitmanesque release of the body, Molloy's body assumes the form of "leaves of grass."

Molloy resigns himself to a dreamy torpor in the garden, lying on his back, side or stomach, and becoming one with it. In this union, he imagines words as mere sounds bereft of meaning, and the entire world collapsing endlessly into death. His own sounds become like the buzzing of an insect, and he can no longer understand language. He feels he can no longer distinguish smells and tastes or even judge distances. The felt boundaries of the body are so endlessly variable, indeterminate, or even absent, that it is unclear to Molloy whether the stars seem to tremble or it is his hand upon his knee.

Molloy's experience of a Nirvana-like oceanic experience in Lousse's garden is closely related to Molloy's desire to return to his mother. There is no explicit textual connection between Molloy's experiences at Lousse's house and the quest for his mother. However, the yearning for his mother is, in fact, part of the oceanic, boundary-transgressing definition of his self which he experiences in Lousse's garden. Molloy's sense of merging with the life in the garden is also a kind of merging with the womb of the earth, the Magna Mater absorbing him. The desire to return to the mother is, after all, the chief impetus behind Molloy's entire narrative and is narrated with a striking sense of immediacy:

> having waked between eleven o'clock and midday (I heard the angelus, recalling the incarnation, shortly after) I resolved to go and see my mother. (19)

In aptly alluding to the incarnation, Molloy emphasizes the biological aspects of his relationship with his mother. Just as the incarnation reconciles Word and flesh, Molloy's narrative is a secularized version of the integration Molloy experiences in tracing his origins. Molloy never says that he found his mother, but Molloy's consciousness of her is all-pervasive. He observes that his relationship with his mother holds tremendous significance for him: "If ever I'm reduced to looking for a meaning to my life . . . it's in that old mess I'll stick my nose to begin with, the mess of that poor old uniparous whore and myself the last of that foul brood, neither man nor beast" (23).

Molloy admits that his life has been a series of attempts to arrive at some final resolution about "that old mess." These attempts are the result of a voice Molloy often hears and submits to. The voice frames imperatives to which he says he responds by virtue of the "two fools" he contains: "one asking nothing better than to stay where he is and the other imagining that life might be slightly less horrible a little further on" (64-65). The "hypothetical imperatives" broadly converge on the same terms: "they nearly all bore the same question, that of my relations with my mother. . . " (117).

Molloy refers to a special element in his relationship with his mother: "with her alone I—no, I can't say it. That is to say, I could say it . . . yes, I could say it easily, because it wouldn't be true" (24). He cannot explain his preoccupation with his mother clearly because he does not understand it himself. He feels equal to her in age: "we were like a couple of old cronies, sexless, unrelated, with the same memories, the same rancours, the same expectations" (21). His recognition of his mother and himself as "old cronies" results in some hostility in him since he cannot bear to be addressed as "son." In Molloy's terms, "I took her for my mother, she took me for my father" (21). Molloy says of his mother: "I called her Mag, when I had to call her something. And I called her Mag because for me, without my knowing why, the letter g abolished the syllable Ma, and as it were spat on it, better than any other letter would have done" (21). By calling her "Mag," he tries to abolish the maternal relationship at the same time that it "satisfied a deep and doubtless unacknowledged need to have a Ma" (21). The inevitability of this metamorphosis and confusion is not to establish the identity of Molloy, but rather to lead it to dispossession in a universe where the subject is always non-self-identical, its predicates essentially free-floating.

The mother is deaf and lacks the ability for symbolic exchange. She recognizes Molloy by his odour, the least intellectualized of all senses and responds with an animal joy: "She knew it was me, by my smell. Her shrunken hairy old face lit up, she was happy to smell me" (21). Molloy communicates with her by knocking on her head. "Incontinent of faeces and water" (22), she has reached an advanced stage of decrepitude. She is a "deaf blind impotent mad old woman" (24), and reeks of the "odour of antiquity" (24). Molloy lends some pleasure to his old mother by kissing "that little grey wizened pear" (just as later Malone kisses his mother's "old grey pear" occasionally). Molloy's description of his aged mother collapses the pathos that is traditionally attached to the physical process of ageing. Resentment and repugnance toward his mother conflict with an obscurely perceived attraction.

Searching for roots, losing self and locating selfhood is the theme of the "mythological present" to which Molloy's writing is committed. Molloy is thus inextricably involved in beginning and ending. As a continuously expanding present, Molloy finds himself in his mother's room/womb at the beginning of his narrative. The inaugural sentence of *Molloy*: "I am in my mother's room" (7) suggests an anonymous subject who is no longer Molloy and not yet his mother. His anonymity registers the fundamental intersubjectivity of the self in Beckett. Molloy's arrival in his mother's room, after having crawled through slush and darkness, suggests a condition where he can with wry humour accept that "I must resemble her more and more" (7). Molloy is not sure and cannot recall how he got to his mother's room: "I don't know how I got there. Perhaps in an ambulance, certainly a vehicle of some kind. I was helped" (7). The maternal room offers him the nourishing space of the womb. Composing stories as he lies in his mother's bed, and "piss[es] and shit[s] in her pot" (8), he links his creative afflatus with his arsehole, "a link between me and the other excrement" (107). It is a continuously expanding present as well as simultaneously an infinite progression. Even as he writes the word "now" or "it is midnight," the instant of "now" has already vanished and "it was not midnight" (249). The self is dimensionless and Molloy cannot recall whether he is dead or alive: "From things about to disappear I turn away in time. To watch them out of sight, no, I can't do it" (14-15).

Molloy's mother is evidently the origin and the end of Molloy's quest: "And of myself, all my life, I think I had been going to my mother, with the purpose of establishing our relations on a less precarious footing" (118). He imagines being dead and then realizes that "there is no denying it, any longer, it is not you who are dead, but all the others. So you get up and go to your mother, who thinks she is alive" (19). The world dies and to revivify it, one seeks the mother who is the source of life. When Molloy is with her, he says he "left her without having done anything." And without her, he is "on [his] way to her." His point of departure is not the relationship between his presence in a room and the world outside but a symmetrical relationship between his mind and its representations. Molloy's quest includes the dialectic between the idiom of lived experience and that of imaginative fabrication: "Yes, so far as I was capable of being bent on anything all a lifetime long . . . I had been bent on settling this matter between my mother and me. . . ." (87).

The desire for death which Molloy often expresses is a desire to be reabsorbed in his mother's womb. The symbolic death and burial of Lousse's dog inspire Molloy to reflect on how the dog was more fortunate than he: "he at least was dead" (46). It echoes Bakhtin's conception of death as not being final, and burial bringing forth new life from the womb of the earth.

Molloy experiences animosity toward his mother and yet desires a merging with this polymorphous image of his anima. The ambivalent nature of his relationship with his mother stems precisely from the irresolute nature of his self. Molloy describes his progress toward his mother as "a veritable calvary, with no limit to its stations and no hope of crucifixion" (105). A calvary with no end suggests an interminable sense of suffering with no hope for redemption. Setting out to see his mother after seeing A and C, Molloy speaks of leaving "this earthly paradise . . . sheltered from certain winds. . . " (20). He comes upon "a kind of crossroads" (112). It is a kind of center of wholeness, even "a star, or circus." Here "crossroads" evokes the figure of "veritable calvary" again with its Dantesque paradisal overtones. It also helps to explain why the women, Ruth/Edith and Lousse and his mother, merge into the same and one image. It may also help to explain why Ruth/Edith's name is misremembered as Rose. Caught within the incommunicative trap of language, Molloy knows that the search—the question of finding his mother—is in part, the search for the meaning of the self. Tracing an archetypal pattern for the self, the search for the mother is the search for a return to the source, the central core of one's being and self.

Molloy often stops his search with the realization that none of the events actually occurred: "simply somewhere something had changed, so that I too had to change, or the world had to change . . . And it was these little adjustments, as between Galileo's vessels, that I can only express by saying, I feared that, or, I hoped that, or Is that your mother's name" (119). The apprehension that the self will be altered or even lost, is an investigation into the nature of identity, and is a central concern with Beckett. As early as *Proust*, Beckett wrote:

> Man is the creature that cannot come forth from himself, who knows others only in himself, and who, if he asserts the contrary, lies. (49)

To their discomfort, Beckett's characters are assaulted by the fear that their self becomes unrecognizable, or at least, is known only in the other. In cataloging the problems of "self" in Beckett's work, Linda Ben-Zvi acutely observes that "at any given moment the self exists as two separate entities: an outer I, alive in the macrocosm, commingling with the physical world, and an inner me, unseen, unheard, alive only to the I" (*Samuel Beckett*, 5). Beckett's search for selfhood is, in effect, a caricature as he depicts his characters struggling to realize themselves within an abyss of nothingness founded on their hatred of birth, extrojected in the repugnance toward the mother if not all womankind, and ultimately entwined with womb-tomb longing.

The gradual realization of the infinitude of the self collapses the sense of self-transcendence the characters hope to achieve over their bodies which are subject to the corrosive forces of time and space. Concerned with stripping away all external circumstance to lay bare the self, Beckett dismantles everything in order to lead towards the absolute nothingness underlying human life. Though Beckett feigned to despise philosophy, he had some favorite maxims of philosophers, such as Democritus's "Nothing is more real than nothing." And proceeding from this, one can vouch that if Beckett's art is minimalist, it is so in the sense of the naked, unaccommodated images of the physical to which everything is ultimately reduced. The fact that all of Beckett's protagonists, even his later ones, preoccupy themselves with the Hamlet dilemma may explain to a certain extent, why they all consistently fight their births and yearn for death. It is, to my mind, not merely an issue of life and death, but rather of locating the burden of their selfhood, their core identity.

The desire to be finished with living is one more manifestation of the biological in a Bakhtinian form—the celebration of the flux of life not in its Bakhtinian medieval incarnation, but in a more modern variant of a grotesque body. Obsessed with birth and death, Beckett's characters often imagine themselves, like Malone, born into death: "The feet are clear already of the great cunt of existence. . . . My head will be the last to die" (114). The dying Moll of Malone's fiction manifests symptoms of pregnancy, and the Unnamable's gradual recession into his womblike jar is almost akin to death. One way the protagonists try to apprehend the self is through their engagement with death. Death is, of course, a perpetual challenge in Beckett's world. Murphy concludes that raising Lazarus from the dead was "perhaps the one occasion on which the Messiah had overstepped the mark" (180). And like the protagonist of the short story, *First Love*, who prefers the odour of corpses to "what the living emit" (11), Watt comes almost to like the smell of death. The life-death continuity is underscored in such suggestions of coming and going, appearance and disappearance. The sense of constant becoming assaults any notion of absolute reality. Implicit in Beckett's depiction of the body then, is the sense of the imminence of death in an infinite landscape of potentiality.

Death would threaten and at the same time endorse the experience of the body. Molloy is thus not sure whether he is alive or dead. Although his "wanderjahre" is terminated, he feels that

> the confines of my room, of my bed, of my body, are as remote from me as were those of my region in the days of my splendour. (88)

From this premise, he proceeds to explore issues of selfhood, existence, and mental processes. Beckett's Molloy serves as a complex variant of Bakhtin's idea of the grotesque body. Molloy's abandonment of his body to the natural phenomena around him allows for a Bakhtinian kind of transcendence. "All I know is what the words know," Molloy states, "and the dead things, and that makes a handsome little sum, with a beginning, a middle and an end, as in the well-built phrase and the long sonata of the dead" (41). His physical journey being terminated, his existence becomes "interminable" (16). Molloy, Malone, and even the Unnamable are uncertain whether they are dead or alive. Not only is Molloy unsure whether his mother was dead or not when he last saw her, he is uncertain about his own existence. Caught unawares, he is sure that "that may come in useful," and that "it is only since I ceased to live that I think of these things" (32). He is really not so sure, however, if "total freedom" is only possible in a world "without end." As he remains resilient toward extinction, beyond time, beyond the cosmos, he remains unaware that time and movement are really not rigidly conditioned by Watt's "law of series": "From things about to disappear I turn away in time. To watch them out of sight, no, I can't do it" (14-15). And so Molloy is able to freely confess that

> death is a condition I have never been able to conceive to my satisfaction and which therefore I cannot go down in the ledger of weal and woe. (91)

One of the most persistent trends in philosophical exploration has been an exclusive concern with the self, as distinguished from man in general, the endeavour to reduce all experiences to the experience between man and himself. The alienation from the self, or alternately, the withdrawal into the self, are typical phenomena which compel one to question the logic of what constitutes the "self." For both Bakhtin and Beckett, traditional ontology and epistemology are inadequate in explaining the nature of the self and of empirical existence. Like Bakhtin, Beckett seems uncomfortable with such constructions, and is certainly critical of traditional philosophical categories where the human subject perceives itself as a timeless and self-adequate "ego." Beckett's world always hints at meaning but never encompasses meaning. The Beckett protagonists are caught between the external and the internal: "neither one side nor the other" (134).

The "self" for Bakhtin, is constituted through the conflicting network of social practices which is continuously mobile. The possibility of a self-contained consciousness is completely ruled out by Bakhtin for whom discursive interaction with another "I" begins from birth itself. Bakhtin writes in *Problems of Dostoevsky's Poetics*: "To be means to communicate. Absolute death (non-being) is the state of being unheard, unrecognized" (287) implying that every aspect of consciousness constitutes a multiplicity of communicative gestures. Bakhtin's conceptualizations are helpful in eroding, even synthesizing, the inane dichotomies of subject and object, form and content, individual and society as they have bedevilled concepts of the self, language and society. The dynamism involving the constitutive dialectic of continuous social interaction circumvents any kind of psychological reductionism. As a socially constituted entity, the self, according to Bakhtin, spurns the rational, autonomous, and of course, the incorporeal being postulated by Descartes. Through his deployment of carnivalized metaphors and Menippean scenarios, Bakhtin works out the vacuous consequences of the fundamental beliefs and principles of Western culture. Hence, the self in a perpetual state of becoming is "decentered" and the opposition of the social to the individual is transcended. Indeed, it would be fair to state that the Bakhtin of the *Rabelais* book has little use for selves or for individuals. The construction of the self is really of little moment to his conception of the "grotesque" body, and although it is inscribed in the "classical" body, Bakhtin does not seem to have much to say about it, or even in its favour.

While Beckett turns or tropes upon the same configuration of features suggested by Bakhtin, Bakhtinian postulations are not just a template for perceiving their application in Beckett. In appropriating Bakhtinian themes and concept for constructing my argument, I am not suggesting a complete blending of their views. While the intellectual interaction of Beckett and Bakhtin I have shown is very strong, the dangers of oversimplification in the comparison as well as the hemorrhaging of credibility in straining any further, can also not be ruled out. Beckett's pronounced affinity with the themes and concerns of contemporary philosophy reveals that in many respects, he cannot be associated with the more "value based" legacy of Bakhtin. While the metaphysical contraries in Beckett as well as Bakhtin's vision often lead to indiscrimination, Bakhtin is, in my view, certainly the more metaphysical and idealist of the two. I believe that Beckett's poststructuralist decentering of the subject is in important respects different from the decentering carried out by the Marxist socializing of the subject that we find in Bakhtin. Nonetheless, despite the inherent pitfalls of an extended comparison, there are ways in which Bakhtin's theorizations do give us insight into Beckett's understanding of what constitutes the self.

In accordance with Bakhtin's idea of the inversion of social, physical and semantic hierarchies, Beckett's world is one in which the substance of social identity is dissolved even as the biological is privileged. The self in Beckett, likewise, seems to be a suspect entity, indeterminately placed in the constitutive categories of being. Bakhtin's postulations do help to throw light on the fact of being incarnated in flesh as Beckett presents it, the boundary lines of the body collapsing the distinctions between inner and outer in both Beckett as well as Bakhtin. In the ultimate analysis, the physicality of being as ontologically prior to all other particulars does affect the contingent nature of identity. And in Beckett's ontological scheme of identity, the radical instability of the self provides us with an epistemological basis for claims about physical identity.

CHAPTER THREE

The Body's Disciplining in *Molloy, Godot* and *Catastrophe*

Who perceives, who enunciates the difficulty?
Jacques Derrida, "Cogito and the History of Madness,"
Writing and Difference

Until the subject of a tyrant's will
Became, worse fate, the abject of his own
Percy Bysshe Shelley, *Prometheus Unbound*

In addition to the concern for what constitutes identity, Beckett's writings are also concerned with how the self is disciplined, denigrated, and denied. Beckett's preoccupation with body signifiers reflects his awareness of the regulating and thwarting forces on the body reduced, repressed, and objectified. The repressive nature of impositions on the body, moreover, has political implications for the nature of selfhood. One thing that is noteworthy about Beckett's fictional as well as his dramatic characters is that, very often, they lose all autonomy or ontological status by virtue of this disciplining.

Bodily inscription and the discourse associated with the process of inscribing assume political overtones that, as Sheila Rabillard puts it,

> has essentially to do not with the human being in isolation (if such can in fact be conceived), but with being collective and interpenetrative, each shaped by material and social conditions which each in turn helps to create. ("The Body in Beckett: Dene-gation and the Critique of a Depoliticized Theatre," 99)

The attacks on the body in Beckett's writings—the wounding, lacerating, incarcerating, maiming—represent a kind of politicization of the body. This political investment of the body is bound up in an intricate reciprocal nexus with the social and other forces operating on the body.

In this chapter, I will draw on Michel Foucault's *Discipline and Punish*, and to a lesser extent, Elaine Scarry's pioneering work on *The Body in Pain*, to examine, in some of Beckett's writings, how political power operates interactively through the use of torture and pain to scrutinize and judge, to bend and break the body. For Foucault, as for Bakhtin, the body itself is the site of ideological inscription. If Bakhtin's work is read as a treatise on bodily semiotics, then the carnivalesque subversion it celebrates forms an interesting dialectical relationship with the bodily disciplining found in the conceptualizations of Foucault. Beckett's obsession with bodily experience stems not only from a concern with Bakhtinian freedom and subversion but also from the Foucauldian idea of power as micro-politics and bodily disciplines. Foucault argues that social and institutional powers, channeled through ideological state violence, transform the individual into an abstraction. The disciplinary mechanisms that repress and thereby define individuality substitute the "calculable" for the "memorable" man, thus producing the self as the object of scientific analysis and control..

In questioning the ontology of the human subject, Beckett subscribes to the Foucauldian view that the subject is an effect of power constituted in discourses that link power to knowledge. The decentering, even the rejection, of human subjectivity as an interior or as essence, and the substitution for it of one fabricated by power and knowledge, has powerful implications in Beckett. In Foucauldian terms,

> the body is also directly involved in a political field; power relations have an immediate hold upon it; they invest it, mark it, train it, torture it, force it to carry out tasks, to perform ceremonies, to emit signs. (*Discipline and Punish*, 25)

Foucault offers a historical argument about the onset of the institutional repression and disciplining of the body. In *Discipline and Punish*, he examines the socio-historical methods by which the Enlightenment spirit of inquiry and truth was used for the surveillance and disciplining of individual bodies. His focus is on conceptions of power-knowledge relations and of the body as the object of the exercise of technologies of power. Within sociological analysis, the body has always assumed the form of a natural body, a body that is without either history or culture. In Foucault's work, on the other hand, the body is a central component in the operation of power relations. His genealogical analysis reveals the body as an object of knowledge and as a target for the exercise of power. The body is shown to be located in a political field, invested with power relations which render it docile and productive, and thus politically and economically useful. Although Foucault's discussion addresses the transformation in forms of punishment and the emergence of the modern penal institutions, the principal focus of analysis falls upon the "power and knowledge relations that invest human bodies and subjugate them by turning them into objects of knowledge" (53). Discipline and training can reconstruct the body to produce new gestures and habits, and ultimately new kinds of people. This political technology of the body has no specific institutional locus. Rather, there is a diffusion of particular technologies of power and their interrelationships with the emergence of those forms of knowledge which have the individual as their subject.

Foucault conceptualizes power neither as an institution nor as a structure but as a "complex strategical situation," as a "multiciplicity of force relations," as simultaneously "intentional" yet "non-subjective." In short, power is an inherent characteristic of all human relations. And significantly, Foucault has argued that "where there is power, there is resistance" and that power depends for its existence on the presence of a "multiciplicity of points of resistance" (16). By this, Foucault implies that every relationship of power implies a potential "strategy for struggle." He has used the Greek term "agon" for this confrontation. The implication is that the relatively stable mechanisms through which the exercise of power seems to take place may be displaced by the "free play of antagonistic reactions" (37). Within the various discursive levels at which power operates, the exercise of power is also interactive. One limit to power arises when the subject or individual over which power is exercised is reduced to impotence. The other limit stems from the insubordination, resistance, and consequent freedom of an agent. The relationship between power and the intransigence of freedom is the crucial nexus in the power struggle.

There is a distinct Foucauldian strain in Beckett's work which presents the body as a space on which the tension between self and other, internal and external, is played out. Beckett's writings also represent those beings who endeavour to repress and exercise control over the bodies they can silence. (In this context, W.B. Worthen has discussed at length the corporeal subjection of Beckett's actors, most prominent among whom was Billie Whitelaw performing in *Not I*.) Those who tyrannize deprive the subjected bodies of their elemental rights. Although Foucault is concerned with the historical examination of the biopolitics of power rather than with a Beckettian fictionalized rendering of power, the relevance of Foucault's writings to Beckett's is undeniable. Both can be historically situated in France at the same post-World War II moment. Also, Foucault's writings help us to see the extent to which Beckett's writings are politically engaged, and I shall stress this in the course of my chapter. Foucault's "genealogical" method radically historicizes given patterns and social practices of sexuality and mental ailments as they are controlled by power regimes which have sought to shape, subordinate, suppress, and thereby "naturalize" forms of knowledge. These given patterns of "power/knowledge" emerge in subtle ways in Beckett's writings, which reveal the same hostility as that of Foucault toward the truth-claims of particular regimes as well as the cognitive superiority of their discourses.

The changes in bodily control as part of the "civilizing" process accompanying the development of the capitalist mode of production have been variously commented upon by, among others, Karl Marx, Sigmund Freud, and Norbert Elias. It was Foucault, however, who narrowed the focus from social control to bodily manipulation and control. According to him, the body in pre-industrial times was the vehicle through which the sovereign symbolically projected his power. The body was subject to brute public torture, violence, direct sanctions, executions and mutilations. By the end of the eighteenth century, the body became the focus of various "technologies of power" and increasingly came to be viewed as an instrument for training and manipulation, for extracting energy from it in the most "rational" manner possible. The new control involved

> exercising upon [the body] a subtle coercion, of obtaining holds upon it at the level of the mechanism itself—movements, gestures, rapidity and an infinitesimal power over the active body. (*Discipline and Punish*, 137)

The increasing socioeconomic changes, the large-scale "rationalized" systems of production, further brought in a whole new set of "micro-penalties." This led to further refining of body discipline, imposed both from inside and from outside the body.

The key emphasis is on invisible or subtle control: the use of direct coercion has been replaced by indirect coercion in both the private and the public spheres. The effects of these invisible yet pervasive manifestations of power are quite real and it is with these effects—discernible at the level where discourses take hold on bodies and affect the everyday existence of human beings—that Foucault is concerned above all. Foucault describes

> the set of material elements and techniques that serve as weapons, relays, communication routes and supports for the power and knowledge relations that invest human bodies and subjugate them by turning them into objects of knowledge. (28)

Foucault emphasizes not so much power as unitary or imposed from without, or manipulated through a state apparatus endorsing ideological legitimation, as the more subtle impact on the body of institutional discourses. In the conception of the "gaze of power," he provides a basic explanation for the manner in which power is exercised, thus making the connection between power and knowledge. Foucault's discourse on the various "technologies of power" leads to his insistence on material practices operating interactively at the level of everyday social existence. In this way, he has also provided an understanding of relations of power through his analysis of resistance and struggle.

I turn now to some of Beckett's works, beginning with *Molloy*, to show Beckett's representation of the disciplining of the body as Foucault describes it. In Beckett's prose writings, especially in the trilogy, the tyrant is a dominant figure: the police officer who apprehends Molloy and deprives him of physical rest and mental quietude; Moran who uses his son Jacques as a slave at the same time that he is mesmerized by his own tyrant, Youdi; "the powers that be" in *Malone Dies* who appear, Youdi-like, to confine Malone in his room, as well as Lemuel who exhibits extreme cruelty in killing the innocent sailors and in leaving Lady Pedal to perish; and the unnamed "they" in *The Unnamable*. Both Molloy and Moran feel the stress of a malevolent power playing with their lives. For Molloy, "they" control his writing as well as his life:

> What I'd like now is to speak of the things that are left, say my goodbyes, finish dying. They don't want that. Yes, there is more than one, apparently. But it's always the same one that comes. You'll do that later, he says. (7)

Feeling uneasy whenever he lies down "in defiance of the rules," or when he believes he is "going against an imperative," he realizes that "I have always been inclined to submit to them, I don't know why." His overwhelming sense of guilt about "going against an imperative" leads to his conviction that he "has greatly sinned . . . against my prompters." In the course of his journey through the forest, he feels uncomfortable whenever he rests "in defiance of the rules." The "veritable calvary" involves loss of all sense-perceptions, of the coordinated functioning of mind and body:

> For I no longer know what I'm doing, nor why, those are things I understand less and less, I don't deny it, for why deny it, and to whom, to you, to whom nothing is denied? (60-61)

Moran experiences the same pressure to "crave forgiveness, forgiveness for what?" His assignment is better defined than Molloy's, though Moran speaks of it as "a cause which . . . was in its essence anonymous, and would subsist . . . when its miserable artisans should be no more" (157). The orders are transmitted to Moran through an internalized voice, the voice of the other which Molloy first hears in the ditch, and which "haunts" the Unnamable, filling him like a balloon to such an extent that it is the very "voice" with which he "himself" speaks.

Of all Beckett's characters, Moran is most obviously coerced by institutional discourses. That coercion has been internalized as repression. Moran has repressed certain socially unacceptable and darker qualities about himself, a confession he is forced into after savagely thrashing his son. It is no accident that this anal character lives in a town called Turdy. Tyrannical and overbearing, self-centered but dependent on others—his son, his housekeeper, Youdi—Moran is humorless and punctilious. So deep is Moran's "horror of the body and its functions" (161), that he even finds the physical sight of his son repulsive:

> the prospect was more than I could bear of being unable to move a step without having before my eyes my son's little sullen plump body. (177)

The comic-pathetic attempt of Moran to control a physicality that fascinates and repulses him reveals how inadequate is the pattern of his life as well as his philosophical creed. Moran himself is well-adapted to his society's institutions, and he has also tried to rear his son as a part of his well-ordered universe. He dismisses self-doubts as minor quirks, sinful aberrations in this larger, well-ordered system.

The repression has given him, a brutal child-abuser, a split persona, since there are occasions when Moran displays extreme vehemence and others when he displays extreme solicitude toward his son, Jacques. Moran's son, interestingly, has a presence only in his absence as he is perceived only in the tyrannical subjugation of his bodily self. Moran rightly perceives in his son's body an image of Jacques's essential freedom which he cannot subject to his tyrannical wishes. His son's body represents an element in Moran's fine-tuned existence that Moran cannot control. He cannot comprehend why his son maintains a dull and studied silence with him when he is otherwise very loquacious with his companions. Just as Molloy is oriented toward his mother, Moran is fixated upon his son: "thirteen or fourteen at the time. He was big and strong for his age. His intelligence seemed at times little short of average" (128). When Jacques complains of a stomach-ache, Moran, his father thunders:

> A stomach-ache! Have you a temperature I said. I don't know, he said. Find out, I said. He was looking more and more stupefied. Fortunately I rather enjoyed dotting my i's. . . . As he went out . . . I added jocosely, You know which mouth to put it in? I was not averse, in conversation with my son, to jests of doubtful taste, in the interests of his education. (160-61)

Moran treats his son abominably but justifies his arbitrary severity with high moral principles.

A thorough-bred patriarch, Moran's aggression is reinforced by the phallic objects he uses in imposing his will: the lighted cigar, the enema, the umbrella. He constantly suspects his son of deception and disobedience. He disciplines him unmercifully, ostensibly in the interest of his son, but really because he delights in maintaining his authority. Sometimes he sentimentalizes about being a good father, but shortly thereafter has "a violent scene" with him. On the day of his departure, he is unable to brook resistance from his resisting son whom he beats with a stout umbrella "by the end with both hands." Seized with a maniacal fury, he has a dim perception that he may kill his son: "I hear . . . the benches creaking in the court of the assizes." Hence he leaves the room immediately to chop wood in his shed, and returns to help his son dress, almost as if nothing had occurred. Yet the terrifying vision of his hacking the chopping-block is clearly only a slightly displaced version of his violence against his son. Moran's subsequent remark, that he dislikes both men and animals and that God has begun to disgust him, are further expressions of his anger. However, he does return in a calmer frame and helps his weeping son to dress, as if nothing had happened. His relationship to his son is thus characterized by a mixture of mawkish emotion and sadistic joy.

At the inexplicable bidding of Youdi, Moran takes his son with him on his expedition, but he is unable to quell the conflict in his feelings toward his son. Jacques wishes to take a few treasured stamps with him, but Moran removes the albums on the ground that doing so will teach him life's most valuable lesson—how to do without. Moran deprives and thwarts his son himself but believes that it is his sulking son who is defiant. He begins to appreciate Jacques better as he struggles with the difficulties that overtake him in the course of his mission. Seemingly (at first) a confident parent, Moran gradually acknowledges his dependence on his son: "He took good care of me, I must say. He was clumsy, stupid, slow, dirty . . . but he did not abandon me" (216-17). Although he continues to be an overbearing father, there is an alteration in his feeling if not his conduct.

During the course of the journey, Jacques first aids his father and then abandons him, thereby asserting his own independence. Moran's persisting arrogance compels Jacques to leave his father following an argument in which the patriarchal presumption reaches an excess: "I must have got the better of [the argument] as I always did, thanks to my infallible technique, and brought him unerringly to a proper sense of his iniquities" (219-20). After his son leaves him to fend for himself, Moran is possessed by a "hellish hope" that

> my son, his anger spent, would have pity on me and come back to me! or that Molloy . . . would come to me . . . and grow to be a friend, and like a father to me, and help me to do what I had to do. (222)

Ultimately, he is totally shorn of all means or any expectation of help. The "mollifying" process of Moran begins when he, as an agent exercising power, becomes the obverse, the hopeful object of the empowering agent.

What Moran inflicts on his son is replicated in the infliction he himself suffers. In fact, Beckett draws a neat symmetry between the relationship of Moran and Jacques and that between Youdi and Moran. Just as Moran endeavours to overwhelm Jacques so does Youdi overpower Moran himself. The commands of Youdi, Moran's "employer," are always stated in the future tense ("You shall . . . "), and are always impossible for Moran to disobey or defy in any sense. The undefined Youdi has echoes of Yahweh in his name, and there is something Biblical in Moran's fear of Youdi's anger. When it is recalled that his task is to find Molloy and if, as is abundantly hinted, Molloy represents hidden possibilities within Moran, one can explain and rationalize his behaviour. When Gaber gives him his assignment, Moran cannot explain to himself why Molloy is "no stranger to me," though he knows "nothing of the circumstances in which I had learnt of his existence." Vladimir and Estragon waiting indefinitely for Godot provide a parallel to Moran's predicament. Godot, the object of the tramps' expectation, is a vaguely defined entity in their minds. However, since Moran's uncertainty about Molloy exceeds the tramps' uncertainty about Godot, he experiences a greater form of dread. Finding Molloy is his mission and, soon, his obsession. As in the case of Molloy's imperatives, the command for Moran comes from an undefined external source. Moran must respond to the imperatives of reason, externalized in a presumably "vast organization" (147) of agents, messengers, and authorities. Unlike Molloy's "hypothetical imperatives" (87), Moran feels the compelling requirement of Youdi's "simple prophetic present."

Moran's haphazard planning for the journey is ominous. As he undertakes his obscure mission, he experiences a difficult struggle with himself. In the solitude and darkness, protected from the external world's "spray of phenomena" (151), Moran thinks about the unnamed "him" "who has need of me to be delivered, who cannot deliver myself" (151). In the process of imagining Molloy, Moran begins to change. He assumes an affinity with Molloy, "a kind of connection, and one not necessarily false." He also ascribes him a mythic dimension, "the air of a fabulous being." The mythic Molloy is remote from Moran's world, and yet is at the same time his own personal Molloy. Moran wonders whether he "had invented him, I mean found him ready-made in my head." For Molloy is, in so many ways, the opposite of Moran the rational and meticulous man, pedantically obsessed about his domestic regime and the "falsetto of reason" (147). Moran is not sure whether there is a conflict between the Molloy so inadequately described to him by Gaber in his orders and the "man of flesh and blood somewhere awaiting me."

Even before setting out on his mission, Moran occasionally sheds his complacency and acknowledges his limitations. He speaks of his life within the limits of a rationally-ordered purpose as a "contrivance" (156), an "inenarrable contraption" (156), and a "fatuous clamour" (146). Beyond it lies "the silence of which the universe is made" (166). He knows that the ordinary way of perceiving, like those "who pride themselves on their eagle gaze" (166), is essentially deceptive. His rationally ordered existence is, he knows, a means of avoiding the chaotic flood of sensations: "It is at the mercy of these sensations, which happily I know to be illusory, that I have to live and work. It is thanks to them I find myself a meaning" (151). Moran imagines that there may be an alternative, for his son if not for him, to this life of "meanings" erected on illusory sensations: "I had not struggled, toiled, suffered, made good, lived like a Hottentot, so that my son should do the same" (166). The "Molloy affair" leads Moran beyond these uncertainties, beyond the life of "duty" to a new freedom. Expelled from a comfortable house and garden, from the assurance of a self-definition and a personal identity, Moran and his son turn their backs on the everyday world of material possessions to leave for the Molloy country. They pass through "the little wicket-gate" (174) that leads into "the right road, it of my election" (174).

As Moran begins to move toward the imaginative world of that "fabulous being," he begins to change. He takes on some of Molloy's weaknesses. He is driven through stages of self-diminishment. Numerous parallels suggest a merging of Moran and Molloy: both set out on a quest, both hear a gong, both meet two strangers, and both make use of a bicycle and a crutch. In his search for Molloy, Moran increasingly loses control of his mind and body until he assumes the postures, attitudes and confusions of Molloy on his journey to his mother's room. Subject to the same deterioration as Molloy, Moran experiences visions of an "intruder self," which is at once Molloy and Moran himself (his face "vaguely resembled my own"). Of the many Molloys the rational Moran had tried to conjure up, he does coincide with at least one, the Molloy he had imagined as the opposite of himself. The "fabulous" Molloy had "seemed to be crashing through jungle. He did not so much walk as charge" (154). After his own gradual self-transformation, Moran almost lurches forward, throwing himself against the obstacles in his way: "The more things resist me the more rabid I get." And on his return journey, Moran says, "Bent double, my free hand pressed to my belly, I advanced, and every now and then I let out a roar, of triumph and distress." (228)

What comes into focus in the course of Moran's journeying is this gradual but tremendous change. Moran has two irrational encounters during the course of his search for Molloy: one with a man carrying a massive stick and one, the next day, with a man whose face "vaguely resembled my own . . . same little abortive moustache, same little ferrety eyes, . . . and a thin red mouth that looked as if it was raw from trying to shit its tongue" (206). As Moran perceives this second man reaching out to shake his hand, he strikes out, reducing the man to a pulp, and then disposes of the dead body. It is significant that Moran's leg begins to bend normally for a while after he commits the irrational murder: the murder has been in some sense liberating. Moran also remarks that "he no longer resembled me" (208) once the victim's face has been ravaged. The murder has been a form of suicide, the killing of the socialized, petit-bourgeois Moran, and the emergence of the Molloy element within Moran. It also spells the repudiation of his responsibilities to Youdi. While Moran cannot actually recall the details of the murder, it is significant that it involves the scattering of the "great bunch of keys" that he always carries. He tries to collect these dispersed keys as the visible emblem of a coherent identity. "Finally I said, Hell to it, I'll do with those I have" (209).

The dispersed keys, suggesting the abandonment of relationships he has either presumed or desired (the departure of his son being preeminent), are symptomatic of a new sense of freedom, perhaps a sign of his "growing resignation of being dispossessed of self" (204). Moran may be seen to be disengaging himself from the many identifications that once held him secure. At one point, between the encounters with the two strangers, Moran gazes at his own image in a pool. He perceives himself changed, "so changed from what I was" (203). Looking at his own reflection, Moran perceives himself "ageing as a dayfly." An intense transformation shakes him to the roots: "And what I saw was more like a crumbling, a frenzied collapsing from all I was condemned to be" (203). As he now watches "a little globe" swaying through the depths of the water, he experiences dispossession of self.

In a rare moment of tranquillity, Moran experiences an attraction to a silent shepherd to whom he longs to say: "Take me with you, I will serve you faithfully. . . " (218). But "the shepherd silent and the dog unheeded, the little flock departed" (219). The pastoral idyll is a poignantly wishful investing of his own false securities that he knows he has lost forever: "For I had no illusions, I knew that all was about to end, or to begin again, it little mattered which. . . " (221). Shorn of all imperatives and responsibilities, Moran is born to a new sense of discovery. Deprived of the "illusion" of purposive activity, a life of goals and directions, he experiences a new sense of becoming:

> And I remained for several days, I do not know how many . . . seeing no living soul, powerless to act, or strong enough at last to act no more. (221)

Paradoxically, it entails more courage to relinquish a life controlled by the habits of reason and a regulated regimen than to conform to it. Moran acquires that courage in his new awakening.

It is important for Moran to lose one identity—that of the rational man, devoted to method and principle—in order to gain another, that which accepts "life without tears, as it is wept." His former identity built on rational constructs had made him a victim by summoning him to tasks that were not his own. The identity he thinks he has now gained has actually persisted through external changes:

> the face my hands felt was not my face any more . . . and yet the gist of the sensation was the same as in the far-off days. . . . And to tell the truth I not only knew who I was, but I had a sharper and clearer sense of my identity than ever before. . . .(170-71)

Dispossessed, Moran feels free of all possessions. He is excited to "mighty fits of silent laughter" when he visualizes the spectacle of a distant town where rational men conduct the kind of rational activity he used to. He feels "extraordinarily content, content with myself, almost elated, enchanted with my performance" (223).

Gaber's abrupt order: "Moran, Jacques, home, instanter" (224), suggests another break with his former self. Gaber will not listen to Moran's protests that he is sick and abandoned by his son. He merely repeats the message and asks for beer as he is very thirsty. At the end of their conversation, there is another non sequitur: "I opened my eyes. I was alone. My hands were full of grass and earth I had torn up unwittingly and was still tearing up" (226). Gaber has vanished as mysteriously as he had arrived. The order no longer seems compelling, and Moran discredits the authority of the larger order it serves. He has realized that Gaber, "playing his part of go-between," is no more than a projection of his own hallucinating mind.

Earlier in his narrative, Moran admitted to lucid moments, in which he "came even to doubt the existence of Gaber himself . . . and I might have gone to the extreme of conjuring away the chief too and regarding myself as solely responsible for my wretched existence" (147). The full force of that doubt now comes upon Moran, as Gaber's voice becomes for him the "new voice," the voice he hears internally. Moran begins by thinking of his writing as a kind of "pensum," a task imposed on him. When Moran ejects Gaber from his mind, he says that though he still writes, there is no fear in him. Just as Beckett found his motivating energy in "the obligation to express" although he knows there is no principle or cause for the modern artist, no paint and nothing to paint with, which provides an ultimate validation to his work, Moran perceives his obligation as "the voice." It is this voice which takes over now as Moran explains why he must write a report :

> No, I am still afraid, but simply from force of habit. And the voice I listen to needs no Gaber to make it heard. For it is

> within me and exhorts me to continue to the end the faithful servant I have always been, of a cause that is not mine, and patiently fulfil in all its bitterness my calamitous part. (180)

The new voice keeps Moran to his old tasks, but it gives rise to obedience without loyalty. Exiled from his rational life, he can now hear intimations of an alternative to purposiveness.

Moran wills himself to return home not under the threat of Youdi, but by the process of learning to understand the new voice. Moran's homecoming, under painful duress, can be seen as "fulfilment" through disintegration. There is no sense of closure in his return home. Instead, Moran has a proleptic vision of the aimlessness that lies beyond the disintegration of the rational man he was. He often recalls the dance of his bees; to him, the motion of the bees is meaningful—he has distinguished and classified various aspects of the hum, the figure and height in their dance—but the nature of that "meaning" is completely opaque to him. As he undergoes a transformation, he insists on the distinction between himself and the objects he encounters: "And I would never do my bees the wrong I had done my God, to whom I had been taught to ascribe my angers, fears, desires, and even my body." In this way, his refusal to comprehend them in any sense is a new dimension he adds to his own sense of being free and being human. Both the coherence he himself once so speciously forced on his life and his identity crumble away like the handful of dead bees he pulls from the hive.

Returning home, Moran is able to observe calmly the ruin and destruction that have taken place. His bees and hens have died, and Martha has vanished. His previously well-regulated life has consequently gone. During Moran's absence, the electricity has been cut off. When the company offers to reconnect it, he does not want it. After selling everything that can be sold, he is left only with debts. In this way, Moran has given up all external manifestations of his former identity. He tells the reader of the wonderful summer days in his garden, and the peace within him. His new sense of freedom makes him believe that he has "been a man long enough" (240), and he plans to set out once more on a journey which has no objective or destination or the promise of any achievement.

While embarking on his search for Molloy, Moran had foreseen a "long anguish of vagrancy and freedom." Moran had used the word "freedom" as it was used by Kierkegaard, that is, as a constraining force. Freedom was also connected in his mind with vagabondage, the kind of loneliness and exile that is suggested in Sartre's *Les Mouches*. What Moran experiences, however, is something more liberating. Liberating himself from his false consciousness, it is not surprising that Moran speaks of "the great inward metamorphosis" that he has undergone. By releasing oneself from the questionable character of accustomed intelligibility, Moran releases himself from his previous identity which was signified by material possessions.

Moran's narrative reveals the many ways in which the individual is threatened and diminished by the developed forms of social organization. The various forms of reasoning are synonymous with structures of power and repression. Power is directed at the very formation of the body and of identity. To reconstruct a sense of freedom from the forces of power is to anchor oneself on an endless questioning of constituted experience. To question the self-evidence of a form of experience, of concrete systems of thought, knowledge, or power, is to free it and to open it to new possibilities. The representation of the disciplined body in Moran thus shows Beckett's elaboration of a Foucault-like idea of power struggle within the discourse of Moran's intensely bourgeois world.

Foucault's insights also provide a framework for understanding how Beckett explores the interplay of power and subjection in his drama, of how theatre and power interpenetrate. Through representation on stage, the mechanisms of power and authority are exposed and, often also displaced. The mimetic play of power inflicting impositions in a theatrical spectacle makes the body the object of sensory abuse. Foucault deploys theatrical imagery to show coercive techniques being implemented as the "political technology of the body." The panoptic methods and techniques employed in agencies of power result in control and surveillance so that "the 'physics' of power, the hold over the body, operate according to the laws of optics and mechanics, according to a whole play of spaces, lines, screens, beams, degrees, and without recourse, in principle at least, to excess, force or violence" (177). Whether a public and ceremonial display of power or a new economy of disciplinary technologies, the body is subject to a political anatomy of discipline.

That theatre is primarily a visual medium also bears on Beckett's criticism of the "gaze of power" in his later prose works. For Foucault, the primacy of sight leads to the association between reason and power. When reason is associated with the subject abstracted rather than with its inherence in the world, it results in ordering, empowering, objectifying. Foucault uses the analogy of the "panopticon" to suggest the image of this "eye of power" which is associated with the operations of reason. The "panopticon" is the penal structure which made the inmates of a prison be subjected to unremitting surveillance. The eye of power described by Foucault in The Birth of the Clinic as "the Gaze that envelops, caresses, details, anatomizes the most individual flesh and enumerates its secret bites" (170), is quite close to the image of the remorseless eye in many of Beckett's later writings. In different ways, Beckett's "eye works" (which I will not unfortunately discuss here) like *Play, Film, The Lost Ones, Long Observation of the Ray* and *Ill Seen Ill Said* suggest the gaze of reason and the suffering gaze of the embodied eye. The association of reason with the faculty of vision is an analogue of the idea that reason must maintain an absolute separation from the objects it surveys. That thinking and looking are closely bound is part of the Cartesian heritage of distancing the self from itself, of the division between subjectivity and objectivity. Beckett's critique of the sight-reason conjunction in these prose works is also part of a generic merging of drama and prose in his later work. These prose works almost compel us to perceive them as stage performances, and this has been seen as a hypothetical possibility by many readers.

Within the parameters of this discourse, Foucault defines the exercise of power as a mode of action upon the actions of others. Power, for Foucault, is a relational idea in which there is a struggle between "agonistic" forces within the social network. Society is not a fixed structure; rather, it is a dispersed contention between opposing forces. The victim and the victimizer are simultaneously caught in it as "[power] is produced at every moment, at every point, or rather in every relation between points" (93). Within this theoretical paradigm, there is a constant interchange of effects between the visible area of power and the subterranean, pervasive, and constantly moving power mechanisms. The complexity, or rather, the enigma of power is deep as Foucault does not believe in repression or coercion per se: power is not motivated by the desire to control or repress, but rather to produce the "anatomo-politics" of docile and "useful" bodies. The disciplining forces of power increase the economic utilization of the body. Like Bakhtin, and like Beckett, Foucault conceives of the body as a primary site of ideological discourses; the body is organized and shaped by discursive power relations. Foucault's historicizing of power and theatre—his elaboration on the subject of public execution as a theatre of power and terror—reveals that theatre is a potent locus for projecting, very often literalizing, the tyranny of power. The manner in which power relations operate repressively on both the perpetrator and the victim is an interesting dynamic.

As an agent of theatrical meaning, the body engages the actor, character, and spectator at various levels of subjectivities. Beckett's use of theatre as a phenomenological inquiry into the disciplining of the body assumes complex modes of operation. In this context, William Worthen's article "Beckett's Actor," examines the readjustment of the equilibrium between self and role, interpretation and representation, presence and absence that Beckett's dramatis personae are subject to. Worthen comments that the subjection of the actor's body to acute pain leads to the disjunction between body and text:

> The actor's bodily stress dramatizes the presence of both actors and characters on the stage, and redirects our attention to the text/body dialectic. . . . In histrionic terms, Beckett consistently endows the actor's body with a theatrical quality that suggests the actor's "interpretive" immediacy, while the spoken text articulates the motions of the mind that generally imply the actor's "representational" absence. (419, 421)

As a disjunct, disunified subject, the Beckettian actor is conceived as limited in choice and perspective. While theatre presents an already constituted world, it also draws attention to the processes of its staging as part of the material practices on the actor's body. The dynamic of this theatre of the body becomes a paradigm for Beckett's exploration of power.

Some of Beckett's plays are absorbing expositions of the visual tyrannizing of the body. In Beckett's drama commencing with *Waiting for Godot*, strategies of surveillance and tyrannizing control are central. The examples of the Chinese torturer in *Eleutheria*, the dumb Lucky and the all-powerful Pozzo in *Godot*, the unnatural "bottling" of the parents in ashbins in *Endgame*, Dan Rooney as the prime child-murder suspect in *All That Fall*, Croak in *Words and*

Music, an invisible and sadistic hand in *Act Without Words 1* teasing a mime, the violent attempts at suicide in *Eh Joe*, and the Protagonist's silencing in *Catastrophe* are all paradigmatic cases. The fragmented bodies in his plays, mouth (as in *Not I*) or head suspended in darkness, as well as the stark lighting, costumes and gestures, all focus on Beckett's use of the body as invested with power relations.

A central image of *Waiting for Godot* is that of sado-masochistic bondage. In this play, the bellowing master Pozzo wields his whip over his shackled slave Lucky, who is reduced to a mere pathetic creature, unable to think, to react, or even to know of any existence beyond being bonded to his master. However, being tied to each other by a long rope gives an equivocal dimension to their master-slave relationship: each is linked to the other. Pozzo has many similarities to Moran, who also contemplated tying himself to his son by a rope. Like Moran, Pozzo bullies, smokes (a pipe if not a cigar), dresses well, and eats a good lunch. Eventually Pozzo, like Moran, ends helplessly, "falling to bits."

Pozzo's power is hollow. He is made up of the discourses of power, whose status as *mere* discourses becomes increasingly evident. Initially, Pozzo's theatricality is strident:

> I am Pozzo! (Silence.) Pozzo! . . . Does that name mean nothing to you! (Silence.) I say does that name mean nothing to you? (22)

The flamboyant master exudes force and authority and his encumbered servant displays a cowed submissiveness to him. "I present myself: Pozzo . . . made in God's image!" Styling himself a divinity, Pozzo demands reverential attention. Wielding his whip, Pozzo acts with an overbearing mix of callousness and civility. He brusquely questions the two tramps about Godot and then settles down ostentatiously to relish his dinner. He is full of platitudes about the idea that life is a veil of tears and that one is able to learn something from everyone. He is also full of empty rhetoric, priding himself on his orator's voice, which he cultivates and "inflates" with his atomizer. His speech is replete with imperatives, exclamations, and affected aphorisms alternating between bluster and elocutionary zeal.

That Pozzo is full of insecurities soon becomes evident. With his hyperbolic flourishes, Pozzo appears to be solipsistically content in his make-believe world. He can roar with laughter at the idea of Vladimir and Estragon being his fellows: "Of the same species as Pozzo!" (23), he exclaims. On the other hand, he also appears nervous and vulnerable. He can be lyrical in referring to "torrents of red and white light [which] begin to lose its effulgence, to grow pale" (37), and, alternately, intensely callous to his own slave, even ignoring the alarmed concern of the tramps: "To treat a man . . . like that . . . it's a scandal" (27). Pozzo's disproportionate politeness toward Vladimir and Estragon contrasts with his appropriation of Lucky as worse than an animal. He addresses them as "gentlemen," and the tramps reciprocate his courtesies and apologies. Nonetheless, he displays a more subtle kind of repression in his apparent courtesy. His condescending posture, his supercilious air as well as his inflated gestures complement his sentimental windbaggery, and again form a striking blend of contradictions.

"I am perhaps not particularly human" (19), Pozzo states, "but who cares?" This indifference to one's own human-ness seems to me a desperate attempt at covering a lurking sense of guilt for what he knows to be his hideous actions. Pozzo also has a chronometric obsession as he feverishly calculates the hours of his journey, and often consults his watch, often "cuddling" it to his ear. He is concerned with Estragon's age, and asks the tramps to guess Lucky's age. Intensely time-conscious, when Vladimir states that "Time has stopped," Pozzo protests: "Don't you believe it, sir, don't you believe it. . . . Whatever you like, but not that" (36). Time is of the essence of his contract with himself. Pozzo's melodramatics and literary affectations make him seem to be posturing and speechifying, and his pompous rhetoric assumes shades of grandeur: "I don't like talking in a vacuum" (30). From the start, Pozzo's performance is clearly over-determined, and his authority is revealed to be imposed, factitious not genuine. It is quite evident that Pozzo's oratorical flourishes can make us aware of him as nothing but a collection of discourses.

From within his own comforts, Pozzo hurls monosyllabic orders at Lucky whom he addresses as "Pig" or "Hog," and commands him to hand him his overcoat, hold the whip, and bring the stool or the luncheon basket. While Lucky's plight in responding to the commands, sagging under his weight, or sleeping on his feet at intervals, arouses the tramps' pity, Pozzo remains smugly oblivious to everything but himself. The sheer physical violence involved in Lucky's enslavement is embodied in a kind of circus act. Pozzo is convinced that he does a good act in taking Lucky as his slave instead of "kicking him out on his backside." In spite of Lucky's lifelong dedication and service to Pozzo, Pozzo prepares to get rid of him: "such creatures. . . . The best thing would be to kill them" (32). He tells the tramps that he is "bringing him to the fair where I hope to get a good price for him." The master sees to it that no other will exists but his own.

The inevitable reliance of the master upon the slave for his own definition as master is also brought out in the power that Pozzo imposes on Lucky. Pozzo shouts barbaric commands at his slave, on the one hand, and on the other, acknowledges that it is Lucky—"my Lucky"—who had taught him "Beauty, grace, truth of the first water" (33). He knows that he owes it to Lucky, since "[b]ut for him all my thoughts, all my feelings, would have been of common things" (33). Pozzo remarks that it is only by "chance" that he is Lucky's master rather than vice versa, an amusing twist to their sado-masochistic bondage: "Remark that I might just as well have been in his shoes and he in mine."

At the same time, Pozzo's epicureanism is dependent on the continued enslavement of Lucky. Cleverly enough, like a typical despot, he wishes to earn sympathy for himself even as he dismisses Lucky's weeping as undignified. Although Lucky has the wound, "like a goitre" (26) caused by the rope, Pozzo also claims that, in actual fact, it is Lucky who makes him suffer:

> I can't bear it . . . any longer . . . the way he goes on . . . you've no idea . . . it's terrible . . . he must go. . . . I'm going mad. . . . I can't bear it any longer . . . (34)

This is, of course, contradicted by his own confession: "you may be sure there wasn't a word of truth in it" (34). His mannered outburst about the slave "killing him" is more evidence of the emptiness of his own claims to power. One by one, he misplaces his pipe, his atomizer, his precious watch. When Pozzo and Lucky lie tumbled together on the ground, Vladimir calls out the names of both Abel and Cain, and Pozzo responds to both. Significantly, Estragon remarks, "He's all humanity" (83). Drawn into this fabulously calculated self-presentation, the tramps get a glimpse into what the world outside is really like—all spectacle and fixed purpose.

Beckett relentlessly foregrounds the body of the actor as the space on which the tyranny and the operations of power are inscribed. Lucky is burdened with impedimenta he can put down only on Pozzo's command. Lucky enters, his feet shuffling, movements jerky, his panting ceaseless, his body trembling under the weight of basket and Pozzo's baggage. His decrepit body and the running sore on his neck suggest his mental and physical torture. His victimization strangely contrasts with Pozzo's insistence on Lucky's autonomy. If Lucky does not put down his burden, it is because "He wants to impress me, so that I'll keep him" (31). Nonetheless, Pozzo also follows this with: "Well, that's what I think" (31). The inscription of Lucky's marked, silenced body is seen in the fact that his only mode of expression is a body language which speaks hysterically, negating its muted state. Otherwise known as mental atrophy, Lucky's condition is a state of physical palsy, the mind intricately connected to the bodily abjectness. The tramps observe in sheer disgust his "slobber" and his "panting."

There was a time, according to Pozzo, when Lucky could amuse his master by dancing and by thinking; now his dance has deteriorated to a slouch and a totter. If he speaks at all, his speech is uncontrolled and repetitive, the mind losing all bodily control and the body losing all mental control, so much an evidence of instrumental rationalization that the speech barely clutches at a few rudimentary straws of incoherent meaning. Pozzo's instruction, "Think, pig," ensues in a dance as Lucky cannot remember what "think" means, and when he does, he "remember[s]" it as "language." He displays it in a speech which reminds one in a terribly intense manner of the truth of Vladimir's observation that "What is terrible is to have thought." Like Foucault who held that the comprehensive quality of a discourse cannot be identified within a subject, Beckett seems to insist on language as a "decentered totality" where meaning can be drawn only from the relations between signifiers. If knowledge is power, then Lucky's discourse attacks power. Specifically assailing objective knowledge, it also attacks the knowledge on which the two tramps have based their existence, namely of Godot.

The progressive breakdown of all sense or conviction in Lucky's well-known speech is an apt index of the complementarity of mind and body as both are subject to decay and disintegration:

> Given the existence . . . that man in short that man in brief in spite of the strides of alimentation and defecation is seen to waste and pine waste and pine and . . . shrink and dwindle. (42-43)

Rife with contradictions, Lucky's fragmented and unfinished monologue, more a torrent of words, liberates thought from its own tyranny as well as the tyranny of language which communicates the thought. Weaving in and out of the margins of sense, Lucky's "think" mixes sense and nonsense, asyntactical anarchy with flamboyant repetitions in a transgrammatically grotesque discourse. It is not just nonsense pouring out from an automaton. The violence that he seems to be committing on reason offers another (linguistic) version of the violence that he himself has suffered at Pozzo's hands.

In the second act of *Waiting for Godot*, Pozzo is shown as a changed man, blind and given to oracle-like speechifying on time and destiny. He enters the stage with cries asking for help. He appears to be a much gentler and more thoughtful man in both his words and his action. He has shed his histrionic zeal, and collapses on the ground, helpless to raise himself. Gradually and inevitably, Pozzo's self-definition in his role of a tyrant comes alive to him as really nothing more than a collage of fragmentary voices. Now, significantly, Pozzo is blind and Lucky is dumb. The blind Pozzo is persistently asked when blindness struck him. He replies in extreme agony, "Have you not done tormenting me with your accursed time!" (89). The destroyer destroyed in a mutual sadomasochistic relationship is not really a new phenomenon, and Beckett underlines this fact by foregrounding its ravaging inscription on both the physical and mental dimensions of Pozzo's self. Not only has he lost his memory, he has degenerated in body and mind as well. Begged by the tramps to let the dumb Lucky sing and think once more, Pozzo vents his vexation, and his moments of hysterical groaning culminate in his shouts for help. The truth of his own disintegration dawns on him even as he begins to acknowledge his symbiotic relationship with his victim. The torture that he inflicts on Lucky gradually becomes his own destruction, even as Pozzo is willing to concede that the "good angel" who is "killing" him "used to be so kind . . . so helpful" (34). He is now a "fallen angel" turned "wicked," almost as if the sado-masochistic relationship has turned over on its head.

The flamboyant and bellowing Pozzo and his shackled slave, Lucky, portray a powerful power dynamic. In light of the play's existential theme of lack of freedom, their slave-master relationship does comment on man's constraints. What is man free to do? What is he free to be? More interestingly though, the physical restrictions and scars that Lucky's body suffers as a result of his exploitation by Pozzo comment on the alignment of power and its tyrannizing control of the victim's body. Foucault's analysis of the apparatus of surveillance in the discipline and subjection of bodies relates to the Pozzo-Lucky power equation "in which the techniques that make it possible to see induce effects of power and in which, conversely, the means of coercion make those on whom they are applied, clearly visible" (170). If power insinuates itself into the very discipline constitutive of a rational self, then it is impossible to know rationally one's true humanity independent of power's distorting effects.

In an interesting way, just as Lucky's body has been enslaved to Pozzo, Vladimir and Estragon's minds are enslaved to Godot. This is endorsed in Act One, when Estragon's repeated question about whether they are "tied to Godot" is interrupted by the appearance of Lucky with a rope around his neck. If Pozzo has been seen by many critics as an incarnation of Godot, it is because both are tyrants and power-wielders. In an early essay, Ronald Gray in fact, insists that Godot has arrived in the image of Pozzo and that the tramps have not recognized him. But Beckett has refused any identification for Godot. Godot has defined the physical and intellectual limits of the two tramps just as much as Pozzo defines Lucky. Vladimir and Estragon cannot leave the spot which has transfixed them. If they "dropped him," they believe "He'd punish us" (59). The limits that define their actions and thoughts are almost violent in effect. The boy-messenger keeps reappearing to comment as cryptically as possible: "No, Sir," "Yes, Sir," "he has a white beard." The tramps, in turn, appear to have no idea what they want of Godot. They make a "request," which becomes an entreaty, "a kind of prayer," "a vague supplication." Quite characteristically Godot makes no reply to the tramps' request since the sovereign can make no terms with his subject. His silence conveys to Vladimir and Estragon the true nature of their situation, namely, that they must only submit.

The risk involved in a futile wait is also emphasized early in the play by the failure to clarify the inexorable conditions set by the hypothetical presence of Mr. Godot. Estragon's "if's"—"And if he doesn't come," "If he came yesterday"—and his "until"—"until he comes"—project the anxieties existing in this act of waiting for Godot. As they "canter" about Godot, Vladimir is forced to acknowledge the very real fact that they no longer have any "rights." The overwhelming nature of their apprehension of Godot is suggested by the fact that even the slightest noise, the wind in the reeds or a shout, brings a nameless fear, as if ushering in the coming of Godot. The cry that precedes the arrival of Pozzo and Lucky creates the illusion of Godot's arrival: "Godet. . . . Godot. . . . Godin" (29). The name of Godot is silenced with profuse apologies for having mistaken Pozzo for "him": "Personally I wouldn't even know him if I saw him." The uncertainty and dread about Godot's appearance are offset by such remarks to Pozzo as: "Tell him . . . tell him you saw us." Waiting makes urgent demands even when those who wait begin to lose that sense of urgency. The ritual act of passing the time loses meaning, and the silences become interminably unendurable. Vladimir's hallucination, "It's Godot! At last!" and Estragon's, "Do you think God sees me?" suggest despair and no-exit.

Vladimir and Estragon's fearful sense of anticipation of Godot who has completely swamped their thoughts forms an analogue of the terror that is embodied in Lucky's servile relationship with his master. The tramps' idle chatter acting as an evasive symptom of the unnamed fear of Godot results in the final panic-stricken cry, "I'm in hell." The pathos of Lucky's role—the kicks and counterkicks, his physical enslavement, aphasia and breakdown of thoughts—is a result of Pozzo's constant brutality. The two pairs, Vladimir and Estragon and Pozzo and Lucky find a point of fusion in Beckett's thematic rendition of tyranny.

To come back to Foucault who demonstrated in his *Discipline and Punish* the marks of the legal inscription of culpability on the malefactor's body, we see how the Foucauldian polemic pervades the world of Lucky and Pozzo in *Godot.* Whether discoursing on prisons, sex, or madness, the central thrust of Foucault's writings is the body as the most proximate and immediate aspect of one's being, as a necessary feature of social location and personal "enselfment." Bodies are the surface of emergence for penality. Indeed, the whole point of the opening chapter, "The body of the condemned," in *Discipline and Punish* can be said to be the centering of the body within a political economy of punishment:

> The body now serves as an instrument or intermediary: if one intervenes upon it to imprison it, or to make it work, it is in order to deprive the individual of a liberty that is regarded both as a right and a property. The body, according to this penality, is caught up in system of constraints and privations, obligations and prohibitions. Physical pain, the pain of the body itself, is no longer the constituent element of the penality. (10-11)

The body-punishment nexus is registered in the way Beckett's characters constantly experience what Foucault refers to as the "political economy" of the body. Foucault's distinction between the "intelligible" body represented through discourse and the "docile-useful body" disciplined by social control shows the dual relationship between bodies and their representation. For Foucault, the body is a referential field of signifiers which refuses any distinct and independent sense of individuality, at the same time that it becomes inundated with ulterior meaning. And in Beckett's writings too, the body does not expose the power that a dominant group or culture exerts, as much as the effect wrought through its machinations on the body. Lucky's body is a transparency through which the impressions of his repressed and thwarted consciousness become visible.

The misfits and eccentrics in Beckett's work are distortions of the human body, outrageously bizarre descriptions of the human physiognomy. Schizophrenics, aphasiacs, neurasthenics, dysfunctional beings with phantom limbs—the disfigured and disturbed beings are often indicative of the warping effects on the bodily. What is remarkable about Beckett's fictional as well as his dramatic characters is that very often, they are unable to possess any autonomy or an ontological status. The various forms of tyrannizing of the body, social, familial, ideological, and political, undermines the notion of a stable, teleological notion of the self.

After *Godot*, there are many android creatures in Beckett's writings who reflect Beckett's attitude to the status of selfhood when the sentient body is repressed. In this context, the extremely useful work done by Anna McMullan studies Beckett's later drama in order to show how

> the body is foregrounded as a locus of the struggle for control and mastery, either within the subject who has internalized the laws of identity and authority, or between the subject and the external modes of law and discipline. (17)

Beckett's ontologically mongrelized creatures endeavour to break with and transcend the Cartesian dualisms of body and mind, subject and object. As part of their material reality, however, they experience the material conditions of social existence which are inscribed on their bodies. Once their sensory capacities are thwarted and contract, the embodied subject is displaced by the body as object. As the body is subjected to external repressions, this is the necessary concomitant of the loss of a comprehensible structure which relates one to the world. The indeterminacy of bodily being results from the erasure of identity as it is prescribed and proscribed, disguised and disciplined by political configurations of an increasingly techno-powered world. In this sense, subjectivity cannot be understood as a phenomenon of the essential, interior self, but as an effect of power which has been inscribed upon the body's surface.

The farcical comicality of distorted and automated bodily attitudes is an inherent feature of Beckett's drama, reflecting the relationship between the framework of disciplining and its impact on the body. In *Endgame*, Hamm's body functions are reduced in the extreme: immobilized in his chair, he seems paralyzed, and is also blind. Nagg and Nell grotesquely parody physical impotence and emotional repression. The room itself takes the shape of a "cranial box" where the mind has been blocked and caged. In the play, the dustbins in which Hamm's parents, Nagg and Nell reside are synecdochically associated with the corporeal body of man since man enters life and departs from it in the form of what Murphy calls a "waste product" of the organic processes.

In *Krapp's Last Tape*, the technical apparatus of the tape recorder as a machine becomes one with Krapp's various selves, the younger versions of Krapp, so alike and yet so different from the older Krapp. Beckett instructed the actor Pierre Chabert, in his 1975 Paris production of the play, "to become as much as possible one body with the machine." The relationship between Krapp and the tape is a physical, even a visceral one as Krapp responds to it as a sensual object, body to body. Through the mechanical device of the tape-recorder, Krapp replaces his physical desires with the reason and mind of the gadget. *Krapp's Last Tape*, like the later *Words and Music*, takes off from Proust's vision of the changing self as Krapp talks to another version of himself, his recorded voice from thirty years earlier. In *Play*, Beckett manipulates the spotlight as an arbitrary mechanism of control over the three rigidified heads who are immersed in their own individual revelations of the truth of their lives. Underlying this strategic "play," is of course, the disruption and cleaving of the mind from the body. Beckett's foregrounding of the body situated between human and animal, organism and machine, results in a techno-organic, humanoid hybrid man. Beckett ridicules and flouts Descartes's positioning of the human self above its own body by its ability to think as well as articulate thoughts. It is in this sense that the body and the machine interact in the hybridized world of Beckett, and the body is "rewritten" by the disciplining of the technologies of the self. The body thus becomes a political surface which is distinct from the anatomical body.

The "rewriting" of the body is seen in yet another Beckett play, *Catastrophe*, where the silencing of the Protagonist's voice is a comment on power relations in the political arena. This is presented on a microcosmic scale in the theatrical subjection of the actor's body. The central spectacle of the play consists of the subdued, speechless body of the Protagonist on a cold "plinth," hands limp, head down, faceless, and dressed in the inadequate clothes of black robe and pyjamas. It reproduces another image of Lucky. The body as immediate stage presence is foregrounded as the stage is transformed into a rehearsal space. The Protagonist's movements are strictly restricted to the narrow confines of the plinth on which he is made to stand upright throughout the performance, head bowed and hands buried in his pockets. His clothes are strongly reminiscent of those of a concentration camp victim. That the Protagonist's body is being manipulated is evident in the Director's angry outbursts when his assistant offers to gag and then raise his head:

> For God's sake! What next? Raise his head! Where do you think we are? In Patagonia? Raise his head! For God's sake! (300)

Coercion is also imposed on the body of the Protagonist by the process of whitening his flesh and transforming it into semiotic material. As the natural is replaced by the artificial, the body is substituted for sign, for material to be manipulated and disciplined. His dehumanized body is exposed, manoeuvred and anatomized as a piece of clinical investigation. His skull, hands, cranium, toes and shins become objects of representation as the human body, to quote Foucault again, "enter[s] a machinery of power that explores it, breaks it down and rearranges it" (137-38).

The struggle to possess the image of the Protagonist is intense, as the Director and the Assistant both endeavour to shape the Protagonist in their own image. The main action is the blocking of a theatrical spectacle referred to by the Director as "our catastrophe." The dramatized play putatively concerns the mounting of the play that the audience will see. The Protagonist is constructed by the Director and his Assistant eighteen inches off the floor. He is exposed in all his vulnerability and powerlessness as the Director determines his appearance and controls and subjugates his body as an object. Antony Libera offers an interesting reading of the play:

> Behind the promise of becoming a pure subject lurks the total debasement of Man to the status of object. . . . This is his catastrophe, in both senses of the word: it is his tragedy, and at the same time the last chord of his tragedy. . . . (336)

While Beckett himself objected to Libera's allegorical interpretation of *Catastrophe* as "the ancient myth of the fallen angel," Libera's reading can be usefully applied to my own focus on the repression of the body.

The manipulative pauses between the Director and his Assistant's queries and carefully crafted replies; the Director's threat to alter or subtract or reposition the Protagonist's body, to gradually and successively remove his clothing until he is reduced to his ash-colored underwear—all these are ways in which the body can be subordinated. By minimizing the verbal text, Beckett places the dramatic focus on the Protagonist's body which shivers, trembles, and clenches its painfully twisted hands, but never utters a word. Engaged in presenting the spectacle of the Protagonist, the Director instructs that the light shine on his bowed head only. He exercises despotic authority over the Protagonist who cannot act, but is simply, tyrannically acted upon. Like Pozzo in *Godot*, the Director controls the world on "the board." His use and abuse of his power is absolute as he tries to control the body of his victim. While treating the Protagonist as an object to be controlled and manipulated, he also shows disdain for his Assistant. She lights the cigar for him, repeats the action when it goes out, and prepares the Protagonist for exhibition. The Director asks for further ripping and splaying, since, in his words, the Protagonist "could do with more nudity." The gesture of helpless supplication with which the Protagonist's lowered head goes down even further, the stage light intensifying on the last "molting . . . few tufts" of frizzled hair, his "clawlike" hands and their "fibrous degeneration," his "moulting skull" as the Director exclaims at the achievement of his catastrophe frames the representation of the body transformed by coercion. As Foucault observes, the exhibition and exposure of the body ensures "the subjection of those who are perceived as objects and the objectification of those who are subjected" (185).

Beckett's own need to control, to discipline within a Foucauldian power-apparatus, in short, his role as "director-dictator," has been much debated and discussed. Beckett's stance on directorial non-interference has been perceived to replicate the abusive tyrannizing and so-called "interference" of the Director in *Catastrophe*. However, I do not believe that the Director/Protagonist analogy holds true for Beckett's relationship with his own works. The fact that theatre has exerted coercive power on the body or the fact that directors have been known to be tyrants does not hold true for Beckett. In my opinion, it would be misguided to believe that Jacques Derrida's term, "theological stage," replicates Beckett's exactitude and control over the absolute fidelity in the production of his scripts:

> an author-creator who, absent and from afar, is armed with a text and keeps watch over, assembles, regulates the time or meaning of representation. . . . He lets representation represent him through. ("Choreographies," 235)

Beckett's tyrannizing, domineering ways with the real actors and actresses, tying them up with ropes, straps and braces, cannot be denied. It has become a subject for debate about Beckett's own position as a real-life protagonist for his *Catastrophe*. While on the one hand, he has been taken to task by Shannon Jackson, H. Porter Abbot and others, who perceive his authorial prerogative as autocratic, on the other hand, he can also be identified with the Protagonist. The resemblance first observed by Enoch Brater (146) of the fibrous degeneration of Beckett's hands (Dupuytren's Contracture) with the Protagonist's claw-like hands shows that in this instance, Beckett was the victim rather than the victimizer. While he exhibited an openness to the relativity of perception, he could not simultaneously compromise on his directorial competence and standards of perfection. The play is a parodic version of the Aristotelian concept of tragic theatre, complete with character, a plot rising to crescendo and a final catastrophe. Beckett's masterstroke consists in fusing the tyrannical nature of theatre and state in this play, and not in laying his own self open to attack. The fact that the play is dedicated to the suffering of a particular human being, and not to some abstract concept of "the human" is further revealing of the writer's own commitment. The contradictions within Beckett's position can be reconciled by the awareness of Beckett's open-minded ways in his more personal relationships. I believe that Beckett was indifferent to the absolute certainty about anything, and dramatized this as a basic principle of his plays, even using as the last words of his last play, *What Where*, "Make sense who may. I switch off." As a reduced and diminished signifier of Beckett, the humble figure of the Protagonist hybridizes his own tyrannization with the writer's.

The theatrical world of *Catastrophe* resonates with the Foucauldian metaphors of intimidation, surveillance, and disciplining of the body. It also brings in issues of hierarchy as the Assistant is complicit with the Director's tyrannizing zeal, as well as sympathetic toward the body she colludes in tyrannizing. She wears the lab-coat foregrounded in Foucault's account, while the Director wears a fur coat. While she accepts the Director's power at times, there are moments when she too resists, reminding him that the Protagonist is shivering, or else asking if the Protagonist could "raise his head, an instant . . . show his face . . . just an instant." The Director and his Assistant share their own power play. They relate to each other in rather ambivalent terms and speak in a cryptic style. Despite her compliance, the Assistant is able to express her differences from him. The gesture of brushing the chair after the Director leaves is a minor but a significant body movement, suggesting resistance. The Director, on his part, makes a display of his self-importance by puffing on a cigar, strutting in a fur-coat, with a "fur toque to match," and arrogantly claiming: "I have a caucus."

Beckett purportedly had a political motivation to write this play dedicated to the Czech playwright-turned-statesman Vaclev Havel whose incarceration is symbolized by the Protagonist's body. What reinforces the political significance of the play is the literal flesh-ing-out of what Foucault calls the "prison-machine" which inflicts pain and torture as it secures compliance of the body. Instead of showing the acuteness of torture in its mental dimension, Beckett makes it more direct and more physical. The Protagonist's body becomes accentuated and acquires increasing theatrical force as the Assistant strips it of its black gown and black hat, down to the long underwear, the emaciated limbs, the hollow cheeks, the flesh in all its ashen fleshiness. The abject body of the Protagonist encodes his plight all the more as he is made to hold his arms up, at right angles to his body, while he makes a spectacle of himself, shivering, his body position showing his ultimate humiliation and subjection.

Elaine Scarry's discourse on pain and torture is also relevant to understanding the material presence of the Protagonist's subjugated body. The body in pain is also an important feature of Beckett's works. The intricate nexus between body and self-consciousness appears most overwhelmingly in the experience of pain. An intensely private experience, pain cannot be experientially shared with anyone. In her analysis of the body in pain, Scarry has demonstrated that intense pain often acts as a symbolic substitute for death:

> Each only happens because of the body. In each, the contents of consciousness are destroyed . . . though one is an absence and the other a felt presence, one occurring in the cessation of sentience, the other expressing itself in grotesque overload. (31)

As pain takes hold of the consciousness of the victim, all perceptual reference to external reality is annihilated, and subjective experience is entirely related within. Because pain resists objectification, because pain cannot be completely represented in language, rehabilitation can, as Scarry suggests, be attempted through "socialization of sentience" to at least make the consequences of pain "objectified in language and thus fundamentally transformed to be communicable and sharable" (255). Shock and pain reduce one to a self confined to one's own body, just as, in the process of torture that Scarry describes, pain and threat reduce the individual's world to the parameters of his body in pain (35-36). Scarry observes that pain

> achieves its aversiveness in part by bringing about . . . this absolute split between one's sense of one's own identity and the reality of other persons. (4)

This happens as intense pain is experienced spatially either as "the contraction of the universe down to the immediate vicinity of the body" (35) or as the body magnifying to the dimensions of the whole universe. The embodied consciousness of pain implies that pain exists even if the state of the entire body did not have pain. Pain blocks access to language and becomes a way of deconstructing the self. The self in Beckett is made and unmade through the pain, the maiming and scarring of the character's body. Hence, as Scarry has also argued, pain necessarily reiterates and reproduces the physicality of being.

In the final scene of *Catastrophe*, the pain, humiliation and suppression of the body as object show in a climactic kind of way resistance as well as manipulation of the body—the body controlled, objectified and turned into a mechanism. The title of the play is significant in that *Catastrophe* begins with the "final touches to the last scene," which would be the resolution, a comment on the classical catastrophe. While arranging the mute Protagonist for the tableau, the Director turns to his Assistant, and remarks: "There's our catastrophe. In the bag." He uses the word "catastrophe" in the common sense of a calamity or a disaster. In drama, it indicates a reversal of action which finally produces the conclusion or denouement of a plotted structure. The Assistant's earlier suggestions to make the Protagonist raise his head for a moment, or to place a gag in his mouth, have both been rejected by the Director. All along, the Protagonist has remained mute, passive and compliant about his own body. After several experimental positionings, the Director is finally satisfied with the results he has sought: "Terrific! He'll have them on their feet. I can hear it from here."

At this climactic point in the play, there is the sound of distant applause which is then curtailed by the unexpected gesture of the Protagonist raising his head. He "fixes the audience" and fractures the image of subjection. Bert O. States interprets the audience's moral uneasiness at this moment as "shame" (21) as the running tape of a "distant storm of applause falters and dies." He sees the play itself as "a critique of the artist's weapon" (14). As the Director leaves the stage, strictly forbidding the Protagonist to raise his head, the Protagonist does raise his head and "fixes on the audience" (301). Is this final gesture of raising his head a gesture of resistance? Is it the outcome of sheer fatigue born of the oppressive control required to keep the body still in a narrow area for so long? Beyond "the craze for explication," beyond the urgency that "every i [be] dotted to death," all that can be said is that it is a body movement empowering in its implications of overcoming bodily torture and pain as the body is denied and suppressed. That the body also ultimately liberates and is itself liberating is implied in the Protagonist's final gesture which seems to threaten a subversion of the drama being prepared for him. The inexplicable gesture is also reminiscent of the dumb Lucky's gesture of escape from Pozzo through his "think." Both Pozzo and the Director have tried to restore the illusion of being by stripping others of being. Their tyranny extends to an attempt to capture the attention of others: "Is everybody ready? Is everybody looking at me?" (20). The Protagonist's final gesture is one of refusal to conform to the aims of the Director.

By foregrounding the physical experience of his characters, Beckett redefines the relationship of the individual to the world. The thematics of pain centers on the contents of the consciousness, since everything appears in relation to the self when it reacts to pain. Pain interrupts the dialectic between subject and object by severing the self from the other. Pain transfers consciousness on to its own insistently strong consciousness of the body as being-for-itself. Scarry's argument examines the assumption that the search for truth cannot justify the pain of torture. The relationship of intense pain to the unmaking of the victim's voice is often based on interrogation which gets linked to pain. What the process of interrogation disguises as rationalization is the Cartesian otherness of the body unequivocally delinked from the mind. Scarry characterizes it thus:

> The goal of the torturer is to make the one, the body, emphatically and crushingly present by destroying it, and to make the other, the voice, absent by destroying it. (49)

Body and voice in their interlocked relationships are, according to Scarry, imperative in understanding the way we structure our world. The Protagonist's dumb subjection, and finally, but crucially, his dumb effort at resistance, at defiance, is a way of perceiving how the deconstruction of the body is also its reconstruction. Where torture, as Scarry has hypothesized, unmakes the world, it can also remake it in the struggle between the voice of pain and the muted attempts at making the invisible pain visible within the space of the body. Virtually motionless, and more a statue through the course of the play, only his trembling inscribes the Protagonist's living body, the fact that his subjected body will remake a resisting body. "The applause falters, dies," and a long pause ensues before the lights fade, as the mute voice, as well as the mute gaze of the Protagonist, work along with his bodily subjection to make it the Director's own catastrophe.

The body in Beckett thus becomes a referential field for the signifying system that stems from a struggle of power. Within a Foucauldian paradigm, the body is the space on which the play of forces is inscribed. The body in Foucault's *Discipline and Punish* is the fractured body, inscribed with a multiplicity of objectifying techniques. I have shown the semio-techniques of disciplinary codes and power relations as they operate in the cognitive pairing of Moran and his son Jacques in *Molloy*, Pozzo and Lucky in *Waiting for Godot*, and the Director and the Protagonist in *Catastrophe*, to study the political technology of the body. The corollary of the exercise of power in terms of a set of actions is that opposition or resistance to power is conceptualized in terms of freedom. Intrinsic to the power relationship is the intransigence of freedom which we encounter in the subjection inscribed on the bodies of the victims. Jacques, Moran, Lucky, and the Protagonist suffer pain and the tyranny of power. At the same time, these victims also define the limits of power by their mute gestures of resistance.

CHAPTER FOUR

The Body's Sexual Ambiguity in "Enough" and *Not I*

It follows that in any man who utters the other's absence something feminine is declared: the man who waits and suffers from his waiting is miraculously feminized.
Roland Barthes, *A Lover's Discourse*

The truth is, a great mind must be androgynous, having the characteristics of both sexes, being both poetic and analytical.
Samuel Taylor Coleridge

I am taking up the issue of sexual identity in Beckett's writings in this chapter. In doing so, I ask myself the vexed question, how does gender inform the notion of identity? While philosophical queries relating to identity comprehend the term within such internalized features as consciousness or the capacity to place oneself in linguistic terms, there are certain external, socially instituted features such as one's social context or gender status that may also be regarded as normative markers of identity. In deconstructing the body as a symbolic construct, Beckett dismantles gender predictors or signifiers. The breakdown of gendered divisions becomes a sure if gradual characteristic in the evolution of Beckett's literary career. In mapping the movement of gender behavior from Beckett's early writings to his later ones, one finds oneself becoming uneasy about the ramifications of an unexamined inscription of gender roles. By problematizing the sexual identification of his characters, Beckett leads his reader to a self-conscious foregrounding of just what the inscription of gender entails. The many ambiguously gendered characters in Beckett suggest that the writer uses them as vehicles for an exploration of the question of sexual difference even as they offer a challenge to male privilege. I therefore propose gender ambiguity or anomalousness as yet another aspect of the concept of the body in Beckett. The implications of gender ambiguity are related to issues of gender assignment and the material principle of difference where the body is morphologically distinguished as male or female. By withholding the terms of clear gender identification, or, rather, by creating a sense of confusion in our minds, Beckett forces us to think about, and interrogate, sex-role identity which develops from identification modelling. I am not suggesting that he gives any clear solutions or that he tries to wish away gender divisions from our minds. All I am suggesting is that, by problematizing the whole idea of gender, Beckett enables us to rethink and reexamine many of our tacit assumptions about gender identity. I will make my argument on the evidence of some of Beckett's later writings, and my focus will primarily be on a short, not so well-known prose work of the sixties called "Enough," and a more well-known short play of the seventies, *Not I*.

The idea that the body is a construct has profound implications for the debate about gender and sexuality. In fact, much of the recent theoretical and philosophical interest in the body has been generated by feminists attempting to understand the way the body, considered as homologous to women and their sexuality, has been marginalized as against the mind as equated with man. The interest has been incorporated semiotically into the discursive attention given to issues of sexuality and gender. A major perspective on the sex/gender debate comes from the poststructuralists whose work engages with identity politics and also with the exigencies of terms like feminine and masculine, female and male. Is one's sexuality an intrinsic aspect of oneself or a cultural construct? This is the chicken-and-egg query that has been discussed by theorists such as Michel Foucault, Judith Butler, Mary Douglas, Thomas Laqueur and others, and is still debated widely within the realms of feminism, sociobiology, Marxist historicism, psychoanalytic theory, biologism, and the sociology of knowledge. This chapter aims to make connections between the theoretic polemic of these sex/gender discussions and Beckett's engagement with the issue of gender inscription. In fact, because I consider the nature of the connections between Beckett's inscription of gender and the theoretical debates of Foucault and Butler so crucial to my argument, I will discuss

Beckett's texts only after some comment upon the work of these theorists. I also wish to point out that I use terms like "male" and "female" as referring to biologically identifiable body types, and "woman" and "man" as referring to cultural entities.

Situated at the complex intersection of male and female, the protagonists of some of Beckett's works, especially "Enough" and *Not I*, challenge the binarisms of sexual difference and compel us to the searching question of the constructedness of sexual identity. The body's sexuality and its desires may reflect the structuring of the relation between the individual and the other and between male and female. But by circumventing the idea of difference, by creating a new paradigm for sex-role identity that perceives masculinity and femininity along a continuum rather than as opposites, Beckett makes us rethink the cultural inscription of gender roles. What is crucial about his writings is that he does not take up a reformist position—rather, through his works, he calls for a radical reinterpretation of the body and of sexuality. Moreover, in deconstructing the conceptual universe organized into the neat paradigms of binary logic or dualism inherent in Western thought, Beckett implies that women's bodies have their own representative power. Although the question of Beckett's feminist sympathies is debatable, it is my belief that Beckett's later works do provide space for women by their power to make us rethink the very notions of masculinity and femininity. In what follows, I wish to create a space for Beckett's concern with gender boundaries, the fixities of sexual difference as well as the multivalence of the sexual body.

The increasing tendency in Beckett's writings from a definitive gender polarization to an ambivalent, even a destabilized one, has been observed by many Beckett scholars. Beckett's later prose and drama dispel any notion of a stable selfhood and destabilize any clear sense of identity by confounding all markers of gender, even the front and back of the body. The identities of most characters become socially provisional and sexually indeterminate as the reader moves from his early writings to his later ones.

The reliance on gender is impossible to sustain when approaching the later work of Beckett, where any concept of a stable, determinate identity is disrupted or made provisional. Hence the deliberate desexing in his later plays, *What Where*, *Ghost Trio*, *Ohio Impromptu*, and *Rockaby* where environmental aspects of light and temperature are more intensely foregrounded than the sexual aspects of the body. The tenuous presence of the spirit visitor in *Ohio Impromptu*, the childhood conversations with the self in *That Time* where the multi-tonal voices disperse the boundary marks of gender, and the male and female protagonists in *Play*, "so lost to age and aspect as to seem almost part of urns" (147)—all of these confound sexual identity and shatter the fixities of rigid gender divisions. In his prose works like *Imagination Dead Imagine*, *The Lost Ones* and *Ping*, all vestiges of identity are blurred. The physical being of the characters seems increasingly to disintegrate as they recede into the skullspace, leaving behind only voices. In this sense the oppositions of being and non-being, presence and absence, mind and matter, male and female are undermined. Beckett's minimalist works emphasize only the unspoken, while the insubstantial nature of the characters opens up gaps and spaces through minimal patterns of speech and movement. The complete indifference to gender configuration or specificity is mouthed in Beckett's *Endgame* in Hamm's cryptic but ultimate: "as if the sex mattered" (36).

Interestingly, Beckett also carries out a fragmentation, a morcellation of the body as a whole in order to expose how the discriminating gestures of sex categories fragment and restrict, coerce and reify. Beckett disrupts the idea of the body in different ways. A device he particularly adopts is to focus the audience's concentration on a fragment or a specific part of the body. The fragmented images urge the imagination to fill in the gaps as much as they highlight the wholeness of the body that is missing or absent. The image of May's dragging feet as she paces up and down in *Footfalls* or the tangible image of the "skull-sized white globe" in *A Piece of Monologue* foreground the body through rejecting or disembodying parts of it. The fragments and pieces of body parts in Beckett's later works are so evidently undifferentiated that they completely defy any taxonomic gendering. His treatment of the transsexual body climaxes in the voice of Bam in *What Where* and the representation of Light in *Play* which are impossible to categorize easily within gender frames. In *Quad*, Beckett's stage directions read "sex indifferent," and the cloaking of bodies with gowns and cowls leads to indifferent and indeterminate sexuality. The physically diminished characters are abstracted from their conditions of sexual embodiment. Through negative hypothesis, these later writings emphasize the possibility of a not I, a self alienated from the language of sexuality.

On the other hand, Beckett's early works have occasionally been charged of misogynistic implications. As Susan Brienza puts it

> a concentrated reading of the early fiction reveals a disturbing negative depiction of female characters. . . . Whether paragon or parody, the woman here is limited to the body and to the emotions. (*Women in Beckett*, 91)

To wish away the presence of this fact is to wish oneself a deliberate suspension of disbelief. Feminists have taken objection to the characterization of women in early writings like *More Pricks Than Kicks*, *Murphy* and *Watt*, as "clods," as whores and bitches. Repulsed for their physical unattractiveness or feared for the reverse, the women in the early works retard male intellectual pursuits and generally represent the dark side of humanity. The women in *More Pricks* are objectified through the use of definite articles which are never applied to males: "the Venerilla [that is, little venery], his friend and bawd to be," the Frica, a randy "martyress in rut," the Alba, "Belacqua's current and one and only," and also Ruby Tough (if not the Tough) whose own father calls her "a slut." In Belacqua's eyes, a woman "is either: a short-below-the-waist, a big-hip, a sway-back, a big-abdomen or an average" (52). Lady Ottolenghi, his Dante tutor, does not deserve physical description because she has a sharp mind and is "apart from other women" (16). Grotesque creatures, women often get translated into horses, cats, or apes. In *Murphy*, Celia (a prostitute whose success in her profession is praised by Murphy as "the highest tribute that a man can pay a woman"), Miss Counihan ("quite exceptionally anthropoid"), Miss Dwyer ("the morsel of chaos"), Miss Carriage ("with a smell that not even her nearest and dearest had ever got used to"), Rosie Dew (a "stunted penguin" suffering from Duck's Disease), and even Rosie's pet ("dog or a bitch . . . it certainly had the classical bitch's eye") all suggest man-devouring women. In *Watt*, Tetty is "teats," Mrs Gorman "fishes" for sheets, and Mary only eats.

Aside from the question of how accurate this portrayal of the early Beckett as misogynist is, the question whether there is a clear disjunction between Beckett's early and his later works has been much discussed. If feminist critics claim that Beckett's early fiction proliferates with flesh-bound predators entrapping the male protagonists, they also at the same time concede that there is a definite transition, a shift to the portrayal of women as central characters in the drama beginning with *Happy Days*. I would go further than remarking upon this shift, and argue that Beckett, toward the end of his career at least, seems to be committed to the task of examining the cultural implications of the sexualized body. The increasing usage of fragmented names increases the insignificance of gender constructs and thus frustrates the objectifying processes of identification.

Further, I would argue that gender confusion in Beckett's writings is perceptible to a certain extent even in his early works. Thus in *Watt*, the gender assigned to "other voices, singing, crying, stating, murmuring" (29) is difficult to specify: "It might have been a high male voice, or it might have been a deep female voice" (148). The collapsing of sexual difference is also perceived in the effacing of difference and the repeated cancelling of sexual identity as in *Molloy* (an issue I have already discussed in my second chapter). Molloy's remembered affair with Ruth or Edith underscores an ambivalent sense of sexuality as Molloy speculates whether Ruth/Edith might in fact have been male after all. Malone too ruminates in *Malone Dies* on the contingencies of gender and body inclusiveness:

> Perhaps I shall put the man and the woman in the same story, there is so little difference between a man and a woman, between mine I mean. (3)

The artificial limbs and crutches used as aids for walking do not recognize any gender difference. "Stumps" and prosthetic limbs often replace conventionally conceived erogenous zones as sites of sexual attention. More specifically, the obliteration of pronouns from *The Unnamable* and the use of the pronoun "you" in *Company* are suggestive of Beckett's movement away from gender polarization. In a talk with Lawrence Shainberg, Beckett consciously articulated his search for "the non-pronounial" ("Exorcising Beckett," 134), even as, in his own lifetime, he endeavoured to efface the identity of his own self from his writings. What I am trying to argue here is that the movement from the early to the late Beckett is not the movement from traditionally inscribed gender roles to a transcendence of such inscription so much as it is a movement from a relatively unexamined inscription of gender roles to a conscious foregrounding of the implications of cultural inscription.

The traditional exclusiveness of the masculine/feminine binary in Western thought is a sign of the coercive and regulatory nature of gender divisions. Examining this binarism, Michel Foucault in his *History of Sexuality* has located a univocal sex within matrices of power which emerge from specific historical practices. Foucault has made us reexamine the belief that every individual must have a single, true sex in order to possess a social identity, that one has to be either male or female since the hermaphrodite has a false sexual status. According to Foucault, the structural changes in society corresponding to changes in medical sciences and administrative, juridical and legal apparati have compelled us to have an unambiguously singular sexuality. Even in the contemporary social set up, the idea that ultimately everyone must be either male or female has not been given up. The taboos that still exist against dual sexuality prove that medical knowledge does nothing to abolish sex as a necessary category of identity. As Foucault's "genealogical" account has taught us, the systems of power produce the subjects they subsequently come to represent. Foucault has shown us how power does not so much deny sexuality as produce it. It is only power relations which invest the body with the marks of, or an idea of, natural sexuality. As such, sexuality is an organized system, an effect or consequence of the discourse of power.

Foucault further explores the issue of the imposition of a sexual identity in the story of *Herculine Barbin* where Herculine's hermaphroditic body can be seen as a refutation of the regulative tendencies inherent within sexual polarization. Before Herculine's hermaphroditism is discovered, Herculine lives, according to Foucault, an almost utopian existence outside the law of compulsory heterosexuality and its constitutive genders. Foucault wonders in the introduction to the journal of Herculine whether the concept of a true sex is necessary. Foucault's argument about the univocal and causal nature of the construction of sex, that is, produced in the service of social regulation, takes the body as a sign of, or a manifestation of this "sex." The historical production of "sex" as a category is not present in liberatory models of sexuality which, according to Foucault, do not inquire into sexual difference as a necessary feature of bodily identity. While heterosexual desire constitutes part of a cultural matrix in which only certain kinds of identities can exist, other possibilities and other identities are effectively suppressed.

If individuals are denied their autonomy and perceived as constituted by the power matrix, then the body has no intrinsic merits or powers of its own. Although Foucault has been criticized for his conception of the body as completely transfigured by relentless cultural inscription, the significance of his biopolitics has helped us to conceive of the body as a site of social location. In this context, I would disagree with Judith Butler's criticism of Foucault's representation of the body as a passive medium, as so much inert matter. Butler argues that Foucault's construction of the body is part of his Cartesian inheritance,

> that Cartesian dualism presupposed in phenomenology adapted to the structuralist frame in which mind/body is redescribed as culture/nature. (129)

According to Butler, Foucault seems to consider the figure of the body as mute, as prior to culture, awaiting significance. But to insist, as Butler does, that Foucault takes the body as "a prima facie given" is to blind oneself to the finer points of the Foucauldian project. It may be true that he fails to problematize the body qua body; but Foucault's genealogical critique is more an attempt at exploring those identity categories that are the effects of institutions and their practices than it is a view of the body as a kind of tabula rasa, a clean slate on which institutions inscribe their marks. If in the process of cultural inscription, the body comes under siege, this is not to deny its own role as an interactive agency. In fact, for many thinkers, Foucault's theories have provided ways of beginning to think about the body not as something neutral and natural, but as socially (re)produced and inscribed according to specific practices and discourses.

Judith Butler's own cultural analysis has, of course, been immensely valuable in making the social interpretation of gender identity a significant subject for critical reexamination. In her provocatively exciting book *Gender Trouble*, Butler opines that if there were no political anatomy of the body, no tradition of the sociology of sex, we would not be able to identify a "feminine" or a "masculine" position:

> gender itself becomes a free-floating artifice, with the consequence that man and masculine might just as easily signify a female body as a male one. (6)

The indeterminacy of simple identifications on the basis of an essentialist masculinity or femininity becomes a key point in Butler's analysis. Butler argues that there is no such thing as a natural and essential sex, sexuality, gender, or body. She believes that even the idea of the unproblematic unity of "women" is a myth invoked only to construct a solidarity of identity, and merely reendorses reifications of gender and identity. The distinction between sex and gender problematizes the relationship between the body and identity, and Butler goes on to analyze the extent to which the body is shaped by the marks of gender as it is implicated in regimes of power and knowledge in ways such as those identified by Foucault.

Butler's critique of Foucault extends to the latter's interpretation of Herculine Barbin's situation. Here I think she is a sharper thinker than Foucault, though I do disagree with her when she assails Foucault on the body fixed within the nature/culture paradigm. Her criticism stems from what she perceives as Foucault's failure to recognize that the pleasures in which Herculine has been involved while "unsexed" are themselves "always already embedded in the pervasive but inarticulate law and, indeed, generated by the very law they are said to defy" (98). In other words, Herculine's pleasures can be read as disruptive only within the law of heterosexism, and not, as Foucault seems to assume, within an originally unfettered construct. In Butler's more complex reading of Herculine Barbin's situation, Herculine's sexual ambiguity in the eye of the law was a source of both distress and liberation. For Butler, Herculine's diaries "are subjection and defiance at once" (105). There is no "natural heterogeneity," according to Butler, who concludes that

> Herculine can never embody that law precisely because s/he cannot provide the occasion by which that law naturalizes itself in the symbolic structures of anatomy. (*Gender Trouble*, 106)

In other words, the law is not simply a cultural imposition on an otherwise natural heterogeneity. The law "requires conformity to its own notion of 'nature'"(106).

Herculine Barbin's hermaphroditism reveals the ways in which gender is inscribed on the body as a guarantee of its "lawfulness." For Butler, gender is the discursive practice which subsequently constitutes bodies as "naturally" sexed. To presume the primacy of this binarism is not to account for the construction of its primacy. Questioning the problematic binarism of the sexes in their morphology and constitution, Butler questions why one should assume that genders ought also to remain as two. If one were to abandon the cultural construction of gender, that is, the acquisition of gender identity, that is, create "gender trouble,"

> it does not follow that the construction of "men" will accrue exclusively to the bodies of males or that "women" will interpret only female bodies. (*Gender Trouble*, 6)

Moving in and out of the positions variously taken up by feminists whose theorization she subsequently deconstructs, Butler pursues her idea of how "sex" is a cultural and political interpretation of the body.

Besides revealing the contradictions she perceives in Foucault's theory that I have just mentioned, Butler also points out that phenomenological theories such as Sartre's, Merleau-Ponty's, and Beauvoir's tend to use the term "embodiment" as it is used in theological contexts. The term tends to figure the "body" as a mode of incarnation, and hence to preserve the external and dualistic relationship between a signifying immateriality and the materiality of the body itself. However, whether it is Beauvoir's epoch-making analysis of how "one is not born a woman, but rather becomes one" leading to a differentiation between sex and gender, or Monique Wittig's emphatic denial of any distinction between sex and gender, Butler knows that these terms are discursively constructed systems of signification, oppressive to women. While being sexed and being human are coextensive and simultaneous in the sense that sex is an analytic attribute of the human, the "sex" category does become politically invested when the body acquires the variable cultural dimensions of gender.

Butler derives her definition of the body partly from the anthropologist Mary Douglas's study, *Purity and Danger*. Douglas's stimulating work on the politically regulated boundaries of the body is important for feminists like Butler who examine the relationship between sex and gender as part of a network of signifying practices within a cultural field of gender hierarchy and compulsory heterosexuality through which bodies become sexed "beings." Why should gender be restricted to the usual two, one is forced to ask along with Butler—why the apparent duality of sex? Does not one politicize sex as a category of nature and put it to artificial use? Except for the fact that the division of human bodies into male and female suits the needs of heterosexuality, the oppositional relation is merely a contingent cultural constitution of gendered categories.

Beckett's writings, I contend, represent the forces at play in the writings of these theorists. Beckett's subversions may not suggest any explicit political program; but if political programs shape identity according to the purpose at hand, then the lack of identification of the structures of identity in Beckett clearly has political implications. In his denaturalizing and dismembering of sex categories, Beckett indulges in parodic practices that act as disruptive forces and often lead to the subversion of the hegemonic male-female frame. In doing so, he exposes the heterosexual matrix as the reifying agent for the categories of sexual difference. Even if there is no attempt in Beckett's work to decenter phallogocentrism and heterosexuality, one does begin to have doubts, in the later works especially, whether the terms "female" and "male" are stable categories, their meanings fixed and untroubled. In effect, the patriarchal sexual economy is subject to a critical challenge as the implicit norms that govern the cultural understanding of sex and sexuality are quashed, if not turned upside down.

Beckett repeatedly uses the biological and social merging of gender roles in his writings to reveal the implications of the anatomical asymmetry between male and female. Like Foucault, and like Butler, Beckett in his later writings problematizes the relationship between sex and gender and the normative model of heterosexual desire. In examining one of Beckett's prose works of the transition from his early to his late writings, "Enough" (originally published in 1965 as "Assez"), I wish to show how the convoluted relationship of the wo/man who "belonged to an entirely different generation" (140) and the man who "took [me] by the hand. Barely emerging from childhood" (140) assumes various dimensions and connotations, beginning as that of father and child and soon blossoming into that of two lovers. Often regarded as peripheral to Beckett's main canon, "Enough" is, in my opinion, central to Beckett's philosophical vision of a sexualized body which problematizes entrenched social binaries. Without suggesting any overwhelming, apocalyptic ramifications, I argue that "Enough" is a critique of the mentality that refuses to move beyond the convenient pronominal and gender paradigms.

"Enough" has often been regarded as posing a sexual riddle. Beckett's wonder at his own writing, "I don't know what came over me" (235), has been recorded by John Fletcher. I believe that the thematic nucleus of "Enough," built around the ambivalent nature of a love relationship, riddles us into interrogating the universalizing and essentializing significance of sex. The sexuality of the figure who narrates "Enough" appears neutralized, however "feminine" the tone of voice and however definite the reference to the "old breasts" of the speaker at the climax of this short piece. By relativizing the terms "male" and "female" and by calling into question the frame of the love relationship, Beckett challenges both the gendering of the bodies in "Enough" and the assumptions about sex and sexuality that correspond to it. Since gender is not a reified concept but a practice, the alternative possibilities of gender lie in disrupting such practices. By showing how the discourse of dominance writes its own undoing in the discourse of subordination, Beckett shakes loose the sense of a singular, traditional concept of identity. He works from within patriarchal fictions to unmask and to expose the patriarchal control over feminine identity.

Ruby Cohn was the first who pointed to the narrator as an "androgynous creature with feminine sensibility" (*Back To Beckett*, 243), and many readers have supported this interpretation. Confounding this reading, however, is Beckett's own statement about "Enough" which Linda Ben-Zvi quotes in her Introduction to *Women in Beckett*: "But, of course, they are two men" (xi). To have confusion worse confounded, it is true that, while the first limited edition of "Assez," published by *Editions de Minuit* in 1966, offered glimpses into a non-feminine identity, Beckett in later editions of the text always left gendering non-specific. The almost total absence of the narrator's body from the text has also led to the presumed indeterminacy of the sex of the narrator. But an absent body has, in this case, been considered a feminine one by most readers of "Enough" (Paul Lawley's bland reading of the piece is one such example). Why? Why should absence or lack "naturally" be associated with femaleness?

Let me spell out the pervasive confusions in the text of "Enough." Although the sex of the companion is known from his first appearance, ("I did all *he* desired"), the gender of the narrator, an "I," cannot be specified. One agrees that the body of a literary character cannot appear fully in language; the description of the sexual body within a representational space is always dislocated. Does that justify the reader in perceiving a character as male or female? (Does my name alone, which in any case has the neutral meaning of "night," associate me with a woman to a reader of this book? How can one guess whether it is a woman or a man writing these words? Just as I have referred to myself as a free-floating "I," the "I" in "Enough" can be read either way.) What markers guide the reader to determine the sexual identities of the two characters in Beckett's text? There is one character who is definitively referred to as "he," and the narrator, an indefinite "I" figure, is involved in a long-standing relationship with him. Since Beckett's texts always refuse to accept the notion of selfhood, since Beckett has implied that the very conception of identity is itself a mistake that leads to misery and failure (cf. *The Unnamable*), the difficulty of determining the sexual identity of the "I" figure assumes interesting dimensions.

It is appropriate to question why Beckett should bring the issue of sexual indeterminacy to "Enough." It is my contention that the writer deliberately plays on sex-role identity here in order to examine the whole idea of gender stereotyping. Because the sex of the narrator is rendered problematic, because the voice of the narrator seems to transcend conventional gender assignment, the issue is raised of the cultural inscription of masculine and feminine roles. "Enough" plays on the politics of sexual relationships, of the construction of a woman's identity by affiliation and difference. Traditionally, a woman confronts individual identity in the terms of a man's identity. It is almost as if, through "Enough," Beckett is exploding the prevailing cultural mythos and fear of difference that has bedevilled female identity within a phallocentric economy.

The fact that men and women are not physically identical provides the ground upon which discourse produces its historic justification for male dominance. Difference is a problematic concept. Woman, defined by negation, opposition, limitation, and lack, is appropriated in the service of the male prerogative for definition. Apart from the difference in anatomico-physiological givens, the issue of difference often lends itself to misrepresentation. The real issue should not be of difference per se but of opposition and domination—the form that difference takes in our phallocentric economy. Within the present system of dualistic thought, one cannot constitute difference without opposition and conflict, without one term occupying a position of privilege over the other. Thus the status of the term, difference, politicizes its interpretation. Thus also the image of women in opposition to men is perpetuated. Within the self-confirming phallocentric order, the ideology of difference creates the social effects of difference.

Beckett maps a shadowy territory between difference and sameness in the two figures of "Enough." He also creates confusion of tenses in "Enough." The time orders are jumbled so that one is not sure of the exact order in which events take place. The use of "then" is haphazard, and there is a lack of specificity about the events being recaptured. The story breaks into two parts: a single opening paragraph which narrates the present and then the remainder of the narrative. The indirect narrative technique of the speaker of "Enough"—stating, then amplifying, then reorganizing the same material—adds to the sense of confusion. The net consequence is that what is experiential in "Enough" can only be imagined. One starts out by wondering what one should infer from such sentences as: "There are questions you see but don't ask yourself" (139).

"Enough" presents a speaker who is identified by "its" relation to another being. The narrator is defined primarily by that previous association: "It is then I shall have lived then or never." Everything prior to the meeting with "him" is forgotten or dismissed. The entire text is structured upon the tensions between now and then, between the speaker's present act of narration and the previous life in common. Through words, the narrator contrives to evoke the sensations of the other's presence. And though the narrator wishes to start afresh, and "Enough" begins curiously with "All that goes before forget," the narrative in the final event foregrounds only a reminiscing. Set within a familiar terrain, a recognizable plot, the seven-page piece defamiliarizes our normal ways of reading texts, relationships, and identities.

If there is an element of a "sexual riddle" in "Enough," there will be ways of decoding the riddle. In trying to situate the identity of the narrator, I would like to read the relationship in "Enough" in various ways in order to show that Beckett makes the reader rethink the regulated marks of sexual inscription. Can the relationship be a heterosexual one? There is complete submission in the narrator of "Enough" that may tempt the reader, through sheer force of habit, to take the narrator as a woman. The tendency of (probably) most readers to presume that the narrator is female arises in part from the "feminine" devotion and deference displayed toward the male companion:

> I did all he desired. I desired it too. For him. Whenever he desired something so did I. He only had to say what thing. When he didn't desire anything neither did I. When he was silent he must have been like me. I drew satisfaction from it. (139)

The self-abasement and submissiveness of "I" becomes a troubling element. So abased is I that I's sexuality and gender are determined entirely by the will of "him." The gender identity of "I" is so indeterminate within the story exactly because I allows "him" to define everything. Sex/gender is therefore not a given, so much as it is something entirely in the field of force of the other. The "I" might thus be read as representing woman as non-representation, in Susan Gubar's terms, a "blank page"—an unnamable, undefinable something.

"Enough" becomes a revealing instance of how women, defined only in relation to male terms of self-definition and desire, not their own, render the definition of their own identity always inadequate. The reference to "I" exposes identity as a fiction so long as one's difference and one's identity can only be constituted within a patriarchal order. Constructed within a structure of differentiation known as the Order of the Father, sexual difference can be explored only within phallocentric discourse. Sexual identification is only possible within the structure of differentiation which is determined by the phallus.

The narrative voice in "Enough" confesses that all the calmness of its knowledge derives "from him." It is "he" who is physically described, from his misshapen body to his bloodshot blue eyes. It is "he" who decides when the couple shall halt or move, he who speaks, he who takes the narrator by the hand, he who controls movement even in sleep. The narrator is dependent on the companion for all knowledge and desires: "I only had the desires he manifested." Acting in a unison with "him," the "I" remains a passive follower: "I never asked myself any questions but his" (139), and is so willing to become part of him that "He loved to climb and therefore I too" (142). To an extent, this sense of subjection prefigures the passivity of the woman who enables the inhabitants of the cylinder in *The Lost Ones* to locate themselves. In that sense, the "I" is assumed to be a woman. The narrator of "Enough" is, however, not so completely "vanquished." Further, despite some dimensions of personality which might be taken to indicate the contrary, the narrator is not quite so feminine either. Despite the "feminine" tone of the narrator as well as the allusion to the "old breasts" (which might be an old man's paps) at the conclusion, there is a definite neutralizing of the sexual status of the person who narrates "Enough."

Mercier and Camier can be seen as preparing the blueprint for "Enough." Mercier and Camier sustain and complete each other. They decide together to leave the town because it bullies them both. They travel together by train or on foot, make acquaintances together in an inn, and come back to the town together because they cannot really leave it. The couple also hurt each other together: they love each other but make each other suffer. They need one another but exchange insults and fights. The rites of passage of Mercier and Camier, "as one man" sharing a sack, an umbrella, a handkerchief, a raincoat and a pencil, are reproduced in "Enough." In *Mercier and Camier*, the episodes where the two protagonists reach "the end of the alley where, as one man, they turned back again," and where "now Camier accompanying Mercier (in his fall), now the reverse, and now the two collapsing simultaneously, as one man, without preconcertation and in perfect interdependency" (90, 102), foreshadow what happens in "Enough." Like the unnamed "I" in "Enough," Mercier follows his partner in a tame manner: "I did all he desired. I desired it too. For him. Whenever he desired something, so did I. He only had to say what thing. . . ." Likewise in "Enough," the initiative of one enables the other to act so that the two become a single subject. The language of the earlier text contains the same words repeated in "Enough": "mucous membrane" (121), "up to a point" (7), "take me by the hand" (33), "I did all he desired," and the turning over "as one man" (90). As *Mercier and Camier* helps us to see, "Enough" need not necessarily be read as a woman's narrative.

The line, "When he told me to lick his penis I hastened to do so," need not be read in a heterosexual context alone. Oral sex performed on a male does not signify anything about the gender of the speaker. The penile licking can be considered within the frame of a homosexual relationship also. Beckett challenges us to scrutinize the terms we employ, redeploy, appropriate or invent to describe ourselves or others. Why should objects of desire in heterosexism be treated as implicitly "lawful" and "natural?" In my opinion, what is "lawful" only disciplines and constrains the body and its natural desires and impulses. The reader comes to realize that the need to fix a definitive identity for the narrator as male or female is defeated. The text constantly tempts the reader into looking for a discrete sex that would motivate heterosexual desire. But the sense of gender constantly shifts and is not linked to the fixity of sex differences. The struggle to locate any primary sexual characteristics or to separate them conceptually is an impossible task.

The sexual confusion projected in "Enough" dismantles gender differences. The narrator of "Enough," "upright in the macrocosm, not yet reduced to crawling in the mud" could be a he, a she, a hermaphrodite or any sexually variable creature. The sex of the narrator remains indeterminate, and the genital coupling remains indefinite in its sexual orientation. There are no adjectives or pronouns used for the narrator except the ungendered first person singular; neither are there any verbs used which might necessitate gender agreement. The gender indeterminacy is implicit in the conclusion of "Enough," with even the reference to "old breasts" remaining inconclusive. We substitute our own desire for narrative authority for the writer's persistent denials and evasions and for the text's own essential subversiveness.

In his later work, Beckett divests the body of the cultural sedimenta of gender prejudices, the rigid gender divisions that have become a part of ourselves. If patriarchal institutions have prospered by the binary divisions of subject and object, matter and mind, then Beckett dilutes the impact of such divisions by blending or exchanging them. The fact that there are alternative gendered possibilities becomes evident in the anatomical presence of the bodily ambivalence of the narrator of "Enough." The narrator's anatomy does not violate or fall outside the categories of sex, but rather confuses these categories—the free play has the effect of exposing the misconception that sex is a permanent substrate. It is only from a consciously denaturalized position that we can get a perspective upon how any concept of "naturalness" is assumed and presupposed, formulated and then put into practice. The strange, the outside, the irregular, all destabilize the terms of cultural conventions and compel a rescrutinizing of them.

I now turn to *Not I* to examine the role of anatomical difference as a determining yardstick for gender. In *Not I*, the human condition is stripped to its most essential ingredients as the play exposes the cultural formation of identity as sexuality. The overriding sense in this "godforsaken hole" is that there is something wrong with the arrangement of a gender-dichotomized conceptual universe. The fascination of *Not I*, in fact, rests in its intense expression of the inner experience of a particular subject as well as a network of issues concerning gender and the representation of the "feminine." Through the subjective agency of the Mouth, the play reveals the truth about ourselves: of how our subjectivity has become intertwined with our sexuality, how the truth of our sexuality has become the hallmark of identity. The logic of sex leads to personal identification. However, the capacity of sexual desire to become a revealing sign for personal identification depends upon a cultural formation through which the self is constituted. In my opinion, Beckett's *Not I* succeeds in establishing certain powerful parameters for reexamining the terms of that constitution of the self.

The very title, *Not I*, displays the self-avoidance which Mouth repeatedly demonstrates, but in which Mouth can never fully succeed. After all, "I" is as important a part of the title as "Not." In fact, *Not I* can be situated in the context of a dialectical interplay between individuation and anonymity. Mouth emerges as this "tiny little girl" projected "before her time" into this "godforsaken hole" that is simultaneously the space of the world and the orifice that her presence becomes. Mouth is both a medium of expression and also the object of what is expressed about the "whole being" in *Not I*. In being a physically disembodied self, Mouth attempts an evasion that the very existence of Mouth as "Not I" renders impossible.

In *Not I*, the body, reduced to the fragmented image of a mouth suspended in darkness, raises questions of gender and representation. The only material dimension onstage is a pair of lips. In Stanton Garner's term, it is a "de-anthropomorphized" mouth, like a hand or a foot. As the play opens, an unintelligible voice rises from behind a curtain as the house lights begin to dim. As the audience strains to hear the words in the darkness, the curtain rises to show a disembodied mouth suspended eight feet above the ground. A stream of words pours out without a pause for breath from the orifice. An overrun of lips, teeth, tongue and saliva, the disembodied Mouth is compelling in its presence. A spotlight focuses on the isolated and disconnected orifice opening and shutting in a frenzy. Onstage, Mouth is not a woman at all as the general critical opinion avers. Mouth is only a mouth which is "coming up to sixty . . . what? . . . seventy?" looking "aimlessly" for the cowslips of past years. Gradually, the mouth contorts and takes on a life of its own. As "the whole body [is] like gone," a new species seems to be assuming form. Mouth becomes a new icon in Beckett's oeuvre, a being unable to understand the words it speaks and yet compulsively driven to say. Mouth's words do not "make" sense because they "are" sense, the sense of how a gendered consciousness is represented.

It seems apt to ask why Beckett chose a woman to play Mouth. What is the differential impact created in allowing a male mouth in such a case? The experience of rejection, loneliness, marginalization, and the consequential symptoms of hysteria and madness cut across gender distinctions and can be portrayed through a male mouth also. In terms of social convention, however, the pathological symptom of hysteria is not allowed universalizing features. One well knows that the problem of difference is partly a problem of how we think about others. Difference is perpetuated in social practices of consigning others to exclusionary categories. One organizing category is that which regards women alone as subject to the hysterical syndrome; the very etymology of "hysteria" is of course symptomatic.

It might be argued that Beckett chose a woman because he wished to render the experience of female embodiment. Specifically, the sense of sin, guilt and self-betrayal attached to the evasion of identity inscribes the narrated body with the problematic of feminine identity in a patriarchal context. Pierre Chabert points out in his essay, "Presentation," that Beckett's inspiration for Not I was the "old crones" wandering all over Ireland reproduced in Mouth's self-description as "old hag already" occupied in "walking all her days . . . day after day . . ." Mouth is Beckett's Crazy Jane.

The critical opinion on *Not I* has ranged from the interpretation of the play as a sympathetic portrayal of female marginalization and dispossession to the representation of the female as lack or absence.

As voice-persona, Mouth's language—the broken syntax, the explosive and rhythmic outpouring—has been taken to convey contradictions and lack of logic in feminine speech as against unimpeded or controlled masculine speech. Mouth's interrupted silence, on the other hand, is viewed as the role of a silent receiver of male discourse. The disturbing impact of the image of the Mouth can be linked both to the uncontrollable flow of its utterance and also to its open, "gaping" character.

Mouth's torrent of speech may lead us to question the idea of identity as a construct of language. The instability of Mouth's language suggests the impossibility of a stable identity. Or, rather, the identity which Mouth's story constitutes is an unstable representation, rather than a true revelation, of the self. The fact that Mouth's speech is not accessible to Mouth or to the audience captures the predicament of Mouth as a gendered subject. Mouth's narrative becomes a description of the stage appearance of Mouth: "Whole body like gone . . . just the mouth . . . stream of words." If language is a sign by which gender identity is culturally constituted and maintained, Mouth's language cast as a rapid-fire monologue, both inscribes and disrupts Mouth's gender.

Mouth cannot perceive its own subjectivity as Mouth is not conscious about its own speech: "no idea what she's saying . . . imagine! . . . can't stop . . . no stopping it." Even the pronoun "she" Mouth uses remains an abstract designation of a position. In refusing "I," Mouth refuses to regard herself as subject; she is already objectified within her own language. The me inside an I that can never be merged with the I becomes the most dominant motif in *Not I*. The refusal to say I because of a me that cannot be covered by a personal pronoun and cannot be verbalized explains the vehemence with which Mouth refuses to drop her third person singular position. Is Mouth the "she" of the story? The dislocated persona of Mouth is only able to acknowledge as her own a painful "roar in the skull." The first-person pronoun is associated with a series of lacks and rejections: specifically with the absence of love.

Julia Kristeva believes that Mouth does not so much reject the discourse of the Father as submit to it so fully as to deny herself. In "The Father, Love and Banishment," Kristeva argues that Mouth is haunted by an absent Father, a "paternal shadow binding her to the body and language" (154). I agree with this critical opinion in that Mouth is caught in the classic double bind to conform and participate in, and at the same time, to struggle to depart from the controlling logos. Mouth's anxiety is connected to the inability to escape or to reject the shadow of paternal authority. The refusal of Mouth to recognize the story as its own history engages critical attention toward other signifying operations constructing gender in *Not I*. The emphatic "she" is an implicit response to and rejection of the first person singular that threatens to invade the logorrhoea. In disrupting the process of signification, in refusing to be constituted within the phallocentric constructs of language, Mouth's fragmented identity is protected from being appropriated and subjugated by the univocal desire for a fixed identity.

The image of the mouth detached from the rest of the body is the antithesis of the stable, specular image with which the ego identifies within a Lacanian framework. As Paul Lawley observes, the Mouth has no form: "in itself it is a no-thing, a 'no-matter,' an absence" (412). Surrounded by space and suspended in the dark, Mouth forms an image of lack or incompleteness. There have been compelling arguments which center on a linguistic interpretation of this very lack or absence as an inscription of female identity: the detachment of Mouth from any body whatsoever is perceived as a metaphor for woman. Defined in the Platonic and the Freudian traditions, Mouth, the personified hole, is seen as the configuration of absence, female genitalia inhabited by a "Not I." Mouth can thus be seen to be a dramatization of female identity as absence—female identity as represented through feeling its bodily absence—the body thoroughly despised and discredited, and yet feeling that it has *only* its body, which is so relentlessly *there*.

Mouth's absence or lack is recognized only in its relation to what is present. In Lacanian terms, the female, lacking the phallic organ to exchange for the phallic privilege of subjectivity, cannot assume the "I" without an erasure of her unrepresentable sexuality. The inability to say "I" is the symptom that betrays the patriarchal economy. Mouth's incapacity to say "I" is also the incapacity to represent herself in what Julia Kristeva has termed the socio-symbolic contract. *Not I* is an arresting representation of the negating—the "notting"—female "I" by the Law of the Father.

If the voice of Mouth, based on stage traditions of the play, suggests female gender, the mouth does not. The mouth is a human organ and it is not gender-specific. It can be a male mouth too. (Enoch Brater has observed in *The Drama in the Text*, how the actress, Billie Whitelaw, who has played both the narrator of "Enough" and Mouth in *Not I*, has given a definitive feminine perspective to the two monologues [58]. However, many viewers who watched her perform have also commented on how her voice and even her body seemed to be playing against her perceived femininity). Mouth cannot be seen as deriving gender from the oral spectacle of word-parturition. In *A Piece of Monologue*, the male soliloquiser describes the word-birth as "Feel soft touch of lip on lip. Lip lipping lip. Then parted by cry as before" (268). Mouth is thus any inscribable sign of anatomy tied to any person. This is not to deny that Mouth can*not* be constituted as a sign of the specifically female body. But only as an inscribed piece of anatomy does gender become an issue. Mouth's exaggerated, grotesque form as an ungendered figure takes issue with inscribable representation. If we allow the mouth to be dissociated and bracketed off from its conventional status as a subject or object of its own discourse, one can also see it simply as a moving organ.

The audience of *Not I* is positioned so that it experiences a similar displacement. On the one hand, the theatrical space privileges the spectator's gaze on the fragile image of Mouth. On the other hand, however, the theatrical space also privileges the menacing image of the Mouth. Mouth's monologue allows no distraction from the gaping mouth at the center of the stage as the audience experience a radical sense of dislocation. The audience is, in fact, an integral component in the play, as experiencing the energia from within. They are made to strain their perceptual and cognitive resources to comprehend the torrent pouring out and viscerally share the experience of the almost inaudible Mouth. The range of the spectators' projections on the Mouth is unlimited under such conditions.

While the audience in a traditional drama remains in a privileged outside position, Beckett's audience for *Not I* constructs and interprets Mouth's narrative. Beckett undermines the authority of the audience as they are unable to comprehend a large part of Mouth's speech. Like Mouth, they are trapped in the framework of theatre and find themselves in the struggle to make sense and order of Mouth's logorrhoea. The spasmodic activity of Mouth's insistent "imagine" frees the spectator's imagination to interpret the kinaesthetic stimuli and the recurrent catch words like "the odd word." The audience is forced to confront the identity of Mouth through language which disrupts the apparati of perception and judgement that would otherwise empower the audience in a position of authority.

The relationship of the Auditor and Mouth is ambiguous. The presence of the stage listener, the Auditor with his gestural expression of "helpless compassion," acts as a bridge between the spectators and Mouth. On a visual level, the juxtaposition of Mouth and Auditor is clearly that of speaker and receiver. The Auditor's onstage position makes the character the representative of the audience. But the posture and stature alienate the Auditor who cannot connect to the Mouth just as Mouth cannot connect to the self. The Auditor thus contributes to the conceptual ambiguities that *Not I* effects. H/she also draws attention to the ambiguous role of the audience in reflecting the audience's role back at them from within the performance they are barely able to hear or understand. While apparently offered as spectacle, Mouth's performance disrupts the apparatus of perception and judgement which would enable the audience to exercise any position of authority; the audience is as helpless as the Auditor.

In some ways, *Not I* seems a compacted and dramatized version of *The Unnamable*; it is almost possible to see the play as an excerpt from that narrative. Amid the fragments of narration, a human being's only story, indeed one's identity itself, becomes the act of narration. In *The Unnamable*, there is metaphysical drama in the inability to speak. If one cannot speak about oneself, one cannot be oneself:

> Oh I know, I know, attention please, this may mean something. I know, there's nothing new there, it's all part of the same old irresistible boloney, namely, But my dear man, come, be reasonable, look, this is you, look at this photograph, and here's your file, no convictions, I assure you, come now, make an effort, at your age, to have no identity, it's a scandal. (102)

If the ground base in both texts is a compound of reduction, constraint, and the dispersion of the self, the counterpoint is the return of new beginnings, "tender mercies" as the Mouth would say, "new every morning."

Mouth in *Not I* tries to run away from the first-person pronoun.

All that the mouth acknowledges as its own is the dull, painful "roar in the skull." Mouth insists on being separate from "I" because it reiterates the hope that the narrative will eventually release Mouth from the suffering self: "Try something else," Mouth insists, "think of something else." Likewise, the obsessive relationship with pronouns is also a central part of the Unnamable's narrative:

> But enough of this cursed first-person, it is really too red a herring. I'll get out of my depth if I am not careful. . . . Bah, any old pronoun will do provided one sees through it. Matter of habit. To be adjusted later. (96)

The struggle for a voice leads the narrator to fictionalize his Mahoods, his Basils, his Worms: "What am I doing in Mahood's story, and in Worm's, or rather what are they doing in mine?" Forced to speak through an unfamiliar voice, the Unnamable cannot recognize his own dislocated identity: "perhaps I am a dying sperm, in the sheets of an innocent boy."

Michel Foucault begins "The Discourse on Language" in *The Archaeology of Knowledge* by paraphrasing the last words of *The Unnamable* as a sign of the erasure of his own authority to speak (although Foucault mistakes the words as those of Molloy). The Unnamable defers speaking of "I" because he says he knows nothing of his self. Fictions are lies invented in order to "put off the hour when I must speak of me." Like Mouth, the narrator senses that while he tells the stories of his "dying generation," another voice speaks to him and tells him what to do to escape the need to go on talking. The inaudible voice interrupting Mouth's narrative also directs and edits Mouth's monologue. In this way, Beckett never lets up in his presentation of the agony of the truncated self.

Keir Elam has observed that "*Not I* must be the first drama in history whose central agon has to do with a grammatical category" (*Beckett at 80/Beckett in Context*, 136). If the egocentric particular "I" is the central characteristic of all drama, then Beckett's play is not an "I." The subjectivity that is always dramatized is elusive in this play. The Mouth is neither the speaking-acting first person nor the agential third person who could be spoken about. The relentless insistence on she/it dissociates the self from individuality. The very conditions of subjectivity become encoded as the suppressed "she" or the repressed "I." Mouth's voice is the inner "me" with no way of egress, the incapacity to say "I." The detachment of Mouth from any body whatsoever can be viewed as a metaphor for woman, at once deformed and irrational. Mouth is seen in this light as the persistent reminder of the fragmentation of women's identification by a patriarchal determinism of the social and cultural orders. Mouth displays a persistence to break free of the body, to be liberated through speech, to abreact through the discharge of speech.

Beckett's attempt to make us interrogate the category of sex and the system of binary sex is complex. He plays on lack or even an absence of sexuality and succeeds in defeating the constructed character of sex as a category of identity. The representation of the feminine position as one of lack and exclusion constitutes an attack on the broader cultural economy, the material world as it is ruled by forces that are phallic, libidinal, and oppressive. There is a very powerful woman-within-patriarchy argument here on the simultaneous devaluing of the body and insistence upon it as the woman's only definition. The body is the site where the political interprets the material. The male control of bodies has always been the cornerstone of patriarchy. As the appropriated objects of men, women play out their resistance to this authority in terms designed to locate phallicization where it "erects" itself, in the consigning of women to silence. The feminine corresponds with the silence, absence, or incoherence that discourse represses. To refuse to speak is to reinscribe woman in silence, marginality, and madness. Through the extension of this schema, woman is the absence of speaking; the speaking subject is not woman. Rather, the thinking identity, cogito, is reserved for men.

For me at least, the inversion of selfhood in Beckett's *Not I* has been one helpful way in understanding how one must reject the notion that sexuality is predicated upon a biological given. It has made me think how the autonomy ascribed to "sex" is an effect of the deployment of sexuality. Gender cannot be free of power for it is an effect of the deployment of sexuality, of the exercise of technologies of power over life. The very materiality of the body is invested through and through by relations of power and knowledge. The emphasis on the construction of gender has also resulted in the bolstering of the myth of feminine passivity—of women composed and written by social forces which men control. What determines the superstructure of masculine and feminine identity is a moot issue. The biological sexual distinction between male and female is often assumed to pre-exist as some natural reality prior to the more problematic construction of gender. Beckett's later writings lead to the point where one can examine sexual difference as something that can be explained on grounds other than those of the innate divide between sexes.

If the gender possibilities disrupt the binary structure as in "Enough," this logically leads to the destabilization of the binary. On the other hand, transcendence of sex binarism is also achieved by exclusionary means by refusing to construct a particular identity as in *Not I*. Like Herculine's "happy limbo of a non-identity," does Mouth's isolated, sequestered existence result in a specific formation of sexuality, we ask ourselves? To counter the universalist heterosexist episteme, to strip the mask of a prior ontological reality, Beckett deconstructs the arbitrary relation of signifier and signified, namely, the body and the body's sexual identity.

The variable identity positions postulated by Beckett likewise shape the movement of his writings and the sexual as well as textual indeterminacies in them. It is in this sense that, as Anna Mcmullan correctly observes, Beckett's works challenge

> the dominant epistemological systems and values of Western patriarchal history, opening up the spaces erased or repressed by the dominant languages of that history. (*Theatre on Trial*, 1-2)

Through the neutered modalities of his writings, through the displacing of the traditional feminist lexicon, Beckett denigrates and disparages any sex-role attribution that would consign women to stereotypical behavior. The last word on this subject has perhaps aptly been made by the embodied performances of David Warrilow and Billie Whitelaw who have actually experienced moving beyond "gender or age" (Ben-Zvi, *Women in Beckett*, 4) while enacting a Beckett play. The body, grossly sexual, irrational, spasmodic, uncontrolled, converges human and natural, subject and object.

CHAPTER FIVE

The Body's Absence in *Not I*, *Footfalls* and *The Later Trilogy*

He dreams and in the middle of the dream falls asleep and dreams another dream, so that his sleep is like a series of boxes, one inside another.

Milan Kundera, *Life is Elsewhere*

In interrogating the concept of identity, Beckett makes subtle distinctions between the concept of identity and the concept of continuity. As a phenomenalist he addresses embodiment by also presenting disembodied characters. Through his disembodied characters, he forces us to trace connections between the former embodiedness of the characters and the spatio-temporal continuity with the disembodied beings. What is the time taken to traverse the distance between this world and the world of the disembodied beings? Is disembodiment a derivative, secondary concept of identity? Is identity interrupted and discontinued after death, and is identity then continuous with bodily identity? In this chapter, I intend to tackle the issue of identity through the theme of physical absence as it is represented in Beckett's *Not I, Footfalls*, and the later trilogy comprising *Company, Ill Seen Ill Said*, and *Worstward Ho*.

On the Cartesian dualistic view that the mind and its contents are non-spatial rests the conviction that what is essential about people is, broadly speaking, mental. The desire for and belief in immortality, or at any rate, the survival after death and dissolution of the body, according to Descartes, shows that the criterion of personal identity cannot be related to bodily continuity. The main premise of Descartes's theorization was that what can be imagined is possible. As Hume later expounded it, "nothing we imagine is absolutely impossible" (32). Nonetheless, Descartes has confused the issue by his idea of an unchanging substance or identifier as the indispensable basis of identity through change, and of the real or objective nature of things as a distinct substratum. This kind of atomistic doctrine explains change as a rearrangement of eternally unchanging things. All arguments about identity which rely on the notion of essential property are inspired by the desire for interrogating Descartes's dualist model. Beckett makes us think about what constitutes identity in terms of the mind-body problem by dislodging and disembodying the mind in many of his writings. He thereby forces us to ask how we are related to our bodies. Is the specific body that the characters inhabit no longer the basic thing that existed independently? Must immateriality and disembodiment be connected to expanses of the mind and imagination?

By destroying the perimeters of the self in space as well as in time, Beckett forces us to ponder beyond temporal identity. By giving a related series of experiences in purely mental terms without any specifically persisting body, Beckett inverts the Cartesian modal argument by showing identity as not ceasing to exist after death. As he writes in *Proust* about the insistence that "the dead annex the quick as surely as the Kingdom of France annexes the Duchy of Orlens" (25). The gradual attrition, the reaching toward what is now commonly known as 'minimalist' writing in his later works, is a matter for some debate. While scholars like Steven Connor perceive a new style, calm, austere, almost disconcertingly deliberate in Beckett's later writings (93), there are other Beckett scholars like Judith Dearlove who find the new style prefigured in all his earlier works, as emerging from the concept of an integral self being collapsed into an impersonal voice, what H. Porter Abbot calls "radical displacements" (224).

In my view too, the transition from the early writings to his later ones, is only a transition in focus from the protagonists' ultimate realization of the limitations of the mind to their discovery of the manner in which the mind tries in vain to reconstruct itself in order to survive bodily extinction. The shift, as well as the point of transition, becomes perceptible in the reduction in *The Unnamable* of everything to a mere voice. By making the Unnamable's existence dependent on a voice and not a specific body, Beckett forces us to ponder on the issue of identity. Whereas in his earlier pieces, Beckett expresses from inside the experience of Molloy's "delicious instants, before one's eyes get used to the dark," in his later works, he tries to express the experience from the outside, where the experience loses in content so assuredly that it ultimately reaches a state of complete absence. Rather than proving the logical possibility of a person's survival of death, Beckett's later works constitute a 'reductio ad absurdum' of the mental criterion of personal identity which requires that mental states do not necessarily involve bodily behaviour.

In Beckett's 'ghost' plays and prose, the attrition which renders man in the interface of life and death, human and subhuman, the vital being and automaton, leads to the corresponding attrition of corporeality. Consequently, there is a progressively increasing stripping away of the flesh from the later works of Beckett. The mutilated, fragmented bodies of Beckett's early works have dwindled and shrunk, and are either lost and rendered anonymous as 'bodies' in a vast populace or become 'ghostly' voices in space or in unconventional settings. There are, on the one hand, the lost bodies roaming in a cylinder in *The Lost Ones*, the "two white bodies" within a rotunda in *Imagination Dead Imagine*, the "little body" surrounded by ruins in *Lessness* and the "body" occupying "a place" in *Worstward Ho*. The androgynous narrator of *Enough* evokes life in the shape of an old hand on old breasts while the imploring eye in *Ping* evokes a response in an otherwise lifeless scene.

In Beckett's dramatic writings, on the other hand, the body is reduced to mere speaking voices like that of the Mouth in *Not I*, the shrouded head in *A Piece of Monologue*, two ghostly hands in *Nacht und Tràume*, the shadowy figures in *Quad*, the 'Remains of a mind' in *Worstward Ho*, a sigh in *Breath*, and the voice of the Listener in *That Time* split into three selves voicing various phases of his life. In *A Piece of Monologue*, the male speaker remembering a female loved one is agonizingly alive to her and equally agonizingly absent, slipping into the grave as well as his failing memory.

In the transmutable landscape of Beckett's later works in particular, self and other slip in and out of the range of visibility, while the interplay of absence and presence intermixes with the spheres of life and death. The male in *A Piece* begins his speech with the word "Birth"—"Birth was the death of him"—and ends with the term "gone"—"Alone gone"—as he exists in a "black vast" and eternally dwindling universe. The Monologue is delivered by an old man who relates in third person singular his birth: "Birth was the death of him." His life, "two and a half billion seconds," was a progress from "funeral to funeral of . . . he all but said of loved ones" (265), and the images he describes are of "Ghost light. Ghost nights . . . Ghost rooms. Ghost graves. Ghost . . . he all but said ghost loved ones" (269).

The minimalist text of the play evokes absence through the spaces of light and darkness as well as the spaces between speech and movement. Existing in the borders between the visible and the invisible, presence and absence, and caught between sound and silence, the shifting identity of the old man foregrounds perceptual indeterminacy.

Beckett makes an intensive exploration of this theme by playing up the fears about the disappearance of his characters. Maddy Rooney's significant plea: "Do not imagine, because I am silent, that I am not present" (25), reveals the precariousness of existence against the sense of absence or disappearance. In another play, *Ohio Impromptu*, an old man sits listening to a man dressed as his double reading to him about an old man who sits listening to a man dressed as his double. The spirit visitor in this play is as reassuringly present and absent as the shadowy Beatrice in Dante's work: "Seen the dear face and heard the unspoken words, stay where we were so long alone together, my shade will comfort you" (286). Similarly, . . . *but the clouds* . . . shows an enigmatic communion with a woman perpetually slipping out of grasp:

> Then crouching there, in my little sanctum, in the dark, where none could see me, I began to beg, of her, to appear, to me . . . No sound, a begging of the mind, to her, to appear to me. (260)

And in *Ghost Trio*, the protagonist has lost even the illusion of individuality. Languishing in his room like the rest of the Beckett heroes, Molloy, Malone, Krapp, and Hamm, he is merely labeled F for 'figure,' and does not seem to have even the name of The Unnamable. In all this Beckett registers the loneliness of the body when even the sense of the self is gone.

In the dramaticule *Come and Go* Beckett presents the image of three women sitting and murmuring confidences about the dark future. What is perceived, however, has to be set against what is communicated in the silences of Vi, Ru and Flo who have no individual identity of their own. They are no more than three shades and their voices are no more than echoes of each other as they sit on a bench which is meant to be invisible to the audience. Gliding in and out, they seem wraithlike, 'ghostly' figures. Their gestural movements and interweaving of hands accentuate their absence in presence. The indeterminate figures are purged of all sense of the tangible flesh. Flo (Flower), Ru(e), and Vi (Violet) portray mortality in their 'rings' of growth and ageing on their lineaments—just as much as male protagonists of other plays incarnate mortality. The three hardly speak and their subjectivity is hence hardly pronounced. And yet, in the enclosing darkness, there is a sense of Death lurking. Echoes of Schubert's "Death and the Maiden" which also forms the central core of Beckett's *All that Fall* give the weight of mortality to this dramaticule which uneasily intervenes between the absence of the bodily and its overwhelmingly evanescent presence. The insistence of the physical, and its precedence over the perception of mortality is thus defined by its very reduction.

This tendency is evidenced again in a play like *Embers* which is cast in the invisible medium of a radio play. Whether Ada is actually a presence or exists simply in Henry's head is confounded by Henry's fictionalizing: "You will be quite alone with your voice, there will be no other voice in the world but yours" (116). Like the image of a dysfunctional corporeality located in the sounds of the alienated Mouth, Henry in *Embers* contextualizes his physicality through his stories. Ada remarks that Addie has heard Henry speaking "in the lavatory" just as Mouth in *Not I* vents her stream of words in the "nearest lavatory." The disembodied nature of these voices are reembodied by the remembrance of gross physical acts, of the animalistic sensations of lovemaking whose byproduct was Mouth, and of Henry's recollections of "hammering away at it" (101) until "we did it in the end" (101). Although he is not sure if "the hole is still there," he does still relish the virile physicality of his father's "trying to toast his arse" (95), and his own "hammering" which "was not enough to drag her into the world" (99).

Beckett also shows a tricky ambiguity in *Cascando* where Woburn's identity cannot be authenticated. And in *Rough for Radio II*, physical identity is further sublimated by making one of the characters mute. In all these plays, there is no definable meaning located within the text as there is no physical space within which the contents of the drama are played out. It is only the body of the actors that forms the physical space within which the narrative is enacted. The theatre, in fact, offers Beckett a context for representing images of the self, and also for investing the self in others. In the theatre itself, the performing bodies of the artists foreground the physical presence of the characters. Despite the epistemological lie of the fictional character of theatre, the continuing presence of the artists grounds the experience of the audience in the concrete particularity of the bodily. Alain Robbe-Grillet's concept of "thereness," of "being-there" or "realism of presence" was meant to demonstrate the intensely embodied nature of Beckett's theatre.

What I wish to emphasize here is that Beckett has, as if by inversion, made the body the agency for grounding the material reality of the self by often denying the self its bodily, palpable and concrete existence. Beckett, in fact, plays on the epistemic nature of the visibility of bodies in order to explore to what extent is this fleshly flesh human. In this context, it seems relevant to quote Lois Oppenheim who expresses his concern that

> though much has been offered in the way of critical interpretation of Beckett's preoccupation with the dismembering of the body, little, if anything has been written on disembodiment as such in Beckett's texts. (220)

Pertinent to this observation, I wish to examine here how the body in Beckett is simultaneously absent and present. The tenuousness of presence set off by increasing invisibility, even absence, serves to emphasize and foreground the sentient phenomena by directing attention to what is not there and what should be there. By either withholding or giving an excess of sensory data, by making the body subjectively experience suffering, pain, ageing and illness, Beckett treats the body as much more than a figural presence.

Beckett's phenomenological treatment of embodiment necessitates the corollary truth of bodily absence or concealment. The close nexus of corporeal absence with modes of presence reinforces the fact that it need not be considered spiritually derogatory to identify the self with the body, to locate one's identity in the material being as it has traditionally been looked upon by the Western philosophical tradition. The interconnections and not the mutual exclusiveness of them should be recognized in an effort to perceive how the essential self is not just a manifestation of an incorporeal mind. The hermeneutical approach that Beckett adopts toward understanding modes of bodily disappearance are really a way of obscuring the deep and fundamental unity of experience and action. In addressing the issue of how the body can be absent from experience despite human experience being rooted in the bodily Beckett shows the body's tendency toward self-concealment. The self-effacement of the visceral processes leads us to forget the organic basis of life. Bodily disturbances or disruptions of motility, perception, or other vital functionings, foreground the mutual implicativeness and homonymity of these phenomenological modes as they interact in the relationship between body surface and the visceral depths. The correlativity of the body's recessive aspects with its more pronounced ones have significant theoretical implications as absence or as iconic nothingness. Beckett uses the representational medium of theatre to play on the densely iconic suggestiveness of physical invisibility or absence. His manipulation of absence points directly toward the viscerality of the body as the attempt to make the visible invisible is a paradoxical reendorsement of the visible.

Beckett disrupts the idea of the bodily self in different ways. A device he particularly adopts is to focus the audience's concentration on a fragment or a specific part of the body. The fragmented images compulsively urge the imagination to fill in the gaps as much as they highlight the wholesomeness of the body that is missing or absent. The image of May's dragging feet as she paces up and down in *Footfalls* or the tangible image of the "skull-sized white globe" in *A Piece of Monologue* compulsively foreground the body in rejecting or disembodying parts of the self. Can we then read disembodiment as literally being divested of being, as a social being cast off from Being-in-the-world, as ontological separation and isolation? I will illustrate my point through Beckett's *Not I* once again and also through *Footfalls*.

The severance of the old woman's body in *Not I* from her voice, of Mouth from her physicality constitute a displacement of bodily being, an absence. On the other hand, the visual shock of the fluorescent mouth perched high up on the stage of *Not I* in darkness writhing and emitting its disordered and chaotic flow of words has a stark "realism of presence." The asymmetry of the theatrical image from the mouth without a body to the body apparently without the mouth is so deeply devastating that one does not know how to associate it with or dissociate it from Mouth. The Mouth in *Not I* collapses the boundaries between inside and outside thereby carrying far-reaching implications for the body which is displaced and manipulated, fragmented and devoured, as it is reduced to a mouth. Synecdochically, the Mouth recalls the power of presence by insisting on absence just as much as it mimics the denial of the 'wholeness' of the body. A mouth without a body or a face, the mouth is merely an orifice from which a voice emanates even as everything else is reduced to the bare essentials of the mortal self. Her fragile mortality as Mouth in *Not I* is in stark contrast to the gross vulgarity of the flesh.

The mouth illuminated in the surrounding darkness utters an almost incomprehensible and incoherent stream of words with a confessional urgency that forms the narrative of the play. A kind of phenomenology of orality, it metonymically represents a character and an unseen body, though by itself it forms an iconic idea of lack, absence, or incompleteness: "Whole body like gone . . . just the mouth." The rejection of the fragmented self is expressed in the rejection of the first-person pronominal expression of individuality.

The dramatic action in *Not I* emerges from the mouth's inability to accept the experience it narrates as that of its own self. The relinquished self in *Not I* cannot identify with the I-voice: "not knowing what . . . what she was . . . what? . . . who? . . . no! . . . she! SHE!" (222). The reluctance to identify with the actions Mouth narrates is also suggested in the disclaimers: "Who? . . . No! . . . She!" The retreat from the self which becomes fragmented and the voice which loses grammatical stability leads to verbal extinction. It results in what Andrew Kennedy calls "a no-longer soliloquy" (30). Even her gushing words, the broken syntax of her explosive babble, suggest and focus on absence: "godforsaken hole called . . . no matter," "parents unknown" as she "stares into space" or "stand[s] there waiting," all of which plays around the idea of nothingness. Mouth as a personified hole can be perceived and configured as absence. In rejecting her own self, it may be claimed that Mouth becomes the iconic "faceless . . . and transpositional subject" (77) in Deleuze and Guattari's terms of expression as the Mouth is implicated in her own perception of becoming.

Mouth conducts an inaudible dialogue with her own monologue. The shrouded figure offers an internal audience to the Mouth, and in their isolation together, they inhabit a world where they both seem to be two aspects of a single being. In a Bakhtinian sense, the grotesque face is reduced to the gaping mouth as the world is swallowed by the mouth as it creates a new world that is ejected out of the lower stratums of the body. Deprived of any sustenance and affection, Mouth is an endproduct of the psychosomatic fragmentation to which her body is reduced, even as the schizophrenic experience may relate to dying or death. As Mikhail Bakhtin in *The Dialogic Imagination* observes that "man's image was distorted by his increasing participation in the mute and invisible spheres of existence. He was literally drenched in muteness and invisibility. . . . The human image became multi-layered, multi-faceted. A core and a shell, an inner and outer, separated within it." (135-36)

It is the very absence of the body thus, reduced to the Mouth, that draws one's attention to the body throughout Mouth's narration. Beckett's oft-quoted desire that *Not I* work on the nerves, and not the intellect of the audience is an insistence on the bodily. The violence of Mouth's discourse frames a body convulsed by "mouth on fire . . . streams of words . . . no idea what she's saying . . . no stopping it" (220). It is interrupted only by "the words . . . the brain" as she rambles on endlessly.

The image of the mouth with its animalistic movement, all saliva, lips, teeth and tongue, and voice cut off from the body, has a paradoxically different impact. Even while the body is bracketted off, the immediacy and haunting presence of her physical being is overwhelmingly there, the brain clashing with the mouth: "hit on it in the end . . . then back." Her apparent discomfiture about the "dull roar in the skull" and the "beam . . . now bright, now shrouded" (221) foreground the whole issue of where her pain emanates from. Although she acknowledges the fact that she suffers no actual pain she writhes and screams in extreme agony with a complete lack of self-consciousness. Unsure of the buzzing in her head: "What? . . . the buzzing . . . yes . . . all silent but for the buzzing" (221), she wonders why her body was still and immovable, and irreconcilable with the buzzing and the screaming in her head. Being suddenly swamped with the sensation of her lips and jaw moving, she hopes she would be "spared that," that her mouth would stop saying it.

While this tussle ensues, her mouth persists in "dragging up the past . . . flashes from all over" (220). She recalls many walking sessions, including the one when directing her steps home, she stops by a little mound in Croker's Acres when she is rendered immobile though her voice compulsively carries on speaking. Despite the re-assertion of her own speechlessness, she is possessed by an urge to communicate, at the same time that communication wrestles with "something in her begging . . . begging it all to stop" (220). The bare traces of language echo the uncontrollable quality of a "mouth on fire . . . stream of words . . . in her ear . . . and can't stop" (220). Her resistance to her bodily assertions constrain her ability to experience herself at the same time that it distances her from her own insensate physicality. The detachment, the conscious absencing from her elemental body nonetheless, serves to reinforce her body's presence with an intensely dichotomous and contradictory magnitude of cathectic interchange between presence and absence.

The insistence of the physical, often grossly so, its precedence over consciousness of anything else, makes it central to defining the material reality of Beckett's world. Although Beckett's monodrama should logically take us into the mind of the narrating Mouth, it is strangely enough, her whittled bodily self reduced to the barest essentials that constitutes the self's awareness of its own being. The duality of mind and body, if there is any such concept, gets so completely nullified in the manifest image of the mouth which collapses and reduces all differences and becomes the common link binding body and its consciousness. And as Xerxes Mehta has remarked, it also "shows only one of the ways in which Beckett plays with the tension between the fixed and the dynamic" ("Ghosts," 43).

Mouth's body does not seem like a representation of herself at all nor does it seem to exist independent of her mind. The psycho-physiological response within the monstrous appearance of the Mouth and the simultaneous disappearance of her body emphasizes both absence and presence. Paradoxically the body's absence insists on and defines its own presence and meaning. It happens so over and over again in Beckett, until as in *Eh Joe,* voices within threaten Joe about the "louse" that might be watching him. The psyche is haunted by presences that lurk around obsessively with narcissistic fears menacing a "dry rotten" heart as he "sit[s] there in his stinking old wrapper hearing himself" (203). The physical being of the characters seems to dilute and increasingly to disintegrate as they recede into the skullspace, leaving behind only voices.

It is in this sense that the metaphysical oppositions of being and non-being, presence and absence, mind and matter, are undermined in Beckett. It leads to Derrida's critique of the logocentricity of "closed" or "centered" structures, that all interest in "presence" are a fallout of metaphysical imagination, at the same time that it critiques Derrida's assault on the notion of presence as pure givenness. In "Structure, Sign, and Play in the Discourse of the Human Sciences," Derrida traces the history of metaphysics as a hunt for a fixed center, a "point of presence" (247). As against this "fundamental ground . . . a fundamental immobility" (249) providing certitude Derrida emphasizes the destruction of such a metaphysical presence in order to "extend[s] the domain and the interplay of significance ad infinitum" (249). The play of significations in an uncentered structure is the interplay of the presence and absence of Being. Beckett's subversion of teleological narrative form does arrive at Derrida's "Nothing" as the recognized condition for Being, but not without revealing the interface of absence and presence.

The common inherence of absence and presence is thus a given fact in Beckett's writings. The ambiguous nature of corporeality is given a deeper accent in Beckett's late writings when bodily presence is minimized to a ghostly aspect of its fleshly self, or rather more an absence rather than presence. This was anticipated in Hamm's lament in *Endgame* that "I was never there" (74). The phenomenology of bodily absence which Beckett delineates so adroitly in his later writings more particularly has been critically studied by Drew Leder who has used the concept of "dys-appearance" for the "alien presencing" of the body. Leder concerns himself with the philosophical implications of corporeal absence since it is absences, the invisible, often inaccessible visceral organs which reveal the essential structures of embodiment. Leder is convinced that "it is precisely the phenomenology of bodily absence that will provide the tool for understanding previous concepts of self" (4). Using the twin concepts of the Korper (physical body) and Leib (living body), he explores the phenomenal body at the points and regions of its absences and perceptual invisibility, like the internal organs or even the back of one's head. He believes that such a phenomenological examination would help critique the Cartesian paradigm with its privileging of res cogito. As a hermeneutic it could break the spell that consciousness has woven over post-Cartesian and post-Kantian philosophy:

> My self-presencing in consciousness will thus be lined by a multiplicity of absences: the unseen sides of the perceiver and

> perceived, the unknown motivators of my action, the indefinite horizons of praxical engagement. (37)

Leder illustrates an interesting phenomenological point about life being allied to "a certain concealment, a withdrawal and protection of its vital center" (45) in order to explore the perceptual characteristics of viscera. Leder uses Foucault's notes in *The Birth of the Clinic* about how nineteenth century medicine made the direct perception of diseased organs an epistemological goal, the corpse, not the live patient "as the paradigmatic figure of truth." This is because, as Foucault tells us, the "anatomo-clinical gaze," that

> which hides and envelops, the curtain of night over truth, is, paradoxically, life; and death, on the contrary, opens up to the light of day the black coffer of the body. (166)

Engaged in the understanding of the basic structures of embodiment, Beckett explores the issue through the modes of absence and decorporealization. The experience of bodily absence in Beckett is not meant to support the Cartesian dualist paradigm of the body as an oppositional or negational mode within the self in any way. Rather it is an effort to comprehend and arrive at a more definitive concept of the self through the mode of presence-absence correlative. The dysfunctioning and subsequent breakdown of the body is a crucial way of authenticating it as the very medium through which the world comes into being. As an integrated being the body as lived structure is the central locus of experiencing the world.

The dynamics of disappearance are thus set against the dynamic reproductions of Beckett's drama on the stage. The simultaneously embodied and disembodied spaces of Beckett's late plays are a means of examining the slippery but nonetheless, close correspondence between inhering in one's physical self-presence and the deanimated, decentered, and dispossessed nature of obliviating oneself from it. Playing with the dialectic of visible/invisible, Beckett shows in his plays how the identity of his characters remains an unresolvable enigma. Just as Mouth's dispossession in *Not I* is echoed in "Whole body like gone," in other plays too, the physically diminished characters are abstracted from their conditions of embodiment.

Footfalls, *Rockaby*, and *Ohio Impromptu* portray absence in the form of a presence—the presence of an other voice or body. In *Rockaby*, the visual image of the woman rocking in the chair is accompanied by the voice who quests for another creature like herself. Trying to rock herself out of her embodied existence and responding to Voice's "Fuck Life" she wants "More." This unusual chant for "More" directly conflicts with the repressed ghost of her self emanating as Voice. The woman in *Rockaby* is further stripped of her identity by having no name, and neither being able to talk or act—her only utterance being the need for "More." Her recorded voice fuses into the voice of the rocking woman: "when she said/to herself/whom else/time she stopped" (275), and the shifting pronouns enable a merging of identity between the mother and the daughter who replicates her life and death. The existential tension in all these late writings between consciousness and self-consciousness plays on the borders and limits of bodily identity and presence.

In *Footfalls*, the dialectical tension between self and other, presence and absence, refers back to the perceptual gradations between the bodily seen and the unseen. As in *Not I* and *Rockaby*, the action is concerned with memories of a past life, but once again, one is not sure of the final stasis of death. The action here again takes place in the mind as the voice explicitly says: "My voice is in her mind." Nonetheless the stream of consciousness that emanates is bodily rather than mental. The disheveled, gray-haired woman pacing the narrow strip on the stage visually evokes only a glimpse of her body. 'Ghostly' in bodily appearance, May is possessed with a poor arm, poor head and poor mind, as well as a poor appetite.

In *Footfalls*, two characters appear on stage, May through the eye, and her dying mother (the Voice) through the ear. May's endless pacing in the dark interrupts the "faint, though by no means invisible" stillness and silence as she appears "a faint tangle of pale grey tatters" (242). The ageing woman May, "dishevelled grey hair, worn grey wrap hiding feet, trailing" (239), has to minister to the physical needs of her ninety-year-old mother. While the voice in the darkness has bodily needs, it also recalls May's bodily afflictions, especially her compulsive pacing. May might be the visible character who paces on and off nostalgically wrapped in thoughts about her mother, but the real character is characterized by absence except in her voice. A strangely phantasmal dialogue takes place between May and her mysteriously absent Mother. This challenges the verifiability of a character's concrete, tangible existence, raising the issue of the meaning of real existence. The two levels on which the dialogue takes place confuses the senses for what is heard—the "semblance" of a story, and what is perceived as a shadowy figure operate at two different levels of consciousness. And yet ultimately, at the deepest levels of meaning, sense and sensibility, absence and presence, merge and confuse one with the other.

As part of a constant becoming, the "absolute absence of the Absolute" (33) which Beckett has discussed in the same essay on "Dante. . . . Bruno.Vico . . . Joyce," May's pacing in *Footfalls* unravels the infinity implicit within the illusion of space and time. An obsessive affair, her pacing is a means of creating meaning for her feet even as it is deeply felt in the mind. The configurations of absence within presence in May's relentless physical pacing recall to my mind what Beckett philosophically pointed out in *Malone Dies*: "The forms are many in which the unchanging seeks relief from its formlessness" (7). The fluidity of such a situation relieves the sense of corporeal integrity. It is bodily death that threatens and yet at the same time "validates" the sensual experience of the body. Implicit in Beckett's depiction of the bodily as we perceive is a sense of corporeality that is enhanced by the immanence of death. Beckett takes bodily identity to the point where he relates it to survival after death, that is, to the doctrine of the resurrection of the body, and secondly, to the immortality of the soul.

Death and dead bodies make the bodily more visible. In rhetorical terms, death equivocates in Beckett's writings, and is never considered a finality within the unchanging structures of the universe. In his early work, *Proust*, Beckett distinguished "our first nature," perhaps death's oblivion, "of a deeper instinct than the mere animal instinct of self-preservation" (11) from what has become second nature. Caught in a constant cycle of change where one is constantly displaced and decentered, the notion of gaining a stable identity in a permanent sense is impossible. This is the world without categories and prior to all demarcations of time. It is the words of *A Piece of Monologue* which haunt us here: "Nothing stirring. Faintly stirring. Thirty thousand nights of ghosts beyond. Ghost light . . . Ghost graves. Ghost. . . " (269).

In *Footfalls*, the specific visual image of "a woman walking up and down" resonates at three levels of signification: the visual, the aural, and the fictional. As the curtain rises slowly, May is perceived as "a faint tangle of pale grey tatters." Dressed or rather enshrouded in a "worn grey wrap" from top to toe, she punctures the "faint, though by no means invisible" silence and darkness by her endless pacing, by the sound of her footfalls. James Knowlson and John Pilling report Beckett's belief that his 'basic conception' of footfalls rested on the centrality of the May image endlessly pacing up and down across the front of the stage:

> . . . the text, the words were only built up around this picture. . . . That is the centre of the play, everything else is secondary. (221)

Her compulsive yearning to hear the sound of her own physical existence leads back to her experience of loss of self: "A little later, when she was quite forgotten . . . when as though she had never been, it never been, she began to walk" (242).

May's tussle with words suggests her incapacity to configure her identity and her presence in representation: "Will you never have done revolving it all. It? It all." Her mother never appears in her own person. Throughout she is a disembodied voice, the voice of an old woman nearing death, one who appears as the voice of a ghost in the second part of the play. The ghostly voice tells her daughter May: "I heard you in my deep sleep. . . . There is no sleep so deep I would not hear you there" (239). This implies that the ghost May describes may well be her own.

The quagmire within which the ghostly voice and the daughter converse hinges on the daughter's query, "Just what exactly, Mother, did you perhaps fancy it was?" (243). Significantly, May's story gives birth to a character like herself, Amy, who the mother, Mrs Winter, insists she had seen earlier at the evening prayers. May herself knows that the "semblance" of her story is only ill seen, ill said, and only ill understood.

May disappears from the stage in section three as she registers the deletion of her self. All that remains is the dim trace of a shadow of encircled light. Her tangible, fleshly presence shadowed by doubt, the voice of the absent-present mother is also interrupted by: "In the old home, the same where she. . . ." And Beckett steps in here to explain, as quoted by Walter Asmus, that "There is a difference. She was never born" (87). In other words, the act of recognition as existential awareness implies a set of defining traits of phenomenon to counterpoise Beckett's theatrical double: the fact that May exists as an object but has not been born or spiritually animated as a human body.

Once again, Beckett seems to have cleverly transformed Jung's lecture on the girl who "was never born" into a powerful dramatic image. As a presence, not a person ever born outside her imagination, May insists: "I was not there" (243). She thus dramatizes Beckett's famous observation on Joyce's *Finnegans Wake* that one must not really be 'about something,' instead, be that 'something itself' (27). The sparse dialogue constantly punctuated by pauses, the careful disjunction between verbal pacing and its physical counterpart, the complex though in some ways, fantastic merging of mother and daughter, subject and object, past and present, all reinforce the superimpositions of absence on presence. "Where is she, it may be asked" accentuates the uncertainty of the figure onstage reduced to the pair of feet in the diminishing stage light and silence as the play ends.

Nonetheless, the silence is pervasive. The faintly lighted stage reinforces presence and the room devoid of objects but for a pair of pacing feet asserts presence. The absence, in short, counterpoints and brings back the interplay of presence. The sense of constant becoming assaults any notion of absolute reality. Implicit in Beckett's depiction of the body, then, is the sense of the imminence of death in an infinite landscape of potentiality. Death would threaten and at the same time endorse the sensual experience of the body.

In another sense Beckett also interrogates the legitimacy of identity in terms of the unrecognizable mutations that characters undergo. The unrecognizable mutations, the metamorphosis that his characters undergo in their physical death is tested out in the melting, dissolving imagery of life after death. If death could revoke to the body the true self that has been concealed or distorted by the erosive processes of life then the transformative processes of death would suggest a peeling away of the complexities appended to the identity acquired in life as well as a return to a primordial sense of enduring, "essential" identity.

The harking back to an unequivocal essence of semiotic purity seems possible only in death. However, in Beckett, we see that the body in death does not suppress the irreducible quality of the living character of the body. It is true that death restores to the body an image of the true self that gets distorted and concealed by the erosions of time and suffering. Nonetheless, the individual as the transitory and ephemeral link in Nature's chain of birth, life, and death, can be identified only in terms of his bodily self which does not get vanquished in bodily death and extinction. The existential and ontological import of the physical event of dying has interesting connotations and Beckett explores it in its intricate interconnections with the body. Like Descartes, Beckett addresses the body as the locus and site of death. But unlike the central Cartesian metaphysic, the soul is not the only binding, persisting link with the mind.

The concept of mortality and death as a specific, the Beckettian ramifications of deaths, or death-longing, murders or suicides, permeate all of Beckett's writings. Belacqua and Murphy's obsessive fascination with death as a possible state of "embryonal repose" was an early evidence of this. Death is ultimately only an annihilation and an abnegation, a fact neatly encapsuled in Pozzo's eloquent statement:

> One day we were born, one day we shall die, the same day, the same second. They gave birth astride of a grave, the light gleams an instant, then it's night once more. (57)

Beckett's conception of physical life as an experience of dying is the obverse of the belief that life does not end with death which is a continuation of life. Death is a metaphor for the infinity, or at least, the longing for an infinite self present in a finite world. As the Unnamable laments, "I'll be born and born, births for nothing, and come to night without having been" (159). Life and death merged in a continuum or flux has no beginning nor no end. The protagonist of *First Love*, preferring the odor of corpses to "what the living emit," states wryly that the earth has "many graves in her giving, for the living" (35). In a similar mood, Watt also comes to almost like the smell "exceptionally foul, and yet at the same time in some way familiar" as the odor of death. Released from Mr. Knott's house, Watt encounters a strange figure he cannot identify as man or woman, nun or priest, and infers here an endless life-death cycle, a continual coming and going.

This leads me back to Descartes for whom the affirmation of his existence took him to an inquiry concerning his nature: granted it is certain that he exists, what sort of thing is he? Descartes holds that the true concept of matter as well as mind is innate in the human mind where they can be 'discovered' once the prejudices of the senses have been removed. In terms of metaphysical certainty, Descartes writes, one can doubt that one has a body. In seeking 'detachment from sense' Descartes paves the path for a doctrine of physical reality that is dependent on innate concepts and a doctrine of mental reality that is both anti-materialistic and anti-empiricist. The *Meditations* call into doubt all the deliverances of the senses, that which concern the existence of nature, and our physical self. Our knowledge of ourselves as thinking beings is primary and non-sensory. Furthermore, the non-sensory awareness of the nature of the body is far superior to what we take to be knowledge gained by direct sensory apprehension. Descartes's development of his argument for the independence of the mind from body stems from this epistemological transparency of thought: our awareness of our thought-processes is immediate and unproblematic.

Descartes apparently leaves us with a completely spiritualized conception of the "I." Since spirit and matter, according to Descartes, are essentially different, there is no connection between them except through God whose creations we are as spiritual beings, the body being irrelevant. Beckett inverts this individualist emphasis by emphasizing invisible and absent bodies, by referring to them as the vast anonymity of the human populace. In doing so, Beckett shows how they cannot operate without, or could be conceived apart from the body in which they are active.

The coordinate body along with its sensory apparatus is an inescapable element in the working of the cognitive faculties of pure intellect, sense and imagination of the human mind. Is it possible then, to conceive of a disembodied person if the contingent form of the body determines the necessity of one's contingency? And in exploring the need for an epistemic assurance about corporeal objects Beckett reveals the phenomenology of absence and wrestles with this problematic in several interesting ways.

Beckett's other later writings continue to use the device of bodily absence in various ambiguous shades to foreground the preeminence of this issue. *Lessness* thus presents an upright naked male body with blue eyes and a beating heart set against fallen walls and grey ruins: "Flatness endless little body only upright same grey all sides/earth sky body ruins" (133). The "body exposed" to the enveloping void seems to encounter difficulty in sustaining itself as it progressively degenerates. From the "locked rigid" body it appears to become a corpse as the hole-like eyes stare from a rotting face. Decomposition increasingly ravages the body which still manages to remain upright with its heart beating. There is a deep sense of desolation that binds the little body in *Lessness* to the other bodies enclosed in narrow interior spaces in *Ping* and similar texts. Absence is thus a pervasive presence in Beckett. If Beckett's early works like *Murphy* examine the issue of dualism by foregrounding the solipsistic impulses of the protagonist, his later writings like *Lessness* effectively collapse the differences between outer and inner as the different parts of the "little body" are seen as constituting a whole: "Little body grey face features slit and little holes two pale blue."

Similarly, the short pieces comprising the late published *Fizzles* embody ghostly figures like the ones walking on dead leaves in "Closed Space," the person in "For to End Yet Again" so rapt in thought that he has no sense of physical selfhood, and the character in "Still" who at nightfall, relegates from visible movement to visible stasis. The bodies in "Closed Space" "appear six times smaller than life" (199). And in "For to End Yet Again," only the image of the box remains: "For to end yet again skull alone in a dark place pent bowed on a board to begin" (179). These are stories where the living are unborn, and the dead do not die, or where physiological degeneration takes place in a lifeless as well as deathless landscape.

Fizzles then mainly presents voices with no faces and bodies which are disfigured, impaired and decayed, recounting past lives and awaiting impending death and disintegration: "skull . . . dark place . . . board . . . skull in the dark . . . void . . . no neck no face . . . remains." "I gave up before birth" is the narrative of a disembodied 'I' who refuses to accept the fact of his bodily existence ever in time: "he'll never say I anymore, he'll never say anything anymore . . . because of me" (32). The 'he' is offered a means to 'end' without truly having been although 'I' concludes that "I'll feed it all it needs" (33). In "Horn came always," the narrator believes that there is 'something' out there "in outer space, not to be confused with the other" (21). In "Old Earth," there is a more definite sense of being rooted in an organic cycle of birth and death: "I've seen you" and "it will be me." And as the narrator makes a 'nightflight,' he is transferred to "other skies, another body" (44). In "He is barehead," the description of a journey from underground to a world 'above' is, in an uncanny sense, reminiscent of Murphy's voyage to his 'third zone' of the 'Belacqua fantasy.' Journeying back to the land of the living, the narrator emphasizes the physical since "the great head where he toils is all mockery," created in a grey place, grey time, a grey body.

That Beckett occupied himself then with writing "ghostly" works in the last two decades of his literary career is a critical commonplace. Interweaving ghostly, otherworldly elements of the dead and the dying challenges one's notions of what constitutes corporeality. Language, words, body, colour—everything is stripped to the minimal. As a phenomenalist, Beckett examines the universe as possibly constituted out of fleeting objects like sense data where nothing could be identified in one sub-system and re-identified in the other. In his materialist reading of the bodily, Beckett brings this into focus through images of the long white hair in the old woman of *Ill Seen Ill Said*, the stark figure of May in *Footfalls*, the male figures in *That Time*, *A Piece of Monologue*, and *Ohio Impromptu*, and the shadows enclosed in *Residua*. While the performing body acquires a physical presence and immediacy in Beckett's drama, in the late prose pieces, there is an equivocal relationship between the narrating consciousness and the object of narration which brings the object alive as an image of its invention, memory, or perception.

The speaker or narrating consciousness persistently undermines its own existence at the same time that the object of the narrative questions it. The woman in *Ill Seen Ill Said* or the old man who lies on his back in the dark in *Company* are only hypothetical presences in works where the interplay of non-existence or absence constitutes the action.

The contrapuntal relationship between the voices in *Company* are set off against the shadowy Figure whose body foregrounds itself in the separation from the voice. The voice, recounting not too savoury memories of his past, is disjunct, objectified, and thereby separated from the perceiving self of the Figure. The phenomenological theme of being and consciousness, subject and selfhood, revealed in the figments Figure posits of the being lying on his back in the dark and the voice he hears is uncannily played out on the absent/present body of the Figure. Caught between memory and imagination, Figure wonders whether there may be someone else with him in the dark. The ghostly presence mesmerizes him as it subtly plays forth the body in Beckett's 'ghostly' works. Caught on the horns of a dilemma, 'mankind' cannot be certain that the world is not of its own making, while on the other hand, the unnamed voice restrains one from slipping into the mental constructs of solipsism. The voice indicates what is before the scene of his inner gaze rather than what is visible to the senses. It endeavours to bridge the fact of disappearance, of the absence of the other, through metonymic substitution of objects. Within the framework of a representational discourse, a Voice caught between memories spanning birth and death, *Company* leads further toward the uncertain status of the other two parts of Beckett's trilogy, *Ill Seen Ill Said* and *Worstward Ho*.

In *Ill Seen Ill Said*, written "in defiance of reason" (19), imagination "makes way for unreason" (23), and "all could be pure figment" (20). "There is," Beckett shrewdly writes, "at least this to be said for mind, that it can dispel mind" (2). *Ill Seen Ill Said* is a fragmented tale of an old spectral figure who, unable to take in the overpowering vision of her own star rising in the heaven, prepares for her exit from "the inexistent centre" of her own absence: "Absence supreme good and yet. . . . If only to the face. Of her tenacious trace" (60). She is fated to remain in a state of suspension between the fixation with the 'ill seen' mirrored image and its 'ill said' representation: "Such equal liars both" (38). In the contrapuntal pull between appearance and non-appearance, the real and the imaginary, a kind of 'confusion' ensues when a woman's lineaments may be confused with another object. The ghostly figure of the woman coming and going, appearing and disappearing, resists the sense of being affirmed as a full presence. Any definitive sense of identity is deliberately withdrawn from an "unalloyed" scenario in which "all could be pure figment" (20), although "the old so dying woman. So dead" (20), is given a sense of mobility. The see-sawing between the one "having no need of light to see" (8), and the other "this filthy eye of flesh" (30), again foregrounds the body-mind, interior-exterior divide. At the beginning then, the vulturine eye of the 'imaginary stranger' sees as "stoop to the prone who must/soon take up their life and walk" the old woman who "from where she lies she sees Venus rise" (7).

As she is conjured by the hungry eye living within the "skull shell of sky and earth," the 'figment' "Averts the intent gaze. Incriminates the dearly won . . . needs nothing. Nothing utterable" (16). Not satisfied with her image alone, 'he' would have her thoughts as well, and yearns to be by her when she 'devours' the ghostly images in her "still shadowy album," "draw[ing] the head lower down still and hold[ing] it in thrall" (14). The confused sense of everything is worse confounded as she is closely examined by a group of "the twelve" ghostly figures. Confronted by the "confusion" that prevails all through the work, the compelling sense of absence begins to strongly insinuate itself in the shape of "neither be nor been nor by any shift to be" (20). A "literalist of the imagination" perceiving the image of an old woman already dead, this seems a strangely paradoxical situation.

Ill Seen Ill Said begins with the evocation of "she," a creature of the shades who still "rails at the source of all life" (7), while she yearns for union with her loved and lost one. Occupying a region on either side of death, she is described at times as belonging to the realm of death, and at others, as still of this world. At times, she appears to be oblivious and bracketted off from this world, and at others, as ever alternating her movements between her hut and the tombstone. The eye that observes her is likewise, an eye of flesh and body that sees in the present, and at other times, the eye of the imagination which conjures phantoms within the confines of the skull: "Say all gone. . . . In the skull all gone. All?" (25).

Just as the action of Beckett's first trilogy was conducted in the narrator's mind, *Ill Seen Ill Said* returns to the speaker's skull—that "ivory dungeon"—where the perceptual faculties of the mind and the eye are unable to sieve out the remembered from the unimagined as they flesh out the obsessive image of a dead old woman: "the long white hair stares in a fan. Above and about the impassive face. Stares as if shocked still by some ancient horror" (28).

The shadowy 'she,' 'already dead,' is the victim of "helplessness . . . she cannot help" and "rails at the source of all life" (7). The old woman is at the same time seen as substantial and spectral, of this world and yet not of it—partaking at once of presence and absence. At one point the woman's face is compared to "a calm slab worn and polished by agelong comings and goings. . . . How serene it seems this ancient mask. Worthy those worn by certain newly dead" (25). The woman combines strength and vulnerability, the strength borne of long years of suffering with the vulnerability of hope still lurking behind "lashes jet black" (25). At her husband's tomb, she is pictured

> From the waist up. . . . White half halo of hair. Face. . . . Voidlike calm as always. . . . Till under the relentless eye it shivers. . . . Rigidly horrent it shivers at last. . . . (29)

Sitting 'dead still' in the 'still air' in a 'voidlike calm,' she initially appears to be enjoying the stasis. However the grass 'shivers' with 'faintest shiver from its innermost' (29), and gradually and imperceptibly, her entire 'old body' appears 'ashiver from head to foot' (30). The rapt fascination with her body is almost complete when he describes her mouth as "Unlikely site of olden kisses given and received" (49).

The female metacharacter here is barely comprehended by the narrative eye: "But quick seize her where she is best to be seized" (15). Subsequently, the intimations of void and absence lead to "vicissitudes of hardly there and hardly gone" (37-38). Despite the visions of the 'eye having no need of light to see' (8), the physical extinction of the 'filthy eye of flesh' (30), or the 'vile jelly' still leaves the mind vulnerable to memories and needs in the 'madhouse of the skull' (20), the ghostly domain 'behind the lids' (39). Nicholas Zurbrugg rightly points out that the terrifying sense of unreality she evokes, caught between life and death, is reminiscent of Beckett's poem "something there" (147). The "farrago of mind and eye" indict each other of treachery: "The mind betrays the treacherous eyes and the treacherous word their treacheries" (48).

The ghostly images in *Ill Seen Ill Said* are akin to those which disturb even the dead with the uncanny feeling of 'something there' as the narrator tries to track down the elusive 'other.' The narrative voice struggles to free itself "of her tenacious trace" (59), to reduce 'she' to fancies or "pure figment" (20). The text of *Ill Seen Ill Said* then develops into a dialogue between the narrator and his imagination which only has a partial autonomy over 'the eye' with which it perceives 'she' compulsively scrutinizing 'a certain spot' (11) in a graveyard near her cabin, 'rapt' and 'riveted' to her ghostly past. The real is not contingent upon the visible, the observable and the external which is always proving less than objectively true. The narrative voice yearns "if only she could be pure figment. Unalloyed. . . . In the madhouse of the skull and nowhere else" (20). He is determined to 'Close-up' (19) and 'enlarge and devour' (23) her image since imagination has only partial control of 'the eye of the flesh.'

Unable to recall her as she existed bodily in the flesh, he dismisses her image as, "not possible any longer except as figment" (30). Nonetheless, the confusion between the 'real' and 'how say its contrary?' persists. The vision of "boots and stockings" (17) or "the flagstone before her door that dint by dint her little weight has grooved" (17-18) summon tears to the "riveted" eye. As "Imagination at wit's end spreads its sad wings" (17) the apprehension that it is a "pure figment" is reiterated: "Not possible any longer except as figment. Not endurable" (30). The dying narrative voice trembles at the brink of a 'deep awakening' while "the mind betrays the treacherous eyes and the treacherous word their treacheries" (48), fusing appearance and its lack, thing and non-thing. The "first last moment" is an appeal to "Grant only enough remain to devour all" (59).

The old woman's death would indicate that the 'tissue' can 'serve' her disappearance by making 'offal' "the whole kit and boodle," though "grant only enough remain to devour all. Moment by glutton moment. . . . Licks chops and basta" (59). The instants of 'deep awakening' resonating between the dead 'she' and the dying 'he' bring back to the mental sphere, the echo of 'something there.' They also bring alive "the farrago from eye to mind" (40), the instant when the reality of the mind is 'ill seen' as 'outward' reality. To the narrator's imagination, everything seems to evoke the 'infinitesimal quaver' as they tremble with "the pathos of . . . dangling arms." What he terms 'the buttonhook and the passim' leads to such that, "in the end the back and forth prevails" (47). Thus while she is 'already dead,' she becomes "alive as she alone knows how" (50). And while 'he' seems to be dying, he is subject to the torment he defines as 'the look' (57). He cannot help admitting that they are 'equal liars both': "The mind betrays the treacherous eyes and the treacherous word their treacheries" (48). And this search for what that 'something' is, what form the encounter with it may take, continues in Beckett's next work, *Worstward Ho*.

The contingent nature of the body is also evident in *Worstward Ho* where the narratorial eye alights "somehow again on back to the bowed back alone. Nothing to show a woman's and yet a woman's" (34-35). "Topless baseless hind-trunks. Legless plodding on. Left right unreceding on" (43). The move toward worstwardness: "First the body. No. First the place. No. First both" (101), is a move toward the paradoxical combination of contraries, of absent thereness. Like the dying narrator of *Ill Seen Ill Said* who is torn between his susceptibility to past 'shades' and the compulsion to 'finish with it all at last' (51), the narrator of *Worstward Ho* only desires to savour "That little much of void alone" (18), as he eagerly awaits his end with "no mind and words" (29). He is merely the 'Remains of mind' (9) narrating from his own 'shade-ridden void' (25), alive as it were, with the dead. On his own admission he preys on such 'remains' (17) as the shades of one, a woman "stooped . . . in that graveyard," somewhat as "old gravestones stoop" (45) until she is headless and trunkless, and the 'twain' of an old man and child walk with 'equal plod' (13) until he severes them as "topless baseless hind-trunks" (43), 'vast void apart' (44).

The voice speaks to itself first of a body which is provided with bones and the "remains of a mind," then a "Head sunk on crippled hands," and finally, of a pair, "an old man and a child" walking together, "Joined by held holding hands" (13). To suggest the "powerful impression of the invisible world engulfing the visible" (254), Beckett correspondingly condenses and reduces words to suggest by way of their negation the presence of being: "First the body. No. First the place. No. First both. Now either. Now the other" (8). The narrator would also ideally eliminate all traces of memories of 'the one' and the 'twain' from his 'skull.' 'Gnawing to be gone' (41), he ultimately abandons the urge for mere 'lessness': "less no good—Worse no good. Only one good. Gone" (41-42). Akin to the narrator of *Ill Seen Ill Said* who believes "Absence supreme good" (58) but cannot escape physical existence, he can only advance 'Lessward' or 'Worstward' until he is reduced to "One dim black hole mid-foreskull" (44), and thence to a diminutive 'pinhole', staring beyond a 'boundless void' (46-7).

As the skull 'secretes' in *Worstward Ho* words 'ooze' from the 'soft' as the 'preying on the remains' and the 'gnawing on these bones' persists. The 'pox on the void' (43) insist on creating in the 'clenched staring eyes' of the skull of which "What left of skull not go. Into it still the hole" (46). The entire quest of *Worstward Ho* is a motivation toward 'On,' in searching for 'the wrong word' with which 'to end yet again.' It thus embodies as well as juxtaposes nothingness and hereness, presence and absence: "On. Say on. Be said on. . . . Till nohow on." For Beckett, the perception of everything is "ill seen ill said," since it is impossible to give a stable presence to oneself despite one's will to imagine. The empirical idea of an inherent reality is as much suspect as the raw and immediate experience of a discursively constructed reality. It is in these paradoxical terms that, the strongest and most intense feeling perceived in any reading of Beckett's works is that of absence. As Stephen Barker critically comments,

> Whether it be the name of the Unnamable, the rest of Winnie's body or Billie Whitelaw's face, or Godot himself, something is perennially absent. Not missing, not non-existent—absent. (181)

The co-existence of absence and presence accentuates the dense correlation of the manner in which the twin thematics interpret each other. This is because, for Beckett, the idea of any meaningful sense of reality is constantly eluded. It is an imagined or hypothetical possibility existing on the threshold between existence and essence, presence and absence, the fleshed interior and the yet unfleshed exterior. Within the collapsible narrative of his writings hovers the potentiality of both presence and absence, more so his later ones, although the germinal content is evident in his early ones as well. Constructed out of these oppositions, the embodied identity of Beckett's characters alternate between difference and indifference, the visible and the invisible. The ineluctable termination of existence, the inevitable annihilation of life, is uncompromisingly interlinked with its corporeality, and not just as a mere bodily tenement to the mind. Thus while both Eastern and Western traditions of philosophy regard the physical body as mere earthly detritus that corrupts and shackles what was referred to earlier as the spirit or soul, and in the post-Enlightenment, post-religious world as the mind, Beckett would transcend these traditions of thought by positing the supremacy of the seamless body even as he would reduce and condemn it. Enoch Brater has said that

> the story Beckett's heroes are determined to tell is always the story of getting itself written, finished before the body gives up, the *Company* is gone, or, as in the case of *Malone Dies*, the pencil (a Venus) runs out. (167)

Ironically, it is the body's negation which becomes the source of its affirmation. Beckett would then start with the assumption that the truth-conditions concerning identity vary and can never be defined in terms of a totality. In the absence of any satisfactory theory of identity, Beckett would deconstruct the essence of all identity as well as the existence of all identity, even as he upholds and champions the truth of bodily identity.

Conclusion

bodies fleshed in hues
mind fleshes as difference
comports and signifies relationships
traced through brittled temporal gaps
flipping a toss through same sidedness
the discursive aspect of kindness
pained
annealed
the body does it better

In conclusion I would like to recapitulate the main points of my argument as well as identify certain loose ends and issues so far unaccommodated in my work. I have argued that the physicality of Beckett's characters is the chief focus of Beckett's writings. Beckett's narratives reveal that their actions are physically motivated, and that their marked bodily presence along with the body's needs, and not the demands of mental questing, largely determine their actions. Their conspicuous interest in things physical, their persistent hunger, and their bodily functions reveal that their identities find significant expression within their bodies. They even value physical survival over the survival of their identity just as much as the narrator of "The Calmative" knows that the self is "bedded in my old flesh" (47). The physicality of experience invalidates their discursive distancings from their bodies.

Beckett's writings reveal how the protean body, subject to hunger, disease, lust, cannot suppress its inner potential in spite of its violent debasing by the mind. Much as they try to avoid and escape it, much as Beckett's narrators address the body as though it were a random possession, the body remains supremely imminent, inescapably inescapable. Increasingly degenerating and afflicted with ailing limbs and body parts, often toothless, sight-and hearing-impaired, memory failing and mobility dulled, the characters in Beckett's early prose foreground human physicality as much as the deformed and disfigured creatures of Beckett's drama.

The intensely physical vocabulary of *Waiting for Godot*—with Vladimir and Estragon munching, urinating, smelling, sleeping, or waiting with dangling arms and aching limbs, and Pozzo and Lucky registering their own physical anguish in turning blind and dumb respectively—is an important facet of the play. Beckett's focus on his characters' remarkable gait, aching feet, sore scalps camouflaged with hats, constipated digestion, corns, cramps, bunions, ingrown nails, and other remarkable and unremarkable maladies points to the fact that the physical can never be ignored. Hamm and Clov, Nagg and Nell in their amputated world in *Endgame*, and Winnie in *Happy Days*, buried and cocooned, losing the use of her hands and neck, are indisputably aware of their bodies. In *Eleutheria*, an unpublished play, the protagonist lies in his bed until the very end, and in *Act Without Words*, a man is stranded on the desert, completely immobile as the play ends. The protagonists are mostly crippled, legless, paralyzed, and impotent, socially and sexually. The symphony of suffering that characterizes all that is bodily is summed up in Maddy Rooney's apprehension, in *All That Fall*, of her vast, vile body: "How can I go on, I cannot. Oh let me just flop down flat on the road like a big fat jelly out of a bowl and never move again!" (14).

Beckett's refusal to explain anything in his writings and his thorough denunciation of critical exegesis are well-known, and are in keeping with his insistence on an anti-intellectual behavior toward his theatre. Beckett's rather nonchalant remark to Alan Schneider about his work as "a matter of fundamental sounds [no joke intended] made as fully as possible" says it all. Beckett has insisted that his drama in particular be apprehended through the senses as his writings are not informed by any philosophical cogitation whatsoever. The plot in his drama is minimized, and dialogue and characterization are also diminished. Although Beckett was able to reject intellectualism by abandoning an academic profession, he lamented that he "was doomed to spend the rest of (his) life vomiting it out over and over again" (352). Instead of pontificating on what it means to breathe, Beckett presents a play *Breath*, which is literally about breathing. Similarly, *Waiting for Godot* is physically about waiting for something to happen, which is transposed into a real sensation. The bodily feeling of sexual envy is literalized in

Play, and the physical sensation of listening to oneself speak and then rejecting that strangely familiar voice is projected in *Not I*. Their condition, their situatedness in their beings, becomes their performance.

Throughout his work, then, Beckett emphasizes the body's needs and desires, its vulnerabilities and its sheer fleshiness, at the same time that he mocks intellectualism and celebrates the corporeality of his characters. By selective appropriation of the theoretical work of Mikhail Bakhtin and Michel Foucault, my argument claims that the body is not a neutral medium. I have developed this idea using some of Beckett's writings as paradigmatic texts for proving Beckett's case for the primacy of the sentient and what happens when the sentient is repressed.

The body as an expression of identity foregrounds the question of the relationship between self and the corporeal frame, the sense of embodied existence and the fundamental sense of physical existence. The role of the body in constructing identity has strong cultural nuances. Identity is an "effect" of certain discursive practices which control and govern our notions of identity—the categories of sex and gender, the body, the political construction and regulation of our understanding of what identity can suggestively offer. For Beckett, a discursive identity is the effect of institutional practices. In this concept, the historicizing effects of the identification process also provide the avenues to resistance. The integration of subject and object in an unstable identity disrupts definition and categorization. It leads to a not-I identification where the cultural disciplines of power, even those of institutionalized gender, do not work.

There are the important queries that overwhelm one in encountering Beckett: does being female or male constitute a biological fact or a cultural construction that produces the body through the categories of sex? Very often in Beckett, the ontological status of what is "biologically natural" assumes prime importance in the debate about gender relations.

Beckett reminds us of the enormous gaps in our conception of ourselves as he attacks the dominant structures of identity. The physical circumscription of many Beckettian characters disillusions one of any coherent notion of identity. The constant displacement, decay and dismemberment of body parts make any sense of identity, even sexual identity, unreliable as the insistent contingencies of the body play with the closure inherent in representations of identity.

The body portrayed in Beckett's writings is shorn of all sense of individuation, and emerges bereft of distinctness or any clear sense of identity. It is only a compendium of prostheses, of body parts which are rendered fragmented, or missing limbs which may suffer mutation or be transformed otherwise. By showing how the body and its desires are refused, by presenting a litany of body parts, Beckett also undermines our trust in a stable identity or any fixed traits of character.

There are many doubts and unanswered queries that still assail my mind as I bring this study to a close. What are the political implications and consequences of a radical deconstruction of the categories of identity? Does the effort to locate a common identity lead to a political construction of identity itself? What are the political ramifications on the nature of selfhood?

Beckett's concept of the disruption of the body is consequent upon an ideology that denies free expression to the bodily. Since all of us suffer repression in one form or another, does this make slaves out of us? And Beckett also makes us do some rethinking on the implications of this to democracy since like Bakhtin, Beckett redeploys the categories of identity within which one asserts oneself. If the points of departure are those points from which politics itself is shaped, is democracy an impossibility in the long history of bodily repression?

Further, can we hope to construct a discrete subject through exclusion? Beyond offering the contingent nature of identity which he would deconstruct at best, and which one may or may not accept, does Beckett's concept of the body lead toward anything constructive? Beckett's methodology does avoid the reductiveness of the Cartesian heritage, and also the hypostatizing consequent upon a complete collapse of the ways of representation. Is there anything positively concrete we can gain from the attack upon Cartesianism?

Moreover, for what reasons has the disjunctive binary of inner-outer acquired a strategic position in public discourse? The categories of identity that social structures produce compel a radical rethinking of the ontological constructions of identity. Gender is also mediated as a social construct of the body where the uncritically accepted foundations of sexual difference are based on exclusionary practices. What are the categories of true sex, of specific sexuality, feminists argue? By making sex differentiation irrelevant, Beckett reveals the sexual body as the specific object of politics. Played as part of the surface politics of the body, the construction of sexual coherence conceals the gender anomalies and discontinuities that pervade heterosexual contexts. "Sex" is a cultural and political interpretation of the body, according to Beckett.

Beckett's texts deconstruct sex binarism, and offer a way to disintegrate the false unity designated by sex. But does not this logically lead to the possibility of a hypothetical "third gender?" If the force of Beckett's fiction is to offer an experience beyond the categories of identity, what happens to the entrenched sexual polarities of male and female? Are we willing to abandon them? Why should the body be denied a clear locus for gender and systems of gender on which political forces mark their strategic interests? Does this kind of semiotic analysis offset the regulation of the female body in any way? How is the idea of breaking down stereotypes and sexual identities inherently progressive or necessarily in the service of women? The common identity that would subsume such a strategy of subordination of sexual difference is, of course, a potential pitfall for this line of thinking. Does it lead to a true or abiding masculinity/femininity constituted as part of a strategy within the discourse of identity? What prescriptive criteria should be used to decide the issue of sexual identity? And if the institution of normative heterosexuality should be inevitable, then can one not risk substituting one norm for another at some indeterminate point when the act of deconstructing the established paradigms of dominance would lead to another set of paradigms of submission associated with another form of hierarchization? Furthermore, if "the body" is not gendered, sexed, racialized, classed, then it is virtually an abstraction. Isn't Beckett guilty then, of constructing the same kind of reification of the body that I suggest his fiction fights against?

Terry Eagleton has written in *Literary Theory* about the "naturalizing" of social reality, how it is the function of ideology to "convert culture into Nature" (135). If the "natural" sign is one of the "weapons" of ideology, the body's "naturalness" is engaged in the service of ideology. While Beckett's works raise many questions in my mind on these issues, I start wondering if the body is and can ever be truly and really free. These problematic doubts threaten to subsume my argument and create the discourse of "trouble" within the discourse of the body. They also threaten to generate a counterargument to my argument. Reserving that for another indeterminate moment in the future, I wish to reemphasize the significance of the body in Beckett.

Bibliography

Citations from Beckett's Works

Beckett, Samuel. "Dante . . . Bruno. Vico. . . . Joyce." *Disjecta: Miscellaneous Writings and A Dramatic Fragment*. Ed. Ruby Cohn. New York: Grove Press, 1984. Beckett's miscellaneous comments cited from *Disjecta*

______. *Dream of Fair to Middling Women*. Ed. Eoin O'Brien and Edith Fournier. NewYork: Arcade Publishing, 1992.

______. *Mercier and Camier*. New York: Grove Press, 1974.

______. *More Pricks Than Kicks*. New York: Grove Press, 1934.

______. *Proust*, 1931. New York: Grove Press, 1957.

______. *Murphy*. New York: Grove Press, 1938.

______. *Molloy*. New York: Grove Press, 1955.

______. *Malone Dies*. New York: Grove Press, 1956.

______. *The Unnamable*. New York: Grove Press, 1958.

______. *Waiting for Godot*. New York: Grove Press, 1954.

______. *Endgame*. New York: Grove Press, 1958.

______. *Watt*. New York: Grove Press, 1959.

______. *Happy Days*. New York: Grove Press, 1961.

______. *How It Is*. New York: Grove Press, 1964.

______. *Stories and Texts for Nothing*. New York: Grove Press, 1967.

______. *The Lost Ones*. New York: Grove Press, 1972.

______. *Ill Seen Ill Said*. New York: Grove Press, 1981.

______. *Collected Shorter Plays of Samuel Beckett*. New York: Grove Press, 1984. References to all other Beckett plays from this collection.

______. *Collected Shorter Poems: 1930-1978*. London: John Calder, 1984.

______. *Collected Shorter Prose: 1945-1980*. London: John Calder, 1984. References to "First Love", "The Calmative," "Enough," "All Strange Away," "As the Story Was Told," "For To End Yet Again," "Ping," "Lessness," "Still," "Imagination Dead Imagine," "Closed Space," "From an Abandoned Work," from this volume.

WORKS CITED

Abbot, H. Porter. "Tyranny and Theatricality." *Theatre Journal.* 1988: 77-88.

Adorno, Theodor. "Toward an Understanding of *Endgame.*" 1961. Rpt. *Twentieth-Century Interpretations of 'Endgame': A Collection of Critical Essays.* Trans. Samuel Weber. Ed. Bell Gale Chevigny. Englewood Cliffs: NJ, 1969: 82-114.

Asmus, Walter D. "Rehearsal Notes for the German Premiere of Beckett's *That Time* and *Footfalls* at the Schiller-Theater Werkstatt, Berlin." Trans. Helen Watanabe. *Journal of Beckett Studies* 2 (Summer 1977).

Bair, Deirdre. *Samuel Beckett: A Biography.* London: Jonathan Cape, 1978.

Bakhtin, Mikhail. *Rabelais and His World.* Trans. Helene Iswolsky. Cambridge, Mass.: MIT Press, 1968.

______. *The Dialogical Imagination: Four Essays.* Ed. Michael Holquist. Trans. Caryl Emerson and Michael Holquist. Austen, Tx.: Univ. of Texas Press, 1981.

______. *Problems of Dostoevsky's Poetics.* Ed. and Trans. C. Emerson. Manchester: Manchester University Press, 1984.

Baldwin, Helene L. *Samuel Beckett's Real Silence.* University Park and London: The Pennsylvania University Press, 1981.

Barkan, Leonard. *Nature's Work of Art: The Human Body as Image of the World.* New Haven: Yale University Press, 1975.

Barker, Stephen. "Conspicuous Absence: Trace and Power in Beckett's Drama." *Rethinking Beckett: A Collection of Critical Essays.* Ed. Lance St. John Butler and Robin J. Davis. London: Macmillan, 1990.

Bataille, Georges. "Le Silence de Molloy." *Critique* 13 (1951): 387-96.

Begam, Richard. *Samuel Beckett and the End of Modernity.* Stanford: Stanford University Press, 1996.

Ben-Zvi, Linda. *Samuel Beckett.* Boston: Twayne, 1986.

_____. Ed. *Women in Beckett: Performance and Critical Perspectives.* Urbana: University of Illinois Press, 1990.

Benson, Michael. "Moving bodies in Hardy and Beckett." *Essays in Criticism* 34, No. 3 (July 1984): 229-43.

Blau, Herbert. *Take Up the Bodies: Theatre at the Vanishing Point.* Urbana, IL: University of Illinois Press, 1982.

_____. "The Bloody Show and the Eye of Prey: Beckett and Deconstruction." *Theatre Journal* 39 (March 1987): 5-19.

Bove, Paul B. "Beckett's Dreadful Postmodern: The Deconstruction of Form in *Molloy.*" *In De-Structing the Novel: Essays in Applied Postmodern Hermeneutics*. Ed. Leonard Orr. Troy, NY: Whitston, 1982: 185-221.

Brater, Enoch. Ed. *Beckett at 80/Beckett in Context*. Oxford: Oxford UP, 1986.

______. *Beyond Minimalism: Beckett's Late Style in the Theatre*. New York and Oxford: Oxford University Press, 1987.

______. "Voyelles, Cromlechs and the Special (W)rites of *Worstward Ho*." *Beckett's Later Fiction and Drama: Texts for Company*. Ed. James Acheson and Kateryna Arthur. London: Macmillan Press, 1987.

______. *The Drama in the Text: Beckett's Late Fiction*. New York and Oxford: Oxford Univrsitty Press, 1994.

Brienza, Susan. "Clods, Whores and Bitches: Misogyny in Beckett's Early Fiction." *Women in Beckett: Performance and Critical Perspectives*. Ed. Linda Ben-Zvi.

Bryden, Mary. *Women in Samuel Beckett's Prose and Drama: Her Own Other*. Lanham, MD: Barnes and Noble, 1993

Butler, Judith. *Gender Trouble: Feminism and the Subversion of Identity*. Routledge: New York and London, 1990.

Butler, Lance St. John. *Samuel Beckett and the Meaning of Being: A Study in Ontological Parable*. London: Macmillan Press, 1984.

Cantrell, Carol-Helmstetter. "Cartesian Man and the Woman Reader: A Feminist Approach to Beckett's *Molloy*." *Women in Beckett: Performance and Critical Perspectives*. Ed. Linda Ben-Zvi.

Cavell, Stanley. "Ending the Waiting Game: A Reading of Beckett's *Endgame*." *Must We Mean What We Say?: A Book of Essays*. New York, 1969: 115-62.

Chabert, Pierre. "The Body in Beckett's Theatre." *Journal of Beckett Studies* 8 (Autumn 1982): 23-28.

______. "Presentation." *Special issue on Beckett of La Revue d'Esthetique*. Spring 1986: 7-21.

Clarke, K and Holquist, Michael. *Mikhail Bakhtin*. Cambridge, Mass. and London: Harvard University Press, 1984.

Coe, N. Richard. *Samuel Beckett*. New York, 1964.

Cohn, Ruby. *Samuel Beckett: The Comic Gamut*. New Brunswick, N.J.: Rutgers University Press, 1962.

______. *From Desire to Godot: Pocket Theatre of Post-War Paris*. Berkeley: University of California Press, 1987.

______. *Back to Beckett*. Princeton: Princeton University Press, 1973.

______. *Just Play: Beckett's Theater*. Princeton: Princeton University Press, 1980.

Connor, Steven. *Samuel Beckett: Repetition, Theory and Text*. Oxford: Basil Blackwell, 1988.

Davies, Paul. *The Ideal Real: Beckett's Fiction and Imagination*. Rutherford, NJ: Fairleigh Dickinson UP, 1994.

Dearlove, J.E. *Accommodating the Chaos: Samuel Beckett's Non-Relational Art*. Durham: Duke U.P., 1982.

De Lauretis, Teresa. *Alice Doesn't: Feminism, Semiotics, Cinema*. Bloomington: Indiana University Press, 1984.

Deleuze. G. and Guattari. *Anti-Oedipus. Volume One of Capitalism and Schizophrenia*. Trans. R. Hurley, M. Seem and H.R. Lane. London: Athlone Press, 1984.

Derrida, Jacques. *Dissemination*. Trans. B. Johnson. Chicago: University of Chicago Press, 1981.

_____. "Choreographies." Trans. C.V. Mcdonald. *Diacritics*, 12 (Summer 1982).

_____. "Structure, Sign, and Play in the Discourse of the Human Sciences." *The Structuralist Controversy*. Ed. Richard Macksey and Eugenio Donato. Baltimore: The Johns Hopkins Press, 1972: 248-49.

Descartes, Rene. *Discourse on Method*. In *Discourse on Method and Other Writings*. Trans. F.E. Sutcliffe. London: Penguin, 1968.

______. *Rules for the Direction of the Mind*. In *The Philosophical Works of Descartes*. Trans. Elizabeth S. Haldane and G.R.T. Ross. New York: Dover Publications, 1955.

Douglas, Mary. *Purity and Danger: An Analysis of the Concepts of Pollution and Taboo*. London: Routledge and Kegan Paul, 1966.

Driver, Tom. "Beckett by the Madeleine." *Columbia University Forum* 4 (Summer 1961): 21-25.

Eagleton, Terence. *Literary Theory: An Introduction*. Minneapolis: University of Minnesota Press, 1983.

Elam, Keir. "Not I: Beckett's Mouth and the Ars(e) Rhetorica". *Beckett at 80/Beckett in Context*. Ed. Enoch Brater. 124-48.

Elias, Norbert. *The Civilizing Process*. Vol. I. New York: Urizen Books, 1978.

Eliot, T.S. *The Waste Land. Collected Poems, 1909-1950*. New York: Harcourt, Brace and World, 1963.

Esslin, Martin. "Three Dialogues by Samuel Beckett and George Duthuit." *Samuel Beckett: A Collection of Critical Essays*. Ed. Martin Esslin, 1965.

Federman, Raymond. *Journey to Chaos: Samuel Beckett's Early*

Fiction. Berkeley: University of California Press, 1965.

Finney, Brian. *Since "How It Is": A Study of Samuel Beckett's Later Fiction*. London: Covent Garden Press, 1972.

Fletcher, John. *The Novels of Samuel Beckett*. London: Chatto and Windus, 1964.

______. "Modernism and Samuel Beckett." *Facets of European Modernism*. Ed. Janet Garton. Norwich: University of East Anglia, 1985.

Foucault, Michel. *The Birth of the Clinic*. Trans. Alan Sheridan. London: Tavistock, 1973.

______. *Discipline and Punish: The Birth of the Prison*. Trans. Alan Sheridan. London: Penguin, 1977.

______. *The History of Sexuality Vol .1: An Introduction*. Trans. Robert Hurley. New York: Vintage, 1980.

______. *Herculine Barbin, Being the Recently Discovered Memoirs of a Nineteenth-Century Hermaphrodite*. Trans. Richard McDougall. New York: Colophon, 1980.

______. "The Discourse on Language." *The Archaeology of Knowledge*. Trans. Rupert Swyer. New York: Harper and Row, 1972.

Freud, Sigmund. *Civilization and Its Discontents*. New York: W.W. Norton, 1961.

Garner, B. Stanton Jr. "Beckett, Merleau-Ponty, and the Phenomenological Body." *Theatre Journal* 45 (December 1993): 443-60. Reprinted in *Bodied Spaces: Phenomenology and Performance in Contemporary Drama*. Ithaca and London: Cornell University Press, 1994.

Gray, Ronald. "'*Waiting for Godot*': A Christian Interpretation." *The Listener* 57 (January 24, 1957), 160-61.

Gubar, Susan. "'The Blank Page' and Female Creativity." *Feminist Criticism*. Ed. Elaine Showalter. New York: Pantheon, 1985: 295.

Harvey, Lawrence. *Samuel Beckett: Poet and Critic*. Princeton, N.J.: Princeton University Press, 1970.

Hassan, Ihab. *The Literature of Silence: Henry Miller and Samuel Beckett*. New York, Alfred A. Knopf, 1967.

Henning, D. Sylvie. *Beckett's Critical Complicity: Carnival, Contestation, and Tradition*. Lexington, Ky: Kentucky University Press, 1988.

Hesla, David. *The Shape of Chaos: An Interpretation of the Art of Samuel Beckett*. Minneapolis: University of Minnesota Press, 1971.

Hill, Leslie. *Beckett's Fiction: In Different Words*. Cambridge:

Cambridge University Press, 1990.

Hoffman, J. Frederick. *Samuel Beckett: The Language of the Self.* Carbondale: Southern Illinois University Press, 1962.

_____. "The Elusive Ego." In *Samuel Beckett Now.* Ed. Melvin J. Friedman. Chicago: University of Chicago Press, 1970.

Homan, Sidney. *Beckett's Theaters: Interpretations for Performance.* Associated University Presses: London and Toronto, 1984.

Hume, David. *A Treatise of Human Nature.* E.L.A. Selby-Bigge. Oxford: Clarenon, 1888. Rpt. 1965.

Irigaray, Luce. *This Sex Which Is Not One.* Trans. Catherine Porter. Ithaca, NY: Cornell University Press, 1985.

Jackson, Shannon. "Performing the Performance of Power in Beckett's *Catastrophe.*" *Journal of Dramatic Theory and Criticism.* Spring 1992: 23-41.

Joyce, James. *Finnegans Wake.* New York: Viking, 1947.

Kennedy, Andrew. "Mutations of the Soliloquy: *Not I* to *Breath*". *Make Sense Who May: Essays on Samuel Beckett's Later Work.* Ed. R.J. Davis and Lance St John Butler. Gerrards Cross: Colin Smythe, 1988.

_____. *Six Dramatists in Search of a Language.* London: Cambridge University Press, 1975.

Kenner, Hugh. *Samuel Beckett: A Critical Study.* Berkeley: University of California Press, 1961.

Kern, Edith. "Black Humor: The Pockets of Lemuel Gulliver and Samuel Beckett." *Samuel Beckett Now.* Ed. Melvin Friedman. Chicago: Chicago University Press, 1970.

Kierkegaard, Soren. *The Sickness unto Death.* Together with *Fear and Trembling.* Trans. Walter Lowrie. Garden City, N.Y.: Doubleday, 1954.

Knowlson, James and John Pilling. *Frescoes of the Skull: The Later Prose and Drama of Samuel Beckett.* New York: Grove Press, 1980.

Kristeva, Julia. *Revolution in Poetic Language.* New York: Columbia University Press, 1984.

______. "The Father, Love and Banishment." *Desire in Language: A Semiotic Approach to Literature and Art.* Ed. Leon S. Roudiez. Trans. Thomas Gora, Alice Jardine, and Leon Roudiez. New York: Columbia University Press, 1980.

Laqueur, Walter T. *Making Sex: Body and Gender from the Greeks to Freud.* Cambridge: Harvard University Press, 1990.

Lawley, Paul. "Counterpoint, Absence and the Medium in Beckett's *Not I.*" *Modern Drama* 26: 4 (1984).

______. "Samuel Beckett's 'Art and Craft': A Reading of 'Enough'." *Modern Fiction Studies* 29 (Spring 1983): 25-41.

Leder, Drew. *The Absent Body*. Chicago and London: University of Chicago Press, 1990.

______."Modes of Totalization: Heidegger on Modern Technology and Science." *Philosophy Today* 29 (Fall 1985).

Libera, Antoni. "Beckett's *Catastrophe*." First Pub. *Modern Drama* (Sept.1985): 341-46. Rpt. Lance St. John Butler. Ed. *Critical Thought Series 4: Critical Essays on Samuel Beckett*. Hants, England: Scolar Press, 1993.

Locatelli, Carla. *Unwording the World: Samuel Beckett's Prose Works after the Nobel Prize*. Philadelphia: University of Pennsylvania Press, 1990.

Marx, Karl. *The Marx-Engels Reader*. Ed. Robert C. Tucker. 2nd ed. New York: Norton, 1978.

McMillan, Dougald. *Transition: The History of a Literary Era 1927-1938*. London: John Calder, 1975.

McMullan, Anna. *Theatre on Trial: Samuel Beckett's Later Drama*. Routledge: New York and London, 1993.

Mehta, Xerxes. "Ghosts." *Theatre* Vol. 24, no. 3 (1994): 37-48.

Moorjani, Angela. *Abysmal Games in the Novels of Samuel Beckett*. North Carolina Studies in the Romance Languages and Literatures. No. 219. Chapel Hill: University of North Carolina Press, 1982.

Morot-Sir, Edouard. "Samuel Beckett and Cartesian Emblems." *Samuel Beckett: The Art of Rhetoric*. Eds. Edouard Morot-Sir et al. Chapel Hill: North Carolina Studies in Romance Languages and Literatures, 1976.

Oppenheim, Lois. "Female subjectivity in *Not I* and *Rockaby*." In *Women in Beckett: Performance and Critical Perspectives*. Ed. Linda Ben-Zvi. 217-27.

Ponty, Maurice-Merleau. *The Primacy of Perception, and Other Essays on Phenomenological Psychology, the Philosophy of Art, History and Politics*. Ed. James M. Edie. Evanston, Ill.: Northwestern University Press, 1964.

Pops, Martin. "The Metamorphosis of Shit." *Salmagundi* 56 (Spring 1982): 26-61.

Rabillard, Sheila. "The Body in Beckett: Dene-gation and the Critique of a Depoliticized Theatre." *Criticism* 34:1 (Winter 1992): 99-118.

Rabinovitz, Rubin. *Innovation in Samuel Beckett's Fiction*. Urbana and Chicago: University of Illinois Press, 1992. The anonymous comment was pub. in *Punch* 29 (1855):19.

Robbe-Grillet, Alain. "Samuel Beckett, ou la presence sur la scene." Trans. Richard Howard. *For A New Novel*. New York: Grove Press, 1965: 111-25. Also Rpt. in *Samuel Beckett: A Collection of Critical Essays*. Ed. Martin Esslin. Trans. Barbara Bray. Englewood Cliff, NJ: Prentice Hall, 1965: 108-16.

Robinson, Michael. *The Long Sonata of the Dead: A Study of Samuel Beckett*. London: Rupert Hart-Davis, 1969.

Rorty, Richard. *Philosophy and the Mirror of Nature*. Princeton: Princeton University Press, 1979.

Sartre, Jean-Paul. *Being and Nothingness*. Trans. Hazel E. Barnes. London: Methuen, University Paperback, 1969.

Scarry, Elaine. *The Body in Pain: The Making and Unmaking of the World*. New York: Oxford University Press, 1985.

Shainberg, Lawrence. "Exorcising Beckett." *The Paris Review* (Fall 1987), No. 104.

Shenker, Israel. "An Interview with Beckett." In *Samuel Beckett: The Critical Heritage*. Ed. L. Graver and R. Federman. London: Routledge and Kegan Paul, 1979. First pub. in *New York Times*, May 15, 1956.

States, Bert O. "*Catastrophe*: Beckett's Laboratory/Theatre." *Modern Drama* 30 (1987): 14-22.

Trezise, Thomas. *Into the Breach: Samuel Beckett and the Ends of Literature*. Princeton, NJ: Princeton Univ. Press, 1990.

Watson, David. *Paradox and Desire in Beckett's Fiction*. Basingstoke: Macmillan, 1991.

Whitaker, Thomas. "Wham, Bam, Thank You Sam: The Presence of Beckett." *Beckett at 80/Beckett in Context*. 208-27.

Wittig, Monique. *The Lesbian Body*. Trans. Peter Owen. New York: Avon, 1976.

Worthen, W.B. "Beckett's Actor." *Modern Drama* 26: 4 (December 1983): 415-24.

Wright, Iain. "'What Matter Who's Speaking?': Beckett, the Authorial Subject and Contemporary Critical Theory." *Comparative Criticism* 5. Ed. E. Shaffer. Cambridge: Cambridge University Press, 1983: 59-86.

Zurbrugg, Nicholas. "*Ill Seen Ill Said* and the Sense of an Ending." *Beckett's Later Fiction and Drama: Texts for Company*. Ed. James Acheson and Kateryna Arthur. Macmillan Press, 1987.